GLOBAL TOURISM AND GAS INDUSTRIES RECESSION FACTORS

JOHN LOK

Copyright © John Lok
All Rights Reserved.

Contents

Preface   vii

Prologue   xi

1. Pollution Factor How Influences Tourism Industry To Experience Decline Life Cycle Stage   1

2. Terrorism Attack And Fuel Price Raising Influences Tourism Industry To Experience Decline Life Cycle Stage   69

3. Tourism Strategy Influences Tourism Industry Reaches Growth Or Mature Life Cycle Stages   82

4. Oil Price Changes Influences Tourism Industry Experiences Growth Life Cycle Stage Or Decline Life Cycle Stage   97

5. Factors Influence Oil Industry Life Cycle Stage   136

Preface

Preface

This book researchs what factors my influence global tourism and gas energy industries will experience recession rapidly . This book concerns to explain how and why tourism industry development will be influenced by these possible factors, e.g. pollution, travel stragegy, illness etc. different factors to cause global tourism development will spend how much time to experience growth stage from birth stage, growth stage to mature stage, even decline stage. For example, I shall explain how to prove environmental pollution will influence to the country's tourism industry will experience decline stage from growth stage. I shall attempt to explain how tourism industry strategies may assist the tourism development to experience growth stage or mature stage in short time rapidly. What are the strengths and weaknesses between online and offline travel agents? How can online travel agents win offline travel agents or how can offline travel agents win online travel? Why do travel consumers either choose online travel agents or offline travel agents to help them to arrange travel trips? What factors will change their mind to influence them to choose to buy electronic air ticket or paper air ticket from either offline travel agents or online travel agents? Any these strategies can assist tourism industry development to spend short time to experience growth, even mature life cycle stage.

To indicate how to apply (AI) tool to predict traveler consumption behavior aspect, This part has these three research questions need to be answered? Can apply (AI) learning machine predict travelling consumer behavior?Can (AI) big data gathering learning machine be replaced to human travelling marketing research method, e.g. survey or traveler psychological and travelling marketing research or travelling environment micro and macro economic human judgement of traveler consumption behavior prediction methods to predict travelling consumer behaviors more accurate? Whether is AI tourism behavioral prediction tool or traditional tourism market research method better to predict tourism market behavior? Can AI can assist tourism industry to spend short time to experience growth, even mature life cycle stage.

In my this part, I concentrate on explain why artificial intelligence (AI) big data gathering tool will be one kind of good traveler consumer behavioral prediction tool to be chose to apply to predict traveler consumer consumption behavior concerns when and why and how their travelling behavior will change. I shall indicate some cases examples to give reasonable evidences to analyze whether (AI) big data gathering tool will be one kind suitable tool to be applied to predict when and how and why travelling consumer behavioral changes. If (AI) big data can be one kind tool to attempt to be applied to predict when and how and why travelling consumer behavioral changes. Will it make more accurate to compare other kinds of methods to predict travelling consumer behaviors, e.g. survey, telephone questionnaire? Does it have weaknesses to be applied to predict travelling consumer behaviors, instead of strengths? Can it be applied to predict travelling consumer behaviors depending on any situations or only some situations? Finally, I believe that any readers can find answers to answer above these questions in this book.I write this part concerns how to apply (AI) tool to predict traveler entertainment behavior issue, I aim to let readers to judge whether it is possible to predict future travel behaviour from AI tool to gather past travel behaviour or traditonal tourism market research method which is better. This book is suitable to any readers who have interest to predict any individal or family or friend groups of travel target's psychological mind to design the different suitable travel packages to satisfy their needs.

In third part, I shall attempt explain whether will future space tourism market development be popular to be accepted one kind of travelling leisure to any travelling consumers in global and it will influence global tourism industry to experience decline life cycle stage, due to space tourism may replace earth tourism leisure? What factors can influence traveler prefer to choose space tourism entertainment more than general Earth tourism entertainment? How to influence future space tourism traveler individual space travel entertainment desire to be more stronger? How to attract travelers to feel space tourism entertainment which is one kind of real meaning of life travel leisure at least one time spending?

This part researchs these space exploration benefits questions:Does it have possible to develop space tourism leisure and brings economic growth?Does it have possible to develop space hospital medical service ?Does it have possible to find new biotechnology and undiscovered energy?Does it have possible to apply space technology to invent new computer technology? I shall indicate space tourism leisure aspect benefit: Whether will future space tourism market development be popular to travelling consumers in global? What factors can influence traveler prefer to choose space tourism entertainment? How to predict future space tourism traveler individual entertainment desire whether it strong or weak? How to attract travelers to choose space tourism entertainment? What entertainment benefits to human to earn when we spend space tourism leisure.

This book fourth part explains what factors may influence oil business cycle life stages. Why can some oil businesses experience growth life cycle stage , then going to mature life cycle stage rapidly? Otherwise, some oil businesses need long time to experience growth and mature life cycle stages. What factors may influence the oil business may reach growth life cycle stage and mature life cycle stage? Why does some oil businesses experience decline life cycle stage rapidly ? I shall explain these issues how and why factors may influence any kinds of oil business develop in their business life cycle stages. Why does COVID 19 human disease can influence global tourism and airline airplane fuel or vehicle gas both industries to experience decline life cycle service stage easiy? My readers will make judgement whether above different factors may influence traditonal tourism marketing and oil energy businesses may spend short or long time to reach growth cycle stage, even mature cycle stage, even decline cycle stage from birth stage.

Prologue

Table of contents

Chapter 1
Pollution factor how influences tourism industry to experience decline life cycle stage

I. Explaining why the Environmental Kuznets Curve indicator method is measured to any country's economic growth and environmental pollution relationship commonly p.4-15

II. Explaining how to measure whether income growth is associated with increasing or decreasing environmental quality to developed or developing countries in long term

III. Explaining how countries can reduce environmental pollution and can raise economic growth at the same time

reference

Quality of human life social loss

I. Why environmental factor and quality of life has relationship p.16-29

II. What is the difference between the quality of life and standard of living.

III. Why environmental factor can influence traveller leisure desire to reduce

(i) How environmental risk factor can influence different groups

(ii) How Afria country environmental pollution influences

(iii) How human adult consumption and environmental quality influences future environment for human survival probability of life expectancy.

(iv) Why social and physical environmental factors have close relationship to influence economic growth

(v) How environmental factor can influence any country's house price.

(vi) How environmental pollution can influence social welfare

Quality of traveler individual leisure need reducing

(i) Why environmental pollution and human right abuses has close relationship to influence traveller individual leisure desire p.30-45

● How oil consumer decisions are impacted
on environment? p.63-80
    Chapter 2
Terrorism attack and fuel price raising influences tourism industry to experience decline life cycle stage
● Terrorism attack influences traveller need p.81-96

Airlines fuel manufacturing supply strategy

● Why tourism and airline industries have close relationship to influence their profitability between of them. p.97-113
Fuel raising price solve methods
● Methods to solve rising air fare p.114-132
prices demand
I. Why will biofuels energy be demanded ?
II. Whether the relationship between terrorism and oil prices has close relationship.
III. What factors will influence airline industry's price elasticity of supply and demand?
Bibliography
    Chapter 3
Tourism strategy influences tourism industry reaches growth or mature life cycle stages

1.1 The main cost related factors to offline or online travel agents
1.2 Airline travel agency AirAsia in the domestic airline low cost strategy
1.3 How consumers select travel service
between online and offline mode in travel industry
1.4 What is the online travel sale service strategy? p.133-163
    Online/offline travel operators (agents) maketing
strategies
    2.1 Offline walk in travel unique segment service strategy
    2.2 Systematic differences strategy applies to offline walk in travel agent
    2.3 Service fees and commission cuts strategy
    2.4 Internet negative influences to travel agents

2.5 Concentrating on business travel marketing strategy

2.5.1 What an e-commerce strategy is used by internet travel websites?

2.5.2 Travel agents vs online booking: Tackling the shortcomings and strengths

Reference

Chapter 4

Oil price changes influences tourism industry experiences growth life cycle stage or decline life cycle stage

● How to develop new economic tourism industry

● How new economic development in oil industry p.164-180

New and old economic theories explain oil is not main factor

to influence tourism income

● Can economic theory explain old price change to influence tourism income?

● How the price of oil changes influences global tourism industry growth or recession?

Chapter 5

Factors influence oil industry life cycle stage

● Reasons cause oil industry experiences

decline life cycle stage p.181-200

● How to raise global gas users need desire ?

Electronic vehicle how influences future gas

vehicle market life cycle stage experience changes

HOW DESIGNING UNDERGROUND MASS TRANSIT RAILWAY TO BRING PASSENGERS

● Designing transportation system advantages

● Underground train transportation needs to

know passenger behaviour reasons

reference

● How to let passengers feel impact of

undergrouund train transport to their working time efficiency

● How underground train MTR can let passengers to feel

catching time reducing .

Artificial Intelligent In Road Transportation Strategy influences

vehicle oil need

How artificial intelligent vehicle may interact intelligent

transportation tools

● Does oil price sudden high rising factor influence global oil industry rapid reaches decline life cycle stage?

Pollution factor how influences tourism industry to experience decline life cycle stage

I shall explain how this study confirms the invested correlation between economic growth and environmental degradation of hypothesis that is at the early stage economic growth which increases environmental degradation, then environmental degradation decreases after reaching a certain level of average income per capita. Moreover, I shall explain how other factors, such as trade openness, industrial extension also cause an increase in environmental degradation. This study also has been investigated the between environmental pollution and per capita income when have close relationship to influence economic falling down in long term.

The key indicators are used to capture the changes in environmental conditions have been developed and used in many countries. A high rate of economic growth has been a primary and permanent goal of government and society, particularly in developing countries. The increase in economic growth is related to an increase in the production and consumption of products and services. Consequently, it may lead to an increase in the multiplied products of the people and income per capita consumption. However, economic growth may produce negative impacts on the environment pollution, overexploitation of natural resources, degradation and loss of wildlife habitat and climate change. Hence, many countries have been facing the decline in environmental quality issue when which neglect to reduce environmental pollution challenge in long term.

I believe that the impact of economic growth on environment quality is categorized through three different channels: The first is the scale effect, the second is the composition and the end is the technique effect. The scale effect means to happen as pollution increases with the size of the economy, the explanation being that even of the structure of the economy and the technology doesn't change, it is assumed that an increase in the scale of economic activity leads to an increase in pollution and environmental degradation, when the composition effect refers to the change in production structure of an economy from agriculture-based to industry and service. The last effect is the technique effect, which captures improvement in the technique of production and adaption of cleaner technologies and hence a reduction in pollution

I. Explaining why the Environmental Kuznets Curve key indicator method is measured to any country's economic growth and environmental pollution relationship commonly

Generally, evidence shows that some environmental pressures have diminished in developed countries, the hypothesis could generalized to the global relationship between economy and environment at all. The hypothesis is called the Environmental Kuznets Curve (EKC) hypothesis because of its similarity with the relationship between the level of inequality and per capita income is posited by Kuznet. According to the EKC hypothesis, it indicated that "at the first stage of economic development environmental pressures increase as per capita income increases, but after a critical turning point these pressures diminish along with higher income levels(Beckerman,1992)". In its most optimistic view, the hypothesis suggests that economic growth is itself the solution to environmental problems, because environmental improvement will be an almost unavoidable.

II. Explaining how to measure whether what income growth associated with increasing or decreasing environmental quality is to developed or developing countries

In fact, energy consumption, environmental protection and economic growth belong to an organic whole. The development of industry plays an important part in the development of the national economy. Meanwhile the development of industry spends lots of energy and makes serious pollution. Energy is a important material basis of human survival, economic development and social progress. Instance, China is promoting energy production and sustainable economic growth. We know that the environmental pollution should be the cost of economic development. Energy consumption and environmental pollution in-depth has a great practical significance for guiding the healthy development of China's economy.

The sustainable economic growth, urbanization and environmental protection in China. China has developed to become the second largest economy in the world next to USA. With fact economic growth , cities in China have been expanding and it is through urbanization to cause serious environmental problems, such as pollution of air, water and solid waste, which have imposed huge challenges to economic growth. In fact, urbanization has led to damage to the environment. So, the China environmental pollution is caused from the relationship between economic development and urbanization and then urbanization is driving economic growth. Also, the major environmental pollution is driving to China's economic growth and the major environmental problems of China are caused by urbanization in China and urbanization will cause negative consequences. However, China industrialization demands are increasing and China economic growth is also increasing, but the environment pollution is also increasing at the same time. Another environmental pollution of country, such as Australia, its economy has grown an average of 3.3 % gross domestic product (GDP) annually the past 40 years, corresponding to an average annual GDP per capita growth rate of 1.3% (ABS, 2014). There are concerns that growth has been accompanied by excessive natural resource use and declines in environmental quality. However, economic growth can also stimulate demand for environmental quality and thus environmental policy has been enabling the development and adoption of new technologies. Whether income growth is associated with increasing or decreasing environmental quality issue for long term, which is a question that varies across environmental quality measures and economies growth. The fact is as the scale of Australia economic activity increase, environmental degradation, including increasing resource use and negative externalities tends to increase as well. On the one hand, econometricians indicated that "starting in the early 1990 year highlights the possibility that for some environmental pollutants there tends to be an inverted "U" shaped development path with respect to income, as measured by GDP, such that pollution tends to after some switching point (Grossman and Krueger, 1991)." This relationship could arise from demand side pressures (environmental quality is a normal product) or supply side pressures (technological and structural changes) . It is possible to bring the relationship between environmental quality and economic growth. On the other hand, nowadays, the conflict between economic growth and biodiversity conservation is concerned from many countries' governments. A more compelling response to the conflict is that may be resolved with technological progress. However, I review the conflict between economic growth and biodiversity conservation in the absence of technological progress. The conflict between economic growth and biodiversity conservation is based principle of ecology, such as trophic levels and competitive exclusion, the human economy grows at the competitive exclusion of nonhuman species in the aggregate. However, the conflict via technological progress has not occurred and is infeasible because of the linkage between technological progress and economic growth at current levels of technology. My supportive reason is that surplus production in existing economic sectors is requires for conducting the research and development necessary for bringing new technologies to market. Technologies also reflect macroeconomic goals, and if the goal is economic growth, technologies are less likely to be developed. As the economy grow, the loss of biodiversity may be partly mitigated with end use innovation that increases technical efficiency, but this type of technological progress requires policies that are unlikely if the conflict between economic growth and biodiversity conservation and other aspects of environmental protection is not acknowledged.

In my discussion concerns that environmental damage has not only created obstacles to economic development, but it is also posing great threats to human health and life, to ecological systems and natural world, and to the socio-cultural environments in which human beings lead their daily lives. Hence, I suggest that different countries' governments need to concern mobilization of political risk and socio-economic resources. The concept of "sustainability" was formulated as a result of the linkage between pesticide use and widespread pollution, of the effects of pollution on the health of humans and other animals and plants, and through proposal for managing resources in a way which doesn't destroy supplies of resources needed in the future. A country is considered "developing" when it is experiencing expansion of its productive capacity, the indicator is used, such as gross national product (GNP), and/or GNP per capita. The well being of all people depends largely on economic growth. However, when a country, such as developing countries Hong Kong and India both countries which populations are increasing, indeed it is difficult to imagine development without economic growth. As a result, however, nature has been scarified in the name of economic development. The pursuit of wealth and exploitation of the planet had taken place on an individualistic basic or collectivist basic, environment problems are began to cause increasing concern in growing segments of societies, mainly in the developed countries, such as India and China.

We emphasizes quality of life, but the bio centric view, gives greater recognition to the planet, regarding the pursuit of wealth through industrial expansion and economic growth as incompatible with the earth's resource base. This view also takes the position that economic growth at the expense of natural represents consumption of what belongs rightly to future generations. However, becomes human kind is seen to be living within ecological constraints, economies will have zero growth in quantitative terms. Instead growth should be measured in qualitative terms, such as clean and healthy natural environment level, in other words, on the basis of quality of living rather than standard of living. Quantitative growth may occur only in certain areas, for example, in developing countries, such as China or India and poor areas of developed countries, such as USA, but there must also be negative growth in areas which are already highly developed.

In General, the economy growth is always the attention focal point to every country. The economy growth impacts the protecting environment, on the contrary, the protecting environment also impacts the economy growth whether the environment is a factor considering the economic growth. In fact, environment not only provides the substance foundation and activity space for human, but also is responsible for production. Economic development not only enhances the integration national power and improves the people's life quality, but brings number of environmental problems, soil degradation, desertification etc.

Concerning how to reduce environment pollution and to raise economic growth at the same time. I shall have these questions to be needed to answer in order to give suggestion to solve this challenge. These questions are such as below:

● Whether does economic growth affect the environment?

● On the contrary, whether also does the protecting environment affect the growth economy?

● Whether is protecting economy and protecting environment a pair of contradiction or not what creates the environment problem?

● Is economic development incompatible with environmental quality?

● What is the effect of an increase in employment or wages on the environment in a particular industry?

● How do environmental conditions or regulations influence firm location and expansion decisions and thus economic growth in a community?

However, I feel that poverty is another factor to cause environmental pollution. Instead of factory manufacturing industry, such as India has many poor people neglect to keep natural river, ocean, hill, farming, and any public places environment to be clean and not direct to use these natural places. Solving this problem is that developing countries' economy how to increase economy under the protecting environment. Analyzing poverty and environmental pollution relationship is the focal point. We need to concern problem formulation, such as what the conflict is between developing economic and protecting environment. For example, the problem is concerned the traffic point problem, such as the environment impact of transportation has now become a global issue. Otherwise, environment impacts from transportation in the developed world are now equalized or exceeded by those in developing countries. It is given the relatively high level of car ownership and use in developing countries, such as developed country Hong Kong, which is a small Asia city, but there are many Hong Kong people who like to buy cars to drive to go to office on the roads every day. Hence, it causes much traffic jam transportation problems to Hong Kong roads every day. Otherwise, developing country, Africa. Because people are poor commonly, so there are less many own cars. The air pollution will be reduced also. However, Hong Kong has higher level of pollution to have a negative impact on employment growth due to the following reasons:

Better environmental quality attracts more skilled workers at lower wages and firms have access to whose more easily in regions where environmental quality is higher. Hong Kong has high level of pollution because Hong Kong firms attracts more skilled works to work in high technological manufacuring industry to case air or water pollution.

Production costs may be lower in regions with higher environmental quality if cleaner air and water result in lower rates of sick leaves and higher worker productivity. Hong Kong firms aim to raise worker productivity, so which uses high technological machines to raise whose productivity, but it also brings oil energy pollution to air or water.

I give a hypothesis is that higher earnings and lower employment growth rates contribute to decrease in pollution growth rates, resulting in better environmental conditions in a country. The usual hypothesis is that earnings and environmental quality are positively correlated. Since as earnings rise, the demand for environmental quality increases through an income effect, as do the public and private resources available for environmental improvement. Otherwise, increase in employment might increase pollution activities in the region, due to a scale effect. The scale effect reflects the increase in the level of economic activity in the relevant constant techniques of production and composition of final product. Hence, it seems Hong Kong income growth associated with decreasing environment quality nowadays. Because Hong Kong is lower earnings and high employment growth rates contribute to increase in pollution growth rates, resulting in worse environmental conditions in Hong Kong.

An empirical research on relationship between economic growth and atmospheric pollution was investigated to one sample developing country, such as China, which was based on the panel data analysis, the report was gathered China's economic and environmental data over 1991 year to 2010 year, it showed that there existed the long run relationship between the emission of pollutants and per capita (GDP) Gross Domestic Product to China. According to the panel estimation results from estimator, the relationship between emission and per capita GDP of China was inverse "N"-shaped. However, GDP relation of China could be considered as inverted U-shaped for the reason that per capita GDP of China of left turning point was to small. The relationship between economic growth and atmospheric pollution in China which was based by Environmental Kuznets Curve hypothesis measure method. It was seemed that Environmental Kuzents Curve hypotheses measure method might be an effective economic method to measure the indicator of relationship between environment pollution influence and economic growth to the sample research country, China. The China economic and environmental pollution sample report aimed to research whether China's economic growth would cause greater damage to regional, national and even global environment or environmental quality could be benefits from the increase of income and wealth to China. Finally, it reflected that China has have a positive impact on employment growth and economic growth, but it has also a high level of pollution at the same time nowadays. Because China is lower earnings and high employment growth rates contribute to increase in pollution growth rates, resulting in worse environmental conditions in China.

In fact, many environmental problems happened, due to many factors caused, such as (external diseconomy, regional development, strategy etc.). However, EKC (Environment Kuznets Curve) provides an alternative solution: the increase of capita income will improve environmental quality at last with the increase of income, the pollution level increases at low income level, but pollution finally reduce high income level. However, I recognize that Environmental Kuznets Curve (EKC) has this weaken point which describes an objective phenomenon, but it can't be used a rule to prove the environmental pollution and the increasing or decreasing environment quality measure absolutely.

In fact, China has not a good performance in environmental protection. It has serious air and water pollution. There is excess industrial waste gas in the air, the air will become toxic gas, which will threat health and induce many diseases. For China economic growth is evident across the country at the cost of environmental pollution in the cities (e.g. air pollution). It is the China government's responsibility to solve the conflict between the economic development and environmental protection. In general, judging from the environmental and economic report in Environmental Kuznets Curve (EKC), it can be seen that, in general, the existence of (EKC) and a few negative the (EKC). Further, the relationship between economic growth and environment pollution can be well characterized by inverted "U" sharp in a long term. But in the short term, it may appear all sorts of wave, such a "U", "N" or other shapes. However, I doubt (EKC) measure method whether is suitable for every country, especially for developing countries, such as China. As Kuznets Curve did research on income gaps, it found that income gap increasing first, and then decreasing as economies grow. The relation between the two variables is known as " Kuznets Curve" with the help of Kuznets Curve, it pointed out that there may have the inverted "u" curve relationship between environmental quality and economic development, that is the increase of economic growth and per capita income will lead to a drop in the equality of the environment in the early stages of economic development. However, once the economic development beyond a critical value point, the improvement of per capita income will help to reduce environmental pollution and to improve environment quality. So, it implied that the developing country, China if its economic development could beyond critical value point, then it is possible that it can improve its per capita income and it will achieve to reduce environmental pollution and it will improve environment quality at the same time in the future.

Further, I shall indicate another developed country, such as America whether what its relationship between bio-diversity and ecosystems and economic growth is. The findings further indicate that changes in the global economy combined with climate change, social change and increasing scarcity of ecosystem services is changing the cost-benefit analysis, so that the conservation of ecosystem services is increasing in relative value to USA. In fact, USA government is hard to focus on economic costs and benefits (direct and indirect) and non use values are intangible and more difficult for USA government to use to compare and to select over direct financial gains from degradation of the ecosystem (economic growth).

In USA farming growth sector is very large to keep it's country GDP amount per year. However, keeping clean natural environment is important to USA. Because air and water pollution can influence natural resource and crops and fruits etc. foods agricultural growing economic benefit, due to farmers can not grow many crops, e.g. rice, vegetables, potatoes, tomatoes etc. crop of foods to raise sale numbers in long term. In long term, USA will have bad influence if whose farmers can't grow any crop kind of foods to sell, due to water and air is polluted to influence good farms to let farmers grow much crops to sell to overseas or local both supermarkets or food stores. Although, the manufacturing industry sector income will be raised, but , it will also cause farming sector income and GDP to be decreased at the same time for USA.

The Environmental Kuznet Curve (EKC) hypothesis is an environmental pressure tends to rise faster than income growth in early stages, then slows down and reaches a turning point to which it tends to decline with further growth. The last phase is referred to as delinking of environmental pressure from economic growth. The EKC hypothesis points towards a trade off between environment and development, i.e. it seems to suggest that underdeveloped countries will have to forgo environmental quality of attaining a higher level of development. It further suggests that environment quality will be taken care of as developing countries attain further care of as developing countries attain further level of development. The Environment Kuznet Curve (EKC) hypothesis is summed up " at low level of development both the quantity and intensity of environmental degradation is limited to the impacts of subsistence economic activity on the resource base and to limited quantities of biodegradable wastes. As economic development accelerates with the intensification of agriculture and other resource extraction and the take off of industrialization, the rates of resource depletion begins to exceed the rates of resource regeneration, and waste generation increases in quantity and toxicity. At higher levels of development, structured and services, coupled with increased environmental awareness, enforcement and higher environmental expenditures, result in leveling off and gradual decline of environmental degradation." (Panayotou 1993). (EKC) studies are based on data of developing countries have not come out as yet, the possibility of such studies refuting the trade-off, the way of the Kuznet;s inverted "U" hypothesis was refuted by such studies that came up in 1970 year can't be rules out. Even if the trade off was valid for the past, experiences its policy implication for future of developing countries may not be very useful. An obvious policy suggestion which can be drawn from the trade off is that developing countries should focus primarily on bordering much about environmental protection in their early stages. Because growth itself will take care of environmental quality at a later stage. However, such a strategy can be mistaken (as the economic growth oriented strategy of developing countries, like India in the early planning without much effort for reduction of poverty, believing that poverty was supposed to be mitigated by trickle down effect of high grown.) Moreover, it is important to note that many components of environmental quality, such as bio-diversity are non-reversible of degradation exceeds a level. Anyway, a developing country today need not go through the same course of development on which th rationale for the EKC hypothesis has been formulated. For instance, countries like India have made the transition from a primary sector dominated economy to a service sector dominated economy without going through the phase dominated by the industrial sector. So, it seems that the developed country, USA and developing country, India income growth associated with increasing environmental quality nowadays. Because Hong Kong and India both countries are higher earnings and low employment growth rates contribute to decrease in pollution growth rates, resulting in better environmental conditions in these two countries.

III. Explaining how countries can reduce environmental pollution and can raise economic growth at the same time

Why countries need to pollute environment to develop economy, such a need for industrialization related environmental degradation in the course of economic development. A country needs and chooses to achieve industry production it can raise technological advancement and adopt technologies, which are substantially less polluting than the technologies used by countries which industry in the past. The environmental development trade off might have existed historically. But it is not bad to developing countries to scarce environment quality for industry development. Nowadays, different countries' governments need to concern how to reduce environmental pollution and to raise economic growth at the same time. In fact, human are facing these challenges, such as energy crisis is from 1970 year is precipitated by oil price jumps, market failure in allocation of environmental resources. At the same time, human are also facing economic development that meets the needs of the present without compromising the ability of the future generations to meet our own needs. Due to natural resource is limited to be supplied in the future, industry needs manufactured, human and natural is left undiminished, so this needs restricting consumption to save natural resources for asset creation and conservation and protection of the natural environment. Efforts and indicators for monitoring sustainability indicates the environmentally adjusted national income or Green Domestic Product (GNP)=NDP less depletion of natural capital-environmental damage and green national accounts indicates degradation of environmental capital is like depreciation of man -made capital. Hence, it implies environmental pollution is a damage cost to any countries. Hence, if the country can reduce or avoid the environmental pollution, then its environmental damage cost will not influence its GDP (Green Domestic Product) income amount indicator to be reduced for the country's national income in the year. Then, it's economic growth will be better in the year. Due to GDP is the country whole year income financial performance indicator. It will concern the country's economic growth level in the year.

Environmental pollution is an important issue in the process of economic growth. Instance, China has obtained remarkable economic growth with an average annual growth rate of 9.6% in gross domestic product (GDP) from 1979 year to 2004 year. Despite the impressive economic performance, the environment qualities have become worse during the past two decades. China government began to concern about to following these questions: will the high economic growth be able to sustain within environmental constraints or without exceeding ecological system? What is the effect of economic growth on environment quality? Are there any tradeoff between attaining high economic growth and protecting environment? And will the environment conditions become improved automatically at higher income level? What should the government do to the environmental degradation? When environmental sustainability, due to the increasing scarcity or overuse of renewable natural resources, arisen non renewable commodities, such as fossil fuels or industrial metals which cause problems, such as water and air pollution, atmosphere or the ozone layer. Thus these bad happening(result) have cause-effect relationship between pollution and public health.

Environmental policy aims at putting environmental resources, such as land, water, air, the atmosphere regime, with clear and enforceable rules. The tools various forms of restriction on activity: access to these resources may be limited, for example, by placing limit values on emissions or their use may be limited (by restricting the kind of activities allowed in natural habitats or drinking water reservoirs) or make subject to specific conditions (such as paying a tax or an environmental levy or the obligation to clean and recycle them after use). Rising incomes and rising pollution have brought with them a rising demand for environmental protection of policies. Market forces themselves have led to a reduction in the pollution in intensity of economic activity of the dynamic growth of the " cleaner" rates of return for local and regional pollution are closer to social rates, then for global commons. However, policy action has nevertheless been strong needed to decouple economic activity and emission levels. In fact, environmental policies cause an adjustment of economic structures. The price of using environmental resources and of exposing the public to health risks should be brought closer with social cost, with consequence that pollution and risks to public health should decline and GDP becomes less pollution intensive. Besides, polluting industries will be held in check when cleaner industries will be boosted and net effects on welfare though not necessarily on economic activity as measured in national accounts statistics. This adjustment comes at th price of fiction between regulated industries, their supplies and customers which could offset potential welfare gains. A cost effective environmental policy should aim to minimize costs incurred in achieving an environmental objective by dynamic character of adjustment needs and cost and benefit can be estimates in the absence of well functioning markets. In this way, it could contribute to significantly relaxing potential trade off between environmental protection and economic growth aim and supporting welfare enhancing structural adjustment.

In conclusion, in the future, environmental behavior change will be limited by unclear solutions and low political profile, but models of human behavior can help in understanding how to support change. I shall recommend three methods to solve environment pollution challenge to influence economic growth for long term at the same time.

The first point, it is practical for example, governments need to promote teaching behavior to let their countries' citizen to know the corrective attitude to putting rubbish to rubbish boxes in streets and to promote recycling schemes to achieve more environmentally friendly products. For example, Hong Kong have 7 million people are living in one small city. If HK citizen put their rubbish to any streets, gardens etc. public places. It will influence natural environment to be worse, then it will influence the flowers, trees plants and bees, butterflies, ants etc. insects which can not be alive, due to their natural environment has been polluted by HK citizen. Hence, human have responsibility to protect their natural environment to let any animals and plants can be alive safely and healthy. If our world could have health and good natural environment which can let human and animals and plants to be alive, then pollution can also be reduced, even our countries' economy can grow fast because product manufacturers can have good and beautiful places to let them to build their plants to manufacture their products every day, due to good natural environment will provide good places to let manufacturers to build their plants, then their workers will also have good health to do their jobs in their plants to raise their productivity and work efficiency. Hence, good natural environment and good places provision to be built plants, then workers will have good health to work, so which has cause and effect relationship closely. Manufacturers need to know their workers should not raise their productivity and work efficiency, even they will reduce their productivity and work inefficiency if their work places are polluted.

The second point, economic and legislative need, for example, fines and incentives, making the polluter pays and international action, for example, debt relief international pollution control. Air pollution is the discharge of waste products into air and main sources are cargo or airplanes exhausts, power stations and industrial process as well as water pollution is the discharge of waste products into river or ocean and main sources are ferry, cargo shipping exhausts and industrial process. Thus, governments ought have legislative force to threaten the product manufacturers pollute air or water during their industrial process in their plants.

The third point, involving and empowering people, for example, local decisions and resources of allocation, such as economic decisions about the uses which should be made of land, labor and capital leading to an overall of resources, which generally matches the pattern of consumer demand. Consumer demand creates profitable opportunities for entrepreneurs to organize inputs of factors of production so as to meet that demand. In this way, the allocation of resources responds to the pattern of demand exhibited by consumers. However, the idea and the allocation of resources can be applied much more widely to a range of decision which may be taken by individual or by governments. Such as, people decide how to allocate their own resources when they choose between work and leisure or whether to save more or consume more. Also, governments make resource allocation decisions when they consider making changes to different categories of spending: they may consider whether to allocate more towards defense or education or towards health care or environment protection or unemployment benefit. However, it is not always which the allocation of resources conforms to the pattern of consumer demand. The manufacturing firms and governments can sometimes control certain aspects of the allocation of manufacture raw material resources through monopoly power or through administrative decisions. It aims to reduce natural resource waste and reduce air and water pollution issues occurrence to any oceans, rivers, lands etc. places.

The final point, different countries' governments can achieve agricultural stabilization policies, such as many governments intervene in some way in agricultural markets. In developed countries, the objective is to raise farm incomes, usually by keeping prices above the world market price, and perhaps to keep out cheap imports. This tends to raise food prices to consumers. Within the EU, most policy decisions are embodies in the Common Agricultural Policy. These policies are unpopular with food exporting countries, especially those that are also developing countries. Some developed countries sell subsidized food to very poor countries, which useful if these is a famine. But it is counter-productive when it reduces farm prices and thus poor local farmers' incomes and their incentive to increase output and productivity. So, this developing countries, governments, such as China, India etc. can allocate the limited land natural resources to give to the farmers to use to help their to grow a lot of rice, potatoes, tomatoes, vegetables or to feed many pigs, cows to keep themselves countries' farming sector long term development to earn overseas or local both GDP income and per capita farmer income for long term. Beside, they do not need concentrate on developing manufacturing industry sector income and their environmental pollution will also reduce, due to there are less lands are supplied to manufacturers to build factories to use for long term.

In conclusion, every country needs to concern how to keep economic growth and to avoid to cause environment pollution challenge at the same time. Because, which economy will not be grew, even will be fallen if their environment is polluted seriously for long term, although which economic growth will be raised for short term.

● Reference

Australian Bureau of Statistics (ABS), 2014. Australian National Accounts: National income, expenditure and product (cat. no. 5206.0). Accessed 2 February 2015. Australia from (abs.gov.au).

Beckerman, W., 1992. Economic growth and the environment: Whose growth? Whose environment? World development 20, 481-496.

Grossman, G. M., and A.B. Krueger, 1991. Environment impacts of a North American free trade agreement. NBER working paper 3914. Cambridge, MA: National Bureau Of Economic Research.

Quality of human life social loss

Why the quality of human life can not be measured by GDP (gross domestic product) statistic method only. There have been numerous attempts to construct alternative, non monetary indices of social and economic wellbeing by combining in a single statistic a variety of different factors that are thought to influence quality of human life. The main problem in all these measures is selection bias in the factors that are chosen to assess quality of life and, even more seriously in assigning weights to different indicators (measured on a comparable and meaningful scale) to conclude a single synthetic measure. Substantive meaning and prices are the objective weights (although there are also very big problems in estimating the purchasing-power partities that have to used instead of market exchange rates in order to express countries' incomes in the same currency). However, some researchers have showed that human rights to identify the factors that need to be included in a quality of life measure. But, even if accepted as a starting point, that still does not point to clear to indicators or how which are to be weighted. So, a technocratic and unsatisfying device that is sometimes used is to recort to " expert opinion".

How to use life satisfaction surveys to measure human quality of life? Some researchers had been carrying on researching a methodologically improved and more comprehensive measure of qualify of life satisfaction surveys. Surveys of life satisfaction is as opposed to surveys of the related concept of happiness, are preferred for a number of reasons, such as GDP statistic method. These surveys ask people the simple question of how satisfied who are with their lives in general. A typical question is on the four point scale used to the surveys studies. For example, on the whole are you very satisfied, fairly satisfied, not vey satisfied, or not at all satisfied with the life you lead? The results of the surveys have been attracting growing interest in recent years. Despite a range of early criticism, such as cultural non-comparability, the effect of language differences across countries, psychological factors distorting responses, tests have disproved as migitated most concerns. One objection is that responses to surveys don't adequately reflect how people really feel about their life. However, responses to questions about life satisfaction tend to be promoted, non-response rates are very low. This simple measure of life satisfaction has been found to correlate highly with more sophisticated test ratings by others who know the individual, and behavioral measures. The survey results have on the whole proved far more reliable and information then might be expected to measure quality of life.

Another criticism is that life-satisfaction responses reflect the dominant view on life, rather than actual quality of life in a country. So, life satisfaction is seen as a judgement that depends on social and culturally aspects, but this relativism is disproved by the fact that people in different countried report similar criteria as being important for life satisfaction, and by the fact that most differences in life satisfaction across countries can be explained by differences in objective circumstances. In addition, it has been found that the responses of immigrants in a country are much closer the level of the local population than to responses in their motherland.

In the view point of economists, who disagree to take the survey results completely at face value and use the average score on life satisfaction as the indicator of quality of life for a country. There are several reasons. First, comparable results for a sufficient number of countries tend to be out -of -date and many nations are not covered at all. Second, the impact of measurement errors on assessing the relationship indicators tends to cancel out across a large number of countries. But these might still be significant errors for any given country. So, there is a bigger chance of error in assessing quality of life between countries if we take a single average life satisfaction score as opposed to a multi-component index. Finally, and most important reason, although most of the inter-country variation in the life satisfaction surveys can be explained by objective factors, there is still a significant unexplained component which, in addition to measurement error, might to related to specific factors, that we want to net out from an objective quality of life index.

Instead we use the survey results as a starting point, and a means for deriving weights for the various determinants of quality of life across countries, in order to calaulate an objective index. The average scores from comparable life-satisfaction surveys (on a scale of one to ten) can be assembled for 1999 year or 2000 year in a multi-variate regression to various factors satisfaction in many studies. Together these variables explain more than 80% of the inter-country variation in life-satisfaction scores. The surveys showed the weights of the various factors, included health, material well-being, and political stability and security. These were followed by family relations and community life. Next, in order of importance were climate (environment factor), job security, political freedom and finally gender equality. The surveys showed that the values of the life-satisfaction scores that are predicted by nine indicators represent a country's quality of life index or the corrected life-satisfaction scores, based on objective cross-country determinants. The method also means that the original units or measurement of the various indicators can be rely on the potentially distortive effect of having to transform all indicators to a common measurement also. The survey results indicate the determinents of quality of life factors, and the indicators used to represent these factors are: material wellbeing, health, political stability and security, family life, community life, climate and geography (environment factor), job security (unemployment rate), political freedom, gender equality. However, a number of other variables were also investigates but, upward trend in average life-satisfaction scores in developed nations, whereas average income has grown substantially. However, there is no evidence for an explanation that it has relationship between increasing incomes and stagnant life-satisaction scores: otherwise, the idea that an increase in someone's income causes enemy or disadvantage and reduces the welfare and satisfaction of others. In the researchers' estimates the level of income inequality had no impact on levels of life satisfaction , life satisfaction is primarily determined by absolute, rather than relative, status (related to states of mind and aspirations).

I. Why environmental factor and quality of
life has relationship

The explanation is that there are factors associated with modernisation that, in part offest its positive impact, such as crime, and drug and alcohol addiction, a decline in political participation and of trust in public authority, the erosion of the institutions of family and marriage. In personal terms, this has also been manifested in increased general uncertainty and personal risk. These pheonomena have accompanied rising incomes and expanded individual choice (both of which are highly valued). However stable family life and community are also highly valued and these have undergone a severe erosion. The survey results also showed that four of the indicators are forecast for 2005 yar (GDP , life expectancy, unemployment rate, political stabiliy); one geography is fixed and the remaining four, which represent slow changing factors and quality of life has relationship.

Thus, the researchers implied that GDP method is not accurate to measure human's quality of life. It ought have those other different methods to measure human's quality of life, such as survey method etc. as well as income is not only one factor to influence material wellbeing of human's quality of life; there are other different variable factor to influence human's quality of life, such as health, political stability, security, family of life, community life, climate and geography (environment factor), job security (unemployment rate), political freedom, gender equality etc. factors.

McGregor & Goldsmith (1998) explained that " quality is life is relative and difference between individuals, but it can be perceived as the level of satisfaction or confidence with one's conditions, relationships and surroundings relative to the available alternatives. The concept of quality of life is multifaceted. Quality of life consists of among other things: hope for the future, land, adequate food, clothing, shelter, income, employment opportunities, maternal and child health, and family and social welfare." The concept of quality of life is indeed multi-dimersional, complex and very subjective. For example, someone who has changed their consumptin habit to better ensure that their choices with make a better quality of life for themselves, the environment and future generations, may be seen by others as having a lower or inferior quality of life since which have removed themselves from the materialistic mainstream characteristics of our consumer society. Someone may feel that an absence of violence and abuse in their life and natural fresh air and clean water good quality supply can lead to even though who have fewer tangible resources, money or shelter; peace of mind and freedom from abuse has increased the quality of their daily life relative to what it was like before.

Otherwise, standard of living is often equated with quality of life, but it is not the same thing. A standard of life is a way of life to which a group of people are accustomed. Some people's standard of living includes only basic food, clothing, shelter and safety. Other people expect to eat at expensive restaurants, wear designer clothes, live in huge homes and travel extensively. Different people expect and want different things, who have different standards, which are very much shaped by values, goals, money, past experience and socialization. However, standard of living are most commonly assessed in terms of annual household income levels and to a lesser extent, wealth, community assistance, family contributions, special family needs, distribution of income within the family or household and geographic location.

Thus, it seems that standard of living or GDP alone is not a good measure of quality of life. Quality of life is a personal and inward looking concept that has both objective (factual) and subjective (perception) components. However, an individual's quality of life is also affected by external factors (build and natural environment; services and facilities) and this directly links quality of life to regional issues. The subjective aspect of quality of life is particularly important as if reflects how people feel about their situation and this can't be gauged from objective indicators. Subjective quality of life is often broken down into seven life domains: standard of living, health, achievements in life, personal relationships, safety, community connection and future security. For example, the measure of domain, such as standard of living includes as on income and wealth and housing aspect. The subjective measures: satisfaction with standard of living, distribution with wealth in the region, perceptions of personal income, wealth, housing affordability, housing density, green space and facilities near to homes. Objective measures may include distribution of income, welfare dependence, levels of housing stress. On health aspects, the subjective measures , satisfaction with personal health, region's health services, self assessed health status, needs and service usage. Objective measures may include services available per capita, suicide rates . It seems environment pollution factor can be one part to influence human quality of life.

Many studies of quality of life suggest that personal relations are an importnt aspect, or perhaps the most important aspect of quality of life. For example, Cornelia, B.F. (1999) found that change in interpersonal relations appear to contribute more heavily to satisfaction with quality of life than does either socioeconomic status or social participation. Who found that quality of life is not related of living, having choices is the productive work that you do is the most important dimension of quality of life. However, on environment aspect, rural development is most effective in increasing quality of life when it can increase diversity, both in the environment and in the economy,which can increase social capital, the norms and networks that provide for a collective identity and mutual respect. It can also increase standard of living. Efforts need to promoted standard of quality of life may have.

II. What is the difference between the quality of life
and standard of living.

In fact, every American community with the problem of balancing environment growth with the need to maintain environmental and social health. For example, efficient agriculture to businesses get information about new technologies to present pollution. Increasing role of quality of life and standard of living took place in countries all over the world, especially nowadays, when numerous affects of the global crisis are felt all over the world. Emerging crisis caused many problems. thereby, in the current situation, it is interesting to examine the level of the quality of life and standard of living. After short overview of general development of concepts of standard of living and quality of life. The different indicators can measure quality of life or standard of living include GDP per capita, shopping basket, GFK basket, households' expenditures, poverty rate, income inequality, life satisfaction and happiness etc. indicators. The measures show an increase in the standard of living and quality of life. Hence, if the result showed the standard of living and quality of life. The high level of human development and the results of the level of satisfaction imply that human are moderately satisfied with their lives and enjoy a rather high level of happiness.

Standard of living and quality of life have been concerning issues in countries for many years, especially nowadays, when numersous effects of the global crisis are felt all over the world. The financial security and prosperity of the economic systems disappeared. The economic storm caused rising unemployment, falling incomes, increasing rates of poverty and declines in overall well-being. Thereby, in the current situation, it is interesting to examine quality of life and standard of living. However, standard of living is defined and the level of welfare available to individual or to the group of people. It concerns products and services, people are able to consume and the recources who have access too. It depends on the quality and quantity of available products and services and the way who are distributed within the population. Otherwise, standard of living is generally determined by indicators, such as real income per person and poverty rate. Quality of life indicates to the overall welfare within a certain society, focused on enabling each member on opportunity of accomplishing objectives. Unlike the concept of standard of living, quality of life refers to not only indicators of material standard, but also to various subjective factor that influence human lives, such as natural environment pollution challenges. However, in the estimation of standard of living and quality of life their are used two types of measures, objective and subjective indicators. Objective indicators are used to determine and to explain the economic segment, when subjective indicators are used as a descriptive indicator of the noneconomic segment of quality of life and standard of living.

Many researchers were done in the field of economics, psychology, clinicial medicine, health care, phiolsophy and social science to measure whether which kind of factors can cause human quality of life to be poor. The understanding of the concepts passed through a long period of evolution. Human need natural resources have enough supply to able to satisfy their needs. It concerns the physical circumstances, such as natural environment in which people live, the products and service who are able to consume and the resources who have access to. So, the good quality of life which depends on the quantity and quality of available products and services and their distribution within the population. Otherwise, the idea of standard of living requires a macro perspective and it is generally measured by standards, such as real income per person and poverty rate. The most common measure is national output per capita, measured such as GDP or GDP per capita. Other measures, such as income inequality and life satisfaction are also used. So, it can be feeling of human intangible measure, psychological feeling to measure quality of life to human. It seems that the environmental pollution can have close relationship to influence human quality of life. Thus, quality of life can be measured by objective as well as subjective indicators. One researcher, Felce and Perry (1995) who defined quality of life is as total welfare which includes objective and subjective evaluation of physical, material, social and emotional welfare, personal development and activity, all together evaluated throughout personal set of values.

III. Why environmental factor can influence traveller leisure desire to reduce

What are objective indicators of standard of living and quality of life? Objective circumstances refer to the economic and material conditions which are important aspects of the standard of living and quality of life. In the assessment, eight different indicators were used: CPI, GDP per capita, shopping basket, household's expenditures, GFIC basket, poverty rate, income inequality and HDI. However, these indicators is one number measure. It can't measure anyone's psychological feeling, such as health, safe emotion. The challenge concerns whether environmental pollution factor, such as air pollution, water pollution can cause human's health to be poor, even goes down human's quality of life and economy loss. I shall indicate some evidences to give reasons to support my conclusion why I believe that environment pollution is a factor to cause human quality of life to be poor , even it can also cause economy will encounter loss too.

In general, measure of quality of life need include human's psychological feeling indicator. I shall indicate, Hong Kong, China countries air and water environmental pollution challenges how to influence these two countries' people quality of life to be poor, even, it will cause their economy loss. Nowadays, China and Hong Kong and India and Afria are encountering health problems arising from damage to lungs, heart and blood vessels. Hong Kong and India and Afria and China e.g. Shanghai city pollution is a significant cause of premature death from cardiopulmonary disorders. Present level of pollution cause injury to the immature developing lings of children and adolescents. This damage will lead to life-long health problems in many and a reduction in life-expectancy. Although, there is no evidence from analyses of trends in pollutants that pollution measures in recent years have reduced pollutant concentrations in a way which will benefits public health.

There are clear indicators that for some pollutants. The problem is worsening. In fact, air and water pollution is Hong Kong and China and Afria etc. developing countries' the biggest cause of social and environmental injustice. It harms not only citizens today, but because its transquenerational effects on the urborn and youngest members of the society, it will cause its will health effects well into the later years of this century, even environmental pollution challenge will cause these countries will encounter economy loss.

Human activities have created forms of air and water pollution, such as gases from fuels, uncontrolled emissons from fossil fuels and other chemical sources have long been recognized as a cause of ill health and premature death. For example, in December, 1930 year, a dense fog affected the Meuse Valley in Belgium. Beginning on December, 3 date, the fog intensified over three days and was associated with laryngeal symptoms, chest pain, coughing, and breathlessness. Some patients showed signs of pulmonary oedema. Overall 60 deaths were attributed to the episode. After a long investigation, the cause was considered to be emissions from high sulphur fuels, including suplhur dioxide and sulphuric acid.

What is the current threat to health? the migigration of air polluton following the introduction of clear air has been followed by a period of unprecedented economic development creating new forms of pollution from the combustion of fossil fuels. For example, in constrast to the relatively large tar laden particulates from burning dirty coal which caused episodes like the London city, UK. Smog , traffic pollution now genertes fine with a different size and composition and gases,such as which may cause injury to the respiratory system and the effects of other pollutants. Such as particulates and drive the formation of the secondary pollutant ozone. The effects of pollution will therefore to some extent reflect genetic, environmental lifestyle and behavioral factors to develop these distance in a population together with the existing prevalence of diseases which may be polluted. Hence, living in polluted urban environments is associated with increased levels of biological markers of inflammation compared with residence in a clean air environment. The damage is caused by air pollution manifests itself through a variety of common and recognized health problems, such as upper complaints heart and lung disease. Because of this, we can use statistical methods as well as clinical studies to detect the signal of changes in health problems and increased health care demands in the population. However, doctors had proved air or water pollution can cause these both curdiovscular or respiratory disease indirectly. Curdiovscular disease includes formation of arterial plaques, coronary artery, heart attacks, irregular heart rhythm, loss of heart rate variability, high blood pressure, stroke etc. disease. Respiratory disease includes inflammation of nasal, throat and tracheal airways with acute, lower respiratory tract inflammation and infection causing bronchitis, reduction long growth and function in young people. So, it seems environmental pollution can influence quality of life to human as well as environmental pollution and illness and poor health problem has close relationship.

On the other side, envionmental pollution can bring health risk, over it will influence social inequalities. Some researchers had found that the evidence has been compiled for six envionmental health challenges, such as air quality, housing and residential location, unintentional injuries in children, work related health risks, waste management and climate change. It seems human need to concern air and drinking water quality, waste management and climate change how to influence our environmental pollution challenge. Although, the evidence base on social inequalities and environmental risk is fragmented and data are often available for few countries only, it indicates that inequalities are a major challenge for environmental health policies. Irrespective of development status, environmental inequalities can be found in any country for which data are available. The valid for the exposure to environmental risk factor is also unequally distributed, and this unequal distribution is often related to social characteristics, such as income, social status, employment and education, even environment risk factor can influence human's quality of life.

(i) How environmental risk factor can influence different groups
However, human need to concern how environmental risk factor can influence inequally health outcomes to different groups. Such as, the first group is social determinants affect the environmental conditions of an individual and may contribute to the fact that specific individuals or population groups more often experience loss adequate or potentially harmful environmental conditions. The second group is the affected population groups could still be more exposed through e.g. the mechanism of education and health behavior. The third group is given socially disadvantaged groups could show more severe health effects of the social disadvantage is associated. The final group is social determinants affect health (what remains unclear is the relative importance of socially determined exposure to environmental risk factors). Thus, human need to concern our behavior can lead environmental pollution to influence poor health to alive. Even, we can not neglect how to protect our natural environment to be clean issue. Due to environmental unhealth poor issue can lead our bodies to be unhealth and to be ill and we have no health to

work to influence our job inefficiency and low productivity if we often need to see doctor to raise workload to my staffs often. Then, our employers will be probable to dismiss and many unhealth employee will lose jobs and unemployment ratio will raise and DP will reduce, it will influence our economic growth . Hence, we can not neglect environmental justice and environmental inequity issue, e.g. indoor air pollution and occupational or exposure to environmental tobacco smoke pollution exposure to high traffic roads or to industrial plants pollution in our society.

(ii) How Afria country environmental pollution influences

Surprisingly, most of above countries , among of them, although Africa is a green and natural environmental country, but Africa has encounted poor natural environmental quality to influence it has poor quality of life to its citizen and poor economy growth to its society both. Why does Africa encounter this natural environmental pollution challenge? Afican have now two potential sources of pollution: consumption and production . This looks reasonable to Africa, since maintenance is completely dedicated to improving the environment, when production generates pollution only as a " by product". Capital implies the possibility of a country being trappical in an economent poverty trap by both a bad environment and low longevity. Some countries (or regions) may even experience other time, both environmental degradation and decay in expectancy. The fact that, in some cases, environmental degradation doesn't imply lower longevity may be due to the fact that economic growth might , at the same time, worsen environmental quality, but generate additional resources that can help increasing (or preserving) longevity. However, these is also evidence of countries where environmental degradation is associated with a reduction in life expectancy. It seems worsen environmental quality will influence any country's economic growth and poor quality of life both. For example, McMichael et al. (2004) identify 40 countries that experienced a loss in longevity between 1990 year and 2001 year (26 between 1980 year and 2001), they also support that the resulting world divergence in terms of life expectancy might be explained by ".... (the growing) health risks consequent on large-scale environmental changes is caused by human pressur, by both bad environment and low longevity, biodiversity and sustainable energy".

(iii) How human adult consumption and environmental quality influences future environment for human survival probability of life expectancy.

I shall assure human adult consumption and environmental quality has relationship to influence the future environment (green preferences) to provide human survival probability, it depends on inherited environmental quality. Thus, human will increase or decrease in the survival probability when we need a higher or lower life expectancy. In general, we depend on these environmental conditions to live, which include quality of water, air and soils etc. and resource availability, biodiversity, forestry, fisheries etc.

It is interesting to analyze different possible strategies to escape from the environmental poverty trap as well as factors that could push some economies back to a low equilibrium characterized. To research whether environment factor has relationship to influence human quality of life. We need to give idea of explaining whether environmental care has relationship to an uncertain lifetime. However, I suppose that an environmental kind of factor can be instead of being defined in terms of GDP per capita, capital accumulation etc. economic factors. Poverty is now related to environmental quality. It should be clear, however, I focus only on one specific mechanism lying behind environmental traps. Just as under development traps may be related to a wide variety of factors, ranging from financial to technological ones, including human capital accumulation and life expectancy. So, I should use this assumption to explain why it has relatively between environmental quality and life expectancy.

This " synthetic" indicator (YCELP, 2006) indicated environmental health is defined by child morality, indoor air polluton, drinking water, adequate sanitation and urban particulates and ecosystem vitality that includes factors like air quality, water and productive natural resources, A key ingredient of our setting is that survival until the last period is probabilistic and depends on the inherited quality of the environments. This survival probability affects the weight of the future environmental quality in human's utility function to achieve interest aim. Final stage, human will have optimal choices depend on life expectancy: in particular, a higher probability to be alive in the third period boosts investment in the environment and reduces consumption. In this case, a given country may be caught in a high morality/poo environment if low income is associated with a deteriorated environment.

John and Pecchenino (1994) were the first to introduce the possibility of multiple identifying, case for a poverty cause characteristic by poor economic performance and environmental degradation, however, life expectancy is assumed to be exogenous and plays no role in their model.

Such as soils deterioration are the like, are all susceptible of increasing human morality (thus reducing longevity). So, the existence of both environmental performance and longevity, with countries being concentrated around two levels of environmental quality and life expectancy respectively. The two-way causes are between the environment and longevity. If the causal relationship between environmental quality and life expectancy involves the existence of an environmental poverty, characterized by both bad environmental conditions and short life expectancy.

Human life stage will encounter generations of three periods to get utility from consumption and environmental quality. During adulthood, when all relevant decisions are taken, adult can work and allocate their income between consumption and investment in environmental maintenance: consumption involves deterioration of the future quality of the environment (through pollution and/or resource depletion) when maintenance helps to improve it. The dynamics of environmental quality may also be affected by external factors on more resourced communities. The most importance, unhealthy physical environments across the region adversely affect everyone, ever though who are likely to be most concentrated in more burdened community which also have less social power to change those environments.

Why life expectancy and the environment has close relationship to influence quality of life? Life expectancy and environmental quality dynamics are jointly determined. Human may invest in environmental quality, depending on how much , we expect to live. However, environmental conditions affects life expectancy. In particular, some countries may encounter in a low life expectancy / low environmental quality. This outcome is consistent with stylized facts relating life expectancy and environmental performance measures. Some expects to live longer, who would be willing to invest more in environmental quality, because who feel which have causal link between life expectancy and environmental quality. However, environmental quality is a very important factor affecting health and morbidity: air and water pollution, depletion of natural resources and quality of life.

(iv) Why social and physical environmental factors have close relationship to influence economic growth

I shall indicate reasons to explain why social and physical environmental factors have close relationship to influence economic growth, even human health of quality of life. The social and economic burdens of poor education, lack of affordable housing and less than self sufficient income affect, not just those individuals and families who have the fewest resources. The social gradient means that not only do whose in the bottom worse health outcomes to bottom of income group and the top income group whose will have poor quality of life influence. The higher rates of disease and disability and lesser productivity among many communities means a higher public and private burden of life years, particularly life expectancy once one reaches age 65. In recent decades, research and has increasingly shown how powerfully social and economic conditions determine population health and differences in health among subgroups, much more so than medical care. It seems that environmental factor can influence human's quality of life.

Los Angeles Country Department Of public Health (2016) indicated a country health rankings model, this department explained these three health factors can cause this health outcomes. These health factors include health behaviors (30%), it includes tobacco use, diet and exercise, alcohol use, unsafe sex; clinical care (20%), it includes access to care, quality of care; social and economic factors (40%), it includes education, employment, income, family and social support, community safety; physical environmental factor (10%) , includes natural environmental quality, built environmental quality. Then these factors can cause this health outcomes, such as morality (length of life):50% and morbidity (quality of life) :50%. SO, it implies that physical environmental factor can influence human's length of life. So, on our social environmental problems result is from a complex interplay of a number of forces. An individual's health –related behaviors , particularly diet, exercise and smoking, surrounding physical environment and health care (both access and quality) all contribute significantly to how long and how well human love. However , none of these factors is as important to population health as are the social and economic environments in which human live, learn, work and play. We refer to these factors can be as the social determinants of health to influence our quality of life. How do social determinants affect our quality of life? In the late

19th and early 20th centuries, public health concentrated particularly on the physical environment. Improvements in, for example, clean water supplies, healthier housing, sanitation, workplace safety and safe food lead to sharp increases in average life expectancy . Also our quality of life needed to be concentrated on expanded access to medical care, resulting in further expansion. So, the poverty tap is now characterized by those elements, such as low levels of : (i) environmental quality, (ii) life expectancy and (iii) human capital.

In fact, environmental degradation can have a significant impact on human health. De Hollander et. al (1999) & Melse & De Hollander (2001) showed that estimates of the share of environment, related human health loss are as high 5% for high income countries, 8% for middle income countries and 13% for low income countries. Air pollution and exposure to hazardous chemicals are important causes of the related burden of disease in countries. The transport and energy sectors are major contributors to air pollution, when important sources of chemical pollution are agriculture industry and waste disposal. Opportunities for reducing environment-related health risks are considerable. The benefits of many environment policies in terms of reduced health care costs and increased productivity significant exceed the costs of implementing those policies. So, the impact of environmental risk factors on health are extremely varied and complex. For example, the effects of environmental degradation on human health can range from death caused by cancer, due to air pollution to psychological problems resulting from noise. So it implies environmental factor can influence our quality of life in our societies. However, many factors can also influence human's health of a population, including diet, sanitation, socio-economic status, literacy and lifestyle.

De Hollander et. al. (1999) & Melse and De Hollander (2001) showed that total burden of disease, with estimated environment-related share expenditure, mid-1990 year. The average income group has 15 daily/1000 capita, the middle income group has 20 daily/1000 capita, the high income group has 10 daily/1000 capita. As regards both total burden of disease and the health conditions related to environmental; degradation. The result indicates the environment –related share of the burden of disease is greatly dependent on income, with higher-environmental shares generally occurring in lower-income countries.

On the one hand, it seems the large environmental share of health problems is primarily, due to factors related to poverty, such as limited to access to proper food, housing, health care and drinking water. Environmental determinants of human health in developing or developed countries are related. On the other hand, those to the exposure to air pollutants (particularly in urban areas and chemicals in the environment than to poor living conditions. Also sources of human exposure to chemicals are many and varied. Chemicals can reach the environments, for example, through emissions from industries, anti-fouling paints on marine vessels, pesticides in agriculture, waste incineration and leakage from waste disposal sites. When emissions of chemicals from industries and other point sources of pollution have lead to poor quality of life, source of chemical exposure. Intensive agricultural production uses chemicals in pesticides and fertilizer and in feed additives and medication for livestock. Residues remain in fruit, grains, vegetables, meats and daily products, all of which can reach the consumer.

Other sources of chemicals in food include bio-accumulative chemicals in the environment, such as heavy metals and persistent organic pollutants, which can be found in fish, meat and dairy products. So, environment pollution can influence human need to eat bad or unhealthy food to cause we have poor quality of life to live, such as the high income group or middle income group or low income group of families in our societies fairly. Other human health risks that have recently received considerable attention include unsafe livestock feeding practices through which toxins reach the food chain unintentionally. Dioxins that have accidentally contaminated poultry feeds that contain diseased animal remains can cause the so-called " mad cow disease" in livestock which has been linked to a new form of disease. The effects on health from exposure to chemicals and air pollutants vary from allergies to cancer. Although, the link between exposure and disease is often not clear, Even at low exposure levels, urban are pollutants can cause, asthma, allergies, respiratory diseases and cardiovascular disease if the exposure is continuous or long term. Heavy metals have been shown to cause neurological disorders and various cancers. In addition to , physical diseases, environmental contamination can also cause psychological problems. Noise, one of the determinants of the quality of urban life can have an impact on human health, decreasing the quality of life and potentially contributing to depression.

For Ireland, UK country example, this country politicians and policy makers believe the role of environment can be used to measure quality of life, concerning on either in its own right or relative to economic and social aspects of quality of life. Agreement on what measures quality of life and how it can be measured by the role of environment, not just in Ireland, but everywhere. The conventional approach is used for policy has been to use measure of gross domestic product(GDP) or regional valued added. However, it is acknowledged that such conventional economic measures have only a partial relationship with societal wellbeing. To the extent that economic measures are related to public products and consumption, there are also pressing issues in relation to public products and the sustainability of economic growth. However, the role of environmental factor can influence resource use and human's behavioral consumption.

Aspects to quality of life other than income include the environment, freedom, health, working condition, leisure, social and family relationship. Economists don't deny that these factors do play a role in quality of life. However, environment factor can be one role to influence other factors to influence our quality of life to be good or bad effect. For example, locations which might be desirable as paces to life (in terms of income earning opportunities or other factors) were also likely to have higher costs of living, particularly with regard to house prices or health or unhealthy air/ water pollution of environment situation of the place to provide human to live. Alternatively, social indicators are based on normative ideals of literacy, low rates of premature mortality or a quality environment. Other measurement of people's personal evaluation of their quality of life, much depends on personal expectations and experience.

(v) How environmental factor can influence any country's house price.

I shall indicate that why environmental factor will influence any country's house price. For Ireland example, citizen average incomes and higher in the east of the country, house prices are lower in the west, who are also more able to afford a property of choices. There are more opportunities to purchase houses, where people own their own houses, who are more likely to have benefits from an appreciation is its value and to consequently perceive a higher degree of health. Generally, levels of property appreciation have been higher in the east. Unfortunately, young people and the more economically active segment of the population are more likely to be faced with rising entry level house prices and the prospect of large borrowings. So, the quality of life, such as education, crime and access to healthcare and living environment are not uniformly better in the west or the east regions. Indeed, many measures of social disadvantage are at their worst in the west regions. Some indicators of environmental quality are , indeed better in the west regions, but there are others, such as drinking-water quality or recreational access that are often worse.

Comparisons can often be reduced to an urban-rural dimension rather than a regional one. Factors such as incomes, house prices, crime levels, air pollution and congestion are all likely to be higher in urban areas in Ireland city, UK country. Why environment and housing price has relationship in Ireland to influence quality of life to its citizen? If Ireland's regional development policy is successful , it will bring with it greater competition in the housing market and greater pressures on the environment in Ireland. Because the forest will be decreased to build house, the natural environment will become wood and steel and stone of housing built environment. In fact, it appears that there is a fair of amount of agreement on the relative rating of factors influencing quality of life. Ability to own one's home and security of income were needed, but respondents also placed almost equal important on clean air and drinking water, low crime were differences. The Ireland's rural respondents appeared to place a slightly greater emphasis on key natural environmental attributes, when urban residents valued absolute incomes and social or leisure activity rather more.

In this respect, the analysis identifies three components to Ireland people of quality of life, each of which was evident in all three locations. There components can be broadly described as domestic security, social/leisure and aspects of the planned environment. The first of these includes indicators, such as security of income, absolute income, house ownership and low crime. As this component includes air and drinking-water quality, it suggests that these indicators may be associated with personal health and well-being. When the planned environment component includes those attributes that affect quality of life over which the authorities have a direct influence, for instance, a clean environment, traffic and reducing vehicle numbers on the roads in busy time.

(vi) How environmental pollution can influence social welfare

Environmental quality has an undefined impact on quality of life and various indicators are used to show regional variations in aspects, such as water quality . There are many measures of environmental quality , but is only for quality of life. Moreover, the measurement of societal welfare is important. Societal welfare is not simply , the sum of the parts, but varies depending on the individual in which people find themselves at any time in their life. In principle, it should be possible to apply weights to each element of societal welfare, but as preferences for each of these vary within the population. In the absence of a method with which everybody is satisfied, GNP and GDP are typically the most popular used measures for quality of life or standard of life. But, these are problems with the data itself to measure quality of life because quality of life is feeling or satisfaction of level to the country's citizen and it can not be seen by numbers or statistic method. For example, GDP ignores household production, such as the effort that goes into the rearing of children, the benefits that this provides for society and the public expenditure that is avoided. Neither are costs treated equally with the benefits. GDP counts all economical activities irrespective on pollution appears to increase. GDP even through it is a degree of double counting. Otherwise, environmental products are good to be measured to quality of life. For example, many environmental products are unpriced. Consequently, environmental products that people value, or which are critical to the sustainability of development, are abused or depleted because of their public products have good characteristics and the absence of a market price signal.

Environmental economists try to work within the economic model to measure quality of life. Rather than questioning the link between utility and consumption or choice, the preferred approach is to add an element into the utility function that represents the value of environmental products or the stock of natural capital. By one means or another , the preservation value of these environmental products is estimated in terms of willingness to pay to protect the environment or as willingness to forego other products in return. It seems the quality of people's environment can be represented by objective indicators. At another, their interpretation will vary and can be represented by subjective indicators.

Objective indicators come in two forms: (i) economic indicators and (ii) social indicators. The former depends on an ability to select the products and services that are desires, in other words, the satisfaction of preferences . The economic argument is that people select the best quality of life, who can obtain commensurate with their resources and personal desires. By comparison, social indicators are based on normative ideals on what could be considered the food life. For example, would be infant morality, literacy, crime rates and social indicators are objective measures. Both have guided, much of the research on quality of life, particularly concerning with the urban environment. Quality of life can include natural a significant influence on local quality of life, for instance, natural beauty spots used for recreation.

Quality of traveler individual leisure need reducing

For environmental quality concept, it concerns with health, safety, wellbeing, residential satisfaction and the physical sustainability can be considered to result from an when live ability can be considered to represent the interaction between the physical and the social domains. As with expenditure on the environment, investment in social capital contributes to quality of life. However, the benefits will again vary amongst individuals, depending largely on the security of their individual circumstance. As with the environment, the government can certainly adopt strategies that provide for public security by taking measures to reduce crime, a measure likely to be appreciated by everybody (except criminal) , at least to one degree or another. In other necessary to enhance social interaction, namely community centers or sports facilities. Furthermore, the creation of social capital has an statement which responds to general social trends to raise Ireland citizen's quality of life.

I shall indicate Ireland to explain whether environmental factor is the main factor to influence our quality of life and economic growth. Is environmental quality higher in the Ireland west regions? And if so, does this compensate for lower incomes in these regions? Is it bad that rural areas are characterized by higher costs of living in areas other than housing by environmental factor? In fact, in Ireland , UK country, population increase has a direct impact on the environment by placing demands on local natural resources, particularly open space and water. It also leads to a sense of crowding that reduces the utility associated with access to the environment. How can environment factor influence economy growth in Ireland? In Ireland, agriculture has gone through a period of significant change that has been accelerated reductions in the amount of mixed cropping and traditional land management. Indeed, changes in the expectations of young farmers will ensure that further change is likely to be characterized by increases in farm size and greater specialization with implications for landscape and wildlife. These characteristics of farm holdings are more familiar in the east regions of Ireland , UK country. As with likely to extend to the west regions as the older generation of farmers retires, although this will probably be accompanied by a trend to more farming of production needs to young farmers. So, good natural environment can provide Ireland young farmers to produce more agriculture to earn income, even who can export more rice, fruits, vegetable etc. agriculture foods to overseas. Hence, Ireland GDP will be raise if it can have good natural resource environment to provide Ireland young farmers to grow foods to sell to domestic and /or foreign agricultural market. Given the rate of economic growth, and its concentration in the east of the Ireland, UK country, it would be easy to presume that the quality of the environment is higher the further away from the mid east one goes. Thus, good natural environment is an important factor to influence the farming industry development in Ireland , UK county to satisfy their needs and to raise their quality of life nowadays.

I shall indicate New Zealand and America two developed countries to explain why which are facing environmental pollution challenge to influence their citizen's quality of life and economic growth nowadays. The first country is NZ, although, New Zealand is a developed and natural environmental country, but it had been envountering air pollution annouance and noise annoyance to influence it's citizen's health-related quality of life. I shall indicate why which has this relationship between of them in New Zealand. Nowadays, New zealand population growth is an increasing demand for consumer products and urbanization have lead to concerns over the lived environments in many of the world's cities, such as Auckland, wellington cities in New Zealand. However, environmental quality is an important determinant of health, such as the bad influence of traffic-related air and noise pollution on health outcomes, specially with respect to at risk groups, both in relation to long term exposure as well as acute effect, from brief exposures. For example, cholesterol levels and in relation to myocardial infaction. Nowadays, New Zealand is encountering the high degree of air pollution and noise annoyance to influence it's citizen's quality of life. Air pollutants can be detected either visually, such as witnessing smoke emanating from a vehicles's exhaust, or by smell, such as when odorants stimulate olfactory receptors. The evidence linking air pollution to adverse impacts on human health.

Many air impacts on human health. Many air pollution health studies have focused specifically on urban area, and vehicle generated pollution in particular, as road vehicles are one of the major sources of pollution across much of the world. Elemental carbon, Nox and ultrafine particles an considered to be pollutants most strongly associated with road traffic emissions. In Auckland and Wellington cities, New Zealand , it has been estimated that 71% of summer and 21% of winter concentrations of fine particulate matter is attributable to motor vehicles. Moreover, poor town planning decisions in Auckland (and in New Zealand in general) over many decedes has meant that may people live in very close proximity to busy road and motorways within " road corridors" and so are the adverse effects of road traffic, including noise and air pollution as well as experiencing on potential for degradation in their quality of life. Such as, New Zealand is highly suitable for studies investigating the impact of roads on the health of its residents. For example, NZ, road traffic noise and aviation noist has been linked to cardiovascular disease, hypertension and ischemic heart disease. It influences NZ resident personal psychological and physical both health challenges. In fact, NZ noise increases morbidity and mortality independently of air pollution exposure, though air pollution constituted a greater burden of disease when arise exposure had a greater impac on quality of life, e.g. NZ road traffic noise and air pollution will be caused from drivers in busy time. Specially in Auckland and Wellington cities. It will influence urban and rural environmental pollution. Some retired old people who will feel annoyance when this road traffic occurs in Auckland or Wellington cities to close to their houses in transportation busy time every day.

Next developed country is America, this country's air pollution is also serious nowadays. Because traffic jam often occurs in New York, Washington, Boston etc. big cities in US. So, U.S. cities' parks and its trees have significant influence to produce fresh air to provide U.S. residents who are living in cities to breach for their body health. David J. & Gordon , M. (2016) indicated " In U.S. these urban parks are estimated to contain about 370 million trees with a structural value of approximately $300 billion." The number of park trees varies by region of the country, but which can produce significant air quality effects in and near parks, related to air temperatures, air pollution, ultraviolet indication and carbon dioxide (a dominant greenhouse gas related to global climate change). Additional open space and other vacant lands in cities, which may contain trees and other vegatation. Contribute significant additional benefits, effects of parks and open space at the city scale can vary significantly depending on the amount of parkland and amount of tree cover within the parkland.

The reasons why parks can reduce air pollution. Parks generally have lower air temperature than surrounding areas. Temperatures are usually cooler toward the center of a park than around its edges. At night, the center of a large park may be 13 degree cooler than surrounding city areas. The cooler air from parks often moves out into adjacent developed neighborhoods. This cooling of surrounding areas tends to increase with park size and percentage of the park covered by trees. So, cooler air temperature is provided by urban parks can have significant impacts on human health. During heat wave events, which can kill hundreds of people, park areas may provide city dwellers with some respite from high air temperture, particularly in the evening, during hot, sunny days tree shade can greatly increase human comfort. Because park influences on air temperature extend to developed areas outside of parks, local energy use for heating and cooling buildings is also effected. Although, the net around effect of parks on energy costs has been by reducing temperature is difficult to estimate at least in the southern United States the effect will usually be a net annual benefit. Futhermore, large park trees will reduce winds and may provide a benefit of winter heating of buildings near the park. Although, the overall economic effect of urban trees and parks on air temperature reduction is not fully billions of dollars annually at the national scale in terms of improved environmental quality and human health.

In fact, trees and vegetation in parks can help reduce air pollution both by directly removing pollutants and by reducing air temperatures and building energy use in and near parks. There tree effects can reduce pollutant emissions and formation. However, park vegetation can increase some pollutants by either directly emitting volatile orgnic compounds that can contribute to ocone and carbon monoxide formation or indirectly by the emission of air pollutants through vegetation maintenance practices, such as operation of chain and use of transportation fuels. David J. & Gordon , M. (2016) showed "Annual pollution removal and economic benefits by U.S. urbank park trees is estimated at about 75,000 tones ($500 million) or 80 pounds per acre of tree cover ($300 per acre of tree cover). Carton storage and annual removal by urban park trees and soils in the United States is estimated at about: carton storage trees: 75 million tons ($1.6 billion), carton storage (soils) : $102 million tons of carbon removal (trees): 2.4 million tons ($50 million)". Park management is recommended by U.S. environment protection department: considering that most of the effects of trees on microclimate and air quality are beneficial for park users and nearby residents; park designs that include a variety of land cover, areas of dense trees, scattered trees and lawn are likely to provide the greatest opportunities for optimum physical comfort of visitors; increase the number of healthy trees (increase pollution removal and carbon storage); sustain existing tree cover (maintains pollution removal levels) and (carbon storage); maximize use of low volatile organic compound emitting trees reduces ozove and carbon monoxide formation; sustain large, healthy trees (large trees have greatest per tree effcts on pollution and carbon removal); using long-lived trees (reduces long term pollutant emissions from removal; reducing fossil fuel in maintaining vegetation reduces pollutant ans carbon emissions)." So, if US had many green parks, then which can reduce air pollution, also it can assist many travellers who prefer to travel to US to raise GDP travelling income growth generally.

(i) Why environmental pollution and human right abuses has close relationship to influence quality of life and economic growth?

In fact, environment pollution and human right abuses has close relationship. It is clear that poverty situations and human rights abuses are worsened by environmental degradation. The result can influence poor human quality of life to the developing countries' people unfairly. There are these several abvious reasons: firstly, the exhaustion of natural resources leads to unemployment and emigration to cities; secondly, this affects the enjoyment and exercise of basic human rights. Environmental conditions contribute to a large extents to the spread of infections diseases. From the 4,400 million of people who live in developing countries, almost 60% lack basis health care services, a almost a third of these people have no access to safe water supply; thirdly, degradation poses new problems, such as environmental refugees. Environmental refugees suffer from significant economic, socio-cultural and political consequences. And fourthly, environmental degradation worsens existing problems suffered by developing and developed countries. David J. Nowak & Gordon M. Melsler (2016) showed" Air pollution , for example, accounts for 2.7 million to 3.0 million of deaths annually and of these 90% are from developing countries. " Hence, our societies need to concern human right law to protect unfair treatment to developing countries people. Firstly, both disciplines have deep social root, even though human rights law is more rooted within the collective consciousness, the accelerated process of environmental degradation is generating a new " environmental consciousness". Secondly, both disciplines have become internationalized . The international community has assumed the commitment to observe the realization at human rights and respect for the environment. Thirdly, both areas of law tend to universalize their object of protection. Human rights are presented as universal and the protection of the environment appears as everyone is responsibility.

Human right and environment law can raise our quality of life because the first approach is one where environmental protection is described as a possible means of fulfulling human rights standards. Here, environmental law is conceptualized as giving a protection that would help ensure the well-being of future generations as well as the survival of those who depend immediately upon natural resources for their livelihood. So, the end is fulfulling human rights, and the route is though environmental law, the second approach places the two sphere in inverted positions, it states that the legal protection of human rights is an effective means to achieving the ends of conservation and environmental protection. Therefore, the presently existing human right is as a route to environmental protection. The focus is on the connection to influence any economy: health, food supply , housing, fresh natural air supply etc. aspects of quality of life issues. Hence, human right and environment law and human quality of life and economic growth has close relationship . We can not neglect to concern how to achieve human right law to protect our nature environment existing in our societies.

What are environmental factors affect human health in important way, both positive and negative? On positive environmental factor aspect, which can sustain health, and promoting them is preventive medicine. They include : sources of nutrition (farming, oil quality, water availability, bio diversity/bio integrity, genetically modified organisms ; hurting, fishing:

wildlife, fish populations; water (drinking, cooking, cleaning,sanitation); air quality; ozone layer (protection from cancers disease etc).; space for exercise and recreation, sanitation/waste recycling and disposal. On negative environmental factors aspect, which are threats to health, and controlling them is public environmental health. They include: environmental conditions favouring disease sectors (endemic and exotic sectors); invasive biota (visuses, bacteria etc.), their hosts and sectors; environmental disruptions: floods, droughts, storms, fires earthquakes, volcanoes; air quality: pollution landing to respiratory disease or cancers; water quality: biotic and abiotic contaminants ; integrity of water transport and intrastructure; monitoring and management of municipal, agricutural, industrial outflows to the environment (gases, liquids, solid waste), human changes of the environment that: create conditions that favour disease; disturb and release noxious levels of previously bound chemicals (e.g. mercury released becomes poison) or bioto (e.g. methane released from thawed peat contributes to climate changes, create temporary, intense, life threatening heat islands (e.g. urban heat waves exacerbated by climate change); result from nuclear; biological or chemical welfare or terrorism, disruption cased by other war and violense.

(ii) What is space and environmental technology?

For example, Cananda is a developed country and it begins to concern environmental pollution challenge to announced $3 million to support the initiative strengthening health and environment linkages: from knowledge to action. The initiative will bring together scientific, technical and socio-economic information on environment and health linkages, and transfer that knowledge to inform decision-making at the local, regional and national levels. Also, Canada is principally concerned with the health of Canadians. This involves health factors in Canada and in biologically shared health regions (shared geography or exposure through trade and travel). Supports international health initiatives, such as determining health risks throught environmental analysis of disease vectors in Africa or Asia.

How can the space and environmental factors affecting health? Environmental information and environmental management contribution to the maintenance and restoration of health. Space based environmental management factors and communications can play roles in: Environmental information is for optimising use of health resources; distribution of and access to health advice and treatment (i.e. to health staff treatment facilities; short range environmental prediction for avoidance of high risk, situations and to guide immediate health system responses. Managing acute risks, adopting to them (e.g. temporary moving of vulnerable elderly monitored; modeling of health impact of environmental parameters; prediction of long term health resource needs and environmental planning and mitigation and adaptation to global changes. Large benefits are possible from attention to environmental factors, e.g. asthma prevention, disease and epidemiology. Benefits need to be quantified. This is of particular interest and relevance to pandemics , such as malasia in underdeveloped countries, potentially saving thousands of lives.

What is space and environmental technology? It can contribute to and keep abreast of environmental health forecasts (using existing models and known parameters); prepare and deliver prospectuses for what space can do in anticipation or response; steer space programs according to real risks and real accumulative health benefits, as long technical investment, don't focus primarily on threats that may have high emotional impact , but are of low actual risk; position space technology and the canadian space program in people's winds, aggressively and realistically, as a first line contributor to foresight and preduction, long term maintenance of well-being and prevention of factors of ill-health ; ongoing delivery of health services and management of current health factors and potentially capable and ready to respond in health emergencies. Finally, making the full business case for investment in space technology and space program contributions relative to the full and public and private cost of health programs. This connects not only to GDP raising, but to indicators of quality of life to any countries.

● Reference

Cornelia, B.F. (1999) Rural development news, the North Central Regional Center For Rural Development vol. no 24 , IOWA.

David J. Nowak & Gordon M. Melsler (2016) " Air quality effects of urban trees and parks." National recreation and park association, USA.

De Hollander, A. E. M., J.M. Melse, Elebret & P. G.N. Kramers (1999), " An Aggregate public health indicator to represent the impact of multiple environmental exposures" Epidemiology: 606-617.

Felce, D. and Perry, J. (1995). Quality of life: A contribution to its definition and measurement, vol. 16, no.1 pp: 51-74.

Los Angeles Country Department Of public Health (2016), Country Health Ranking Model, Retrieved From www.countryhealthrankgings.org/our-approach. USA.

Melse, J.M. & A.E. M. De Hollander (2001). " Human Health And The Environment", background document for the OECD Environmental Outlook, OECD, Paris.

McGregor, S.L. T., & Goldsmith, E.B. (1998). Expanding our understanding of quality of life, standard of living and well-being. Journal of family and consumer science, 90(2), 2-6, 22.

McMichael, A.J. M. Mckee, J. Shkolnikov and T. Valkanen (2004), " Morality trends and setbacks, global convergence or divergence?", Lancet 363, 1155-1159.

Yale Center For Environmental Law And Policy (2006). Environmental Performance Index. Data available on-line at http://epi.yale.edu

Future of sustainable resources
scarcity economic and social loss to oil industry

In economic theory, it indicates two major factors are responsible for the emergence of economic problems. They are (i) the existence of unlimited human wants and (ii) the scarcity of available resources, such as limited numbers of food and natural resource shortage. I feel that human need to solve these two problems before 2050 years. How to balance an optimization approach for human and ecological flow needs ? How to solve climate change environment problem and welfare is for the centrality of human need? Because natural environment factor and natural resource and food shortage and our social economic growth which will have close connection relationship. If natural environment is bad, it will influence a lot of crops numbers can't be grown in farms. The reason of crops shortage will be caused, due to numbers of crops supply to be reduced because bad weather can not grow much crops and overpopulation numbers will increase largely at the same time before 2050 year. It will cause the numbers of demand is more than supply seriously. The result of the prices of foods will be increased by overpopulation and food shortage, so that it will cause every country inflation will be risen, it will occur in developing countries urban areas due to which have , such as India , China, Africa etc. countries have no many farms to provide to farmers to grow foods because air and water pollution and factories are built on farm land , so which need to pay higher price to import crops and foods to provide whose overpopulation to eat from overseas developed countries. Experience of developing countries that have succeeded in the reducing hunger and malnutrition shows that economic growth doesn't automatically ensure success, the source of growth matters too. This isn't surprising since 75% of the poor in developing countries live in rural areas and their incomes are directly or indirectly linked to agriculture. Many countries will continue depending on international trade to ensure their food security. It is estimated that by 2050 year developing countries net import of rice will were than double from 135 million tones in 2008/2009 to 300 million in 2050 year. It seems overpopulation will cause developing countries foods shortages in 2050 years.

Climate change and increased biofuel production represent major risks for long term food security. Studies estimate that the aggregate negative impact of climate change on African agricultural output up to 2080 year to 2100 year could be between 15% and 30%. Agriculture will have to adapt to climate change, but it can also help mitigate the effects of climate change. A recent study estimates that continued rapid expansion of biofuel production up to 2050 year would lead to the number of pre-school children in Africa and South Asia being 3 and 1.7 million higher. Thus, policies promoting the use of food based biofuels need to be reconsidered with the aim of reducing the competition between food and fuel for scare resources. The sharp increases in food price that occurred in global and national markets in recent years, and the resulting increases in the number of hungry have sharpened the awareness of policy makers and of the general public. Hence, different countries governments need to concern safe agricultural system to avoid any foods shortage to supply after 2050 year.

The perspective for 2050 year raises a number of important questions. Are current public and private investments sufficient to ensure adequate agricultural production potential, sustainable use of natural resources, information and communication research for technological breakthroughs to avoid foods shortage for the future? What needs to be undertaken to help agricultural meet the challenges of climate change and growing energy scarcity? What can be done to ensure food security in Africa, India , China etc. developing countries. The facing highest population growth rates,. The severest impacts from climate change and the heaviest burden of HIV/AIDS etc. diseases threats.

Finally, on the changing socio-economic environment hand, the main socio-economic factors that drive increasing food demand are population growth, increasing urbanization and rising incomes. In 2007 year, the USA dept. of Economic and Social affairs indicated that in fact, the developed countries population growth is slower than developing countries. However, all of the growth in the world's population will take place in urban areas. By 2050 year, more than 70% of the world's population is expected to be urban. Thus, scientists need to concern to predict developing countries urban area people foods demand and supply both numbers whether global foods can provide enough supply to urban area people in developing countries after 2050 year. On the other side, human will concern whether there be enough natural resource base of land, water and genetic diversity to meet developing countries needs after 2050 year.

What factors cause the resources scarcity and why human need to solve the resources scarcity before 2050 year

In comparison to the past 50 years, the rate at which pressure are building up on natural resources-land, water, bio-diversity will be increasing during the coming 50 years. An expanded use of agricultural feedstock for biofuels and ongoing environment degradation would work in the opposite direction. Much of the natural resource base already in use worldwide shows degradation . These include capture fisheries and water supply . In addition, actions to other ecosystem services, such as the ecosystem service, food production often cause the degradation of others, soil nutrient depletion, erosion, desertification, deflection of freshwater reserves, loss of tropical forest and biodiversity are clear indicators.

Whether natural resource base should be adequate to meet the future demand at global level. Whether any developing countries should still limit commercial natural resource import capacity to let rural area population to use to protect whose domestic natural industry development when rural area population will be increasing seriously in 2050 year. Biodiversity, another essential resource for agricultural and food production is threatened by urbanization , deforestation, pollution and the conversion of wetlands. As a result of agricultural modernization, changes in diets and population density, humankind increasingly depends on a reduced amount to agricultural biological diversity for its food supplies.Thus major reforms and investments are needed in all regions to cope with rising scarcity and degradation of land, water and biodiversity and with the added pressures resulting form rising incomes, climate change and energy demands.

There is a need to establish the right incentives to protect agriculture's environmental services to protect biodiversity and to ensure food production using new agricultural technologies before 2050 year. For the developing countries, in order to ensure that resources are available in the required quantity and quality and in the urban locations where they are needed, large additional investments need to be made in order to avoid rural people of hunger coincides with resource scarcity before 2050 year. Increased investment incentives and provided stable production growth incentives : land, water and biodiversity of three natural resources. The aim should be to stop over-exploitation, degradation and pollution, promote efficiency gains and expand overall capacities as appropriate . To provide the rural population engaging in ecosystem services with win-win solution to improve the sustainability of ecosystems, mitigate climate change and improve rural incomes. Whether and under what conditions the estimated future food demand can be met and how food security can be achieved. Hence, every country needs to have an effective economy system to attempt to solve the basic economic problems. The function of the economy is to allocate scarce resources among unlimited wants. Moreover, every country needs to have effective economic system to study of its citizen behavior in relation to how scarce resources to allocated and how choices are made between alternative uses of the country government's limited expenditure. Due to our earth has scarce resources, it implies human will scarce natural resources to provide us to use. Our governments need to predict whether what our earth's limited natural resources will be all used in order to solve our natural resources to be used in the short time quickly as well as our governments need to apply effective economic system to design soluble methods to avoid our earth will be not to provide any natural resources to satisfy our daily essential needs in one day.

The average U.S. resident , in a year, consumes 275 pounds of meats, uses 635 pounds of paper and uses energy equivalent to 7.8 metric tons of oil. Before, long years ago, the average American ate 197 pounds of meat, used 366 pounds of paper and used energy equivalent to 5.5 metric tons of oil. In the U.S. there is about one passenger car for every two people. Otherwise, Europeans have about one passenger car for every 3.1 people. On the other side, Developing countries have on average, about one passenger car for every 49 people. What does economics have to tell us about these differences in consumption?

Consume sovereignty means the idea that consumer's needs and wants determine the shape of all economic activities. Is this belief valid? That is are the final goals of economic activity all to be found in the act of consumption. Hence, if one day, our earth scarce any kinds of natural resources to be caused shortage, e.g. water, air, oil, land , gas, solar, gas , unclear , wind energy resources as well as foods e.g. vegetables and meats etc. eating resources. Due to human numbers are increasing, such as China, India and Africa etc. developing countries' people numbers are increasing much than the USA, UK etc. developed countries 's people numbers every year. But, our earth's vegetables and pigs, cows, sheet etc. meats foods numbers are decreasing every year. I believe that our foods and vegetables and natural energy resources prices will be influenced to be rose too much due to human demands (wants) are excessive to compare to our earth natural energy resources and meats and vegetables foods supply numbers. On the other side ,if every country's inflation will be increasing , but our salaries will be decreasing, or our salaries will be kept to stable and no changing, even employers will decide to dismiss employees to cause unemployment ratio rising. In result, global consumers' shopping ability will be falling down and crime numbers will be rising by poor, such as developing countries, e.g. Africa, China, India etc. will have many people feel hungry, or who feel diseases , even who will be sick to die from diseases or will be kill to die by crimes. Also , these other factors include foods scarcity, foods and natural energy prices rising, working and home environment pollution etc. factors , these factors can then cause global economic poor , serious inflation ,unbalance incomes reallocation between rich and poor people, discrimination and unfair threat will be caused between countries, even , the war between countries will be caused. Hence, our governments need to concern how to solve our earth natural energy resources and foods and vegetables scarcity challenge , due to which will be caused shortage to supply to human to consume to use or eat in the future on day occurrence. Thus, above reasons can be concluded that as below:

Nowadays, the numbers of human (every country people) are increasing more than just the increasing numbers of consumers' consumption activities , such as our daily essential consumption include meats and vegetables etc. foods and natural energy resources, such as lands, water, gas, oil, wind, water, nuclear, electricity etc. energy . Moreover, natural resources and foods numbers are decreasing due to overpopulation are increasing in developing countries and the numbers of emigration are rising to developing countries, such as UK, USA, France, Germany poor people numbers are increasing due to war or poor issues occur in the developing countries. Moreover, due to the provision consumption activities are most directly address living standard (or lifestyle) goals, which have to do with satisfying basic needs and getting pleasure through the use of natural resources energy provision service demand and vegetables and foods tasty demand by the developed countries' people needs . Also, these poor issues will occur in the developing countries possibly in the future. Due to these factors, I predict our essential consumption , such as foods, vegetables and natural energy resources service provision price will be increasing in global competitive market due to foods and vegetables and energy shortage will be caused by the overpopulation demands rising up and foods and natural energy resources supply numbers falling down factors. Hence, our governments must need to find methods to solve the problem of our essential natural resources shortage and foods scarcity issues occurrence in the future.

Suggestions to solve resources scarcity methods

● Estimation of growth of rural population and income and expected changes of natural resources supply numbers

I recommend developing countries need to estimate growth of rural population and incomes numbers and expected changes numbers in consumption patterns . Taking into account developing countries' known resource capacities and projected development of yields, input use and technologies and making assumptions about their future trading capacity, estimates are also make of future food production level, land use and natural resource numbers import trade demand of developing countries estimation before 2050 year.

Estimation of water natural resources, such as water scarcity agreement on key definitions, the conceptualization of water scarcity in ways that are meaningful for policy development and decision making, the quantification of water scarcity, policy and technical response options available to ensure food security in conditions of water scarcity, criteria and principles that should be used to establish priorities for action to response to water scarcity in agriculture and ensure effective and efficient water scarcity copying strategies. Thus, developing countries will concern to reduce water resources shortage risk. Why is predict water supply important?

During the twentieth century, large multi-purpose dams have served the needs of agriculture, energy and growing cities, and helped protect population from flood hazards. On farm water conservation, particularly the adoption of agricultural practices that reduce runoff to increase the infiltration and storage of water in the soil in rained agriculture is the most relevant local supply enhancement option that farmers have to increase foods production by increasing water availability and decentralized water harvesting conveniently in rural areas for farmers needs. For example, ground water exploitation has grown or in scale. Ground water's capability to provide flexible, on demand water in support of irrigation has been as a major advantage by farmers in rural areas. Thus, farmers need to learn how to reduce water losses increase water productivity and water re-allocation to avoid natural resource of water shortage after 2050 year.

● Renewable natural resources and foods planting sustainability development

The concept of sustainability has become the current answer to absolving our earth of its environment and economic crises in the 21 ST. century. On the one side, the pessimists, usually ecologists and other scientists, who are convinced the earth can't forever support the different countries' demand of renewable and non renewable resources. On the other side, are the optimists, the economists, who are equally convinced that the earth, with market incentives, appropriate public policies, material substitution, recycling and new technology can satisfy the needs and improve the quality of human welfare. Both views are supporting arguments are explored used and sustainable development. Thus, renewable old energy natural resource can keep old energy natural resource to renew to use or research other new energy resource to substitute old natural resource, it will reduce the risk of energy resource shortage if the other new natural resource can be substituted to the old natural energy resource to use in our daily life , such as inventing one kind of new energy resource can be used to substitute gas to drive cars or drive boats or plans or the old gas can be renewed or cycled to use to drive cars or boats or the oil can be renewed or cycled to use to cook. Also, our earth foods, e.g. fruits, vegetables or meats etc. foods if which can be recopied to grow many numbers planting foods from any one kind food or many kinds of foods, such as one meat can be copied to manufacture two to three same kind tasty meats or unlimited same kind tasty meats. I believe the renewable natural resource energy or recopied foods can reduce our foods or energy shortage after 2050 year.

The application of sustainable strategy
between local and national and regional

of international countries

A redefined concept is of the society as whole system, made up of three concentric circles: the economy is found within the society, and both the economy and society exist within the environment. Sustainability indicators are therefore said to attempt to measure the extent to which these boundaries are respected.

I think sustainability measure as a whole concept environment, society and economy. At the bottom of the triangle is the environment or the ultimate means which represents natural resources as a precondition for decent human life. The economy (which includes technology, politics and ethics) is on the next, is not independent but serves as a vehicle for achieving ultimate ends. At the top is equity or society or ultimate end which refers to the wellbeing of the human being.

According to Daly(1990) who indicated "that the economy therefore succeeds to the extent that it conserves and restores ultimate means the environment, and enables the achievement of ultimate ends society equity. This is the application of sustainable strategies to local, national and regional issues, as well as the role of international agencies in local /national strategies." Our earth occurs issues of overpopulation, diseases and political conflict, developed countries also have to deal with problems, such as pollution and unlimited urban expansion with limited resources. Sustainability is the process suggested to improve the quality of human life within the limitations of global environment. It involves solutions for improving human welfare that doesn't result in regarding the environment. We(human) need to concern living within certain limits of the earth's capacity to maintain life, understanding the interconnections among economy, society and environment and maintaining a fair distribution of foods and vegetables and natural energy resources and opportunity for this generation and the next. Thus, on the one side, our governments need to concern three categories: Social/ political, environmental and economic issues are interconnection. Social issues include poverty, consultation, empowerment and culture. Environmental issues include pollution, natural resources and biodiversity/ resilience and economic issues include efficiency, growth and stability. It seems our governments need to considerate social and environment and economic issues to reduce our natural energy resources and foods and vegetables to allocate to let every country people to use fairly.

Reducing global warming and biodiversity
issue occurrence

It seems that we need to know our society will influence our natural environment good or bad. If our society damaged our natural environment, then it will be possible to influence our foods supply of decreasing numbers. e.g. fishes, pigs, cows, sheep and vegetables and fruits etc. foods . Due to bad climate and air and lands and ocean pollution can influence foods can not be grown easily and successfully in farms or fishes can not be lived healthy in ocean. Then, it will cause our meats, fruits and vegetables etc. foods supply shortage. Even, our gas , oil, water etc., natural resources will cause our oceans and lands pollution if human pollute our oceans and lands. In result, our natural resources used numbers will be reduced due to clean lands and oceans are polluted for long time. Finally, natural resources and meats and vegetables and fruits , rice etc. foods prices will be risen due to which are shortage to supply and developing countries' population numbers are increasing which will cause more demand.

Finally, it shall cause many developing countries' poor people who can't eat enough meats, fruits, rice vegetables etc. foods as well as who can't use enough natural resources to attempt to adapt whose past normal daily life, such as lacking enough oil to help them to cook foods to be heat to eat at home or lacked enough water to be boiled to drink. Even, whose health will be poor , then who get diseases to cause die easily when there is no enough oil to buy or enough water to drink. Hence, these developing countries governments need to concern foods and natural resource scarcity problems which will be occurred if who do not find methods to reduce this issue to be occurred after 2050 year.

As Erekson et. al.(1999) concerns about" loss of resources, such as biodiversity or global weather (climate) warming are pacified with the potential of new technology which will lead to greater investments to the future generations for alternative resources and welfare."

Hence, I recommend our governments need to concern global warming or biodiversity issue because of our foods and vegetables and natural resources, such as water, air will be possible polluted to be caused shortage quickly if our earth's global warming or biodiversity issue occurrence to cause our earth's large oceans or lands areas to be polluted. Our governments can attempt to control natural resources , such as oil, gas, water supply into the market and not though the political special conditions to keep them, without considering the political and social standings, which rule the control power and the use of those resources. Such as developed countries can be able to minimize the impact of foods or/and natural resources production and consumption over the natural resources, they are only mechanisms built within an economic rationality, which should be possible to control its people's demand of natural resources, e.g. oil, gas, water and supply of natural resources get more balance. Then these natural resources sale price won't be raised more every year. When there developed countries' people , such as American and Britain who can control to reduce to spend to use the excessive natural resources too much in any time and any place habitually. Then , I believe the developing countries' governments e.g. Africa, China, India, which can buy those developed countries governments' excessive natural resources to raise those developed countries' natural resources supply numbers to provide to whose people to use as well as the most important benefit is that developed countries can gain foreign income from excessive natural resources expectation. Then, these governments will raise GDP economic growth. Hence, if developed countries could control whose people consume natural resource numbers and they could also control to produce natural resource supply numbers . Then, they can gain more excessive natural resources export chance to achieve to raise GDP economic growth aim for long term. As Kirkby et al., (1995)explained "the complexity of sustainable development our natural environment. If our governments can let our earth natural environment gets creation to maintenance, then our natural environment will be reduced the time to degradation. In the long time result, our society rural and urban economy will be growth , then our different countries' global growth will be caused diversity." Hence, it seems different countries' governments need to concern sustainable development to our natural environment .

How to apply agricultural green bio-economy
concept to solve control sustainable food
consumption and production in a resource-
constrained world

Nowadays, challenges for the global food supply have never been so complex. Between now and 2050 year, it has been predicted that growth in the global population and changing diets in developing countries, special in India and China and Africa etc. developing countries which may lead to an increase of around 70% in food demand. At the same time, depletion of fossil hydrocarbons will increase the demand for biomass for biofuels and industrial materials. Hence, developed and developing countries' governments ought need to coordinated to reduce air and water pollution and approached to lands use planning and oceans use planning to supply enough farms to grow potatoes, vegetables, tomatoes, fruits and let cows, pigs, sheep etc. animals can have comfortable and clean farm to live to produce good tasty meats to provide human to eat as well as to reduce pollution to supply fresh and clean water to let fishes to be lived and provides to human to drink clean water. Due to overpopulation will be predicted by scientists after 2050 year, so it will be caused foods and energy shortage possibly. Hence, different countries' governments need have long term perspectives to prepare to have enough foods and energy supply to provide us to eat and use for our earth with resource constraints and environmental limits, and which includes guideline on agricultural research to achieve foods supply aim.

On the one hand, I believe the knowledge-based bio-economy can play in realizing there challenges in particular the balance demand between foods, feed and fuel and the strategic role new technologies can have upon developing a sustainable an green bio-economy. On the other hand, I also think production of the presently high resource dependence and to build more environmentally begin sustainable agriculture system able to feed 9 billion people by 2050 year. I recommend global governments need to concern all aspects of food security including the total food chain and impacts of other land-use and management as well as non food areas, research areas which can be closed to free resources for new priorities, research to manufacture more new unique natural resources, due to gas, oil etc. resources will be used all in one day. On the energy shortage aspect, Substitution of these oil, gas etc. natural resources are needed . For example, nuclear energy is a kind of new natural resource, it can be used to push machines of rockets to be moved in space. In the future, I hope that nuclear energy can be used to drive cars or ships or trains etc. transportation tools in land. Hence, new natural resource research is essential and valid investment to be improved by scientists in the future.

On the global food supply interconnected challenges hand, including climate changes, energy and water supply are further encountered by the financial and economic changes in an increasingly globalized world. As a result, it is unclear how the growing demand for food and bioenergy (both biomass and biofuels) within a wider bio-economy can be met without further compromising ecosystem services on which all economic activities and social depend. I shall emphasizes the interaction of the economic, social and ecological components of our food systems at various levels, with feed backs increasingly the uncertainty and risks relating to future developments.

We need to face the food requirements of a growing world population have to be satisfied and we also need to the face of increasing resource scarcities, such as water, energy and land and foods etc. with the situation further exacerbated by climate change. Thus, we need to focus on our reducing demand through food consumption behavioral changes and structural changes in food systems and food chains change. Due to some developed countries people often to choose to buy these foods to eat excessively e.g. cow meat and pig meat and drink excessive soft drinks, e.g. man-made color juice. So, these developed countries consumers will feel these excessive foods and soft drinks can be rubbish if these developed countries consumers often drink these man-made color juice and eat pig and cow meats often excessively. It seems who ought to change their diet behavior and food consumption to avoid to spend too much money to buy excessive foods and drinks and who often shall not decide to eat and drink them when who feel not hungry habitually . Hence, changing human diet habit is one important psychology factor to reduce water and foods shortage, due to the meats and juices can be reduced to be rubbish if human can learn how to control their diet habit to reduce to consume excessive meats and vegetables and rice and soft drinks etc. kind of foods and drinks. Then, I believe that food and water drinking numbers will be reduced too much in the future. Hence, different countries' governments need to educate whose people to know that why who will face foods and water scarcity possibly and to let who to know how the issue can be avoided to cause by the changing of their diet habit and consumption behavior. Teaching includes, such as let who to learn why resources scarcities are expected to reduce and defining food security concept, the need is for a better understanding of complexity of vegetable systems, the need to improve the diversity and response capacity of food systems to enhance resilience, the need to address both food consumption and production, knowledge generation and innovation through cross-sector approaches is essential and the need for agricultural knowledge and innovation systems that are fit for farming purpose. After developed countries' people are educated to let who to know why who need to reduce to consume excessive foods and soft drinks habitually to aim to avoid the chance of foods and water supply shortage will be occurred after 2050 year.

On the other side, in the case of biodiversity, the loss of functional biodiversity destabilizes ecosystems and weakens their ability to deal with natural disasters or human induced stresses, such as pollution and climate change. Hence, scientists need to research how to reduce new diseases to cause foods and water pollution, even new diseases cause to influence human health. Due to unpredictable new diseases will be caused foods, fruits, vegetables etc. can't be grow easily , even cows, pigs, sheep etc. animals are not health to cause diseases to be died easily. Then, those new diseases will be decreases our foods supply numbers seriously.

Resources scarcities are expected to define future food security. The predominant form of agriculture, food processing and retailing relies heavily on cheap inputs and the potential impact on this of long term resource scarcity trends has been largely overlooked. Scarcities are either biophysical limits, such as resource supply and availability or environment limits relating to pollution and its impacts on ecosystems and the global climate system. Hence, every country's government ought to educate to let whose citizen to discuss how to protect future food security topic to avoid resource scarcities occurrence after 2050 year. We need to know we are facing pollution (e.g. land, water, energy) and related to environmental limits e.g. climate change, ocean acidification and biodiversity loss. They represent a real threat, not only to future food supplies, but also to global stability and prosperity, through increasing poverty to developing countries and impacts on international trade, finance and investments.

Hence, pollution and environmental limits will have direct relationship to influence every countries' foods supply numbers , then it will influence every country's gross domestic product income if the consumption is reduced by foods inflation. For example, the combined effect of climate change and bio-diversity which makes the food production systems poorly due to a reduced resilience to shocks and changes over the long term , such as the limited availability of ore resources, soil degradation to loss of biodiversity. Both of these require a long term strategic approach to research and an openness to new research directions. These will need to help provide solutions towards more sustainable food consumption and production, some of which will need to break with current farmers or food manufacturers way of producing food methods. For example, research into ecological approaches: foods nutrient and water clean management and replacement of energy intensive inputs are priorities. Research to support energy efficient technologies for use in the food chain is also needed. Industry should assist in tackling the forthcoming challenges with new business models that can support the decoupling of resource use and changing consumption excessive foods behaviors and improving health foods production methods. For instance, changing the foods supply chains) e.g. more local purchasing) may have huge impacts on costs and also on creating closer links and confidence between producers and consumers.

In conclusion, different countries need find methods to solve foods and energy scarcity problem before 2050 year. I recommend that who can attempt to solve earth warm climate, innovate agricultural production and supply system, change human diet habit and food consumption of behavior, co-operate the trade of foods and energy demand and supply between countries fairly and reasonably, reduce food and natural resource waste, renew and recopy new kind of foods, research new natural resource substitution etc. different methods. However, if every country government can attempt to find any one or more of these methods to solve food scarcity to avoid to occur before 2050 year. I believe that the food scarcity challenge won't be occur after 2050 year in the future.

Reference

Erekson, O.H., Loucks, O.L. Strafford, N.C. 1999.
The context of sustainability . In: Sustainability
perspectives for resources and business
USA, p. 3-21.
Daly, H.E. 1990, Towards some operational
principles of sustainable development,
ecological economics, 2(1), 1-6.

Kirkby, J; O' Keefe P., Timberlake, L. (eds.) 1995.
The earthscan reader in sustainable development.
Earthscan Publications Ltd., London, 1-14p.

4.1 Suggestions to solve resources scarcity methods to oil supply

I. Estimation of growth of rural population and income and expected changes of natural resources supply numbers

I recommend developing countries need to estimate growth of rural population and incomes numbers and expected changes numbers in consumption patterns . Taking into account developing countries' known resource capacities and projected development of yields, input use and technologies and making assumptions about their future trading capacity, estimates are also make of future food production level, land use and natural resource numbers import trade demand of developing countries estimation before 2050 year.

Estimation of water natural resources, such as water scarcity agreement on key definitions, the conceptualization of water scarcity in ways that are meaningful for policy development and decision making, the quantification of water scarcity, policy and technical response options available to ensure food security in conditions of water scarcity, criteria and principles that should be used to establish priorities for action to response to water scarcity in agriculture and ensure effective and efficient water scarcity copying strategies. Thus, developing countries will concern to reduce water resources shortage risk. Why is predict water supply important? During the twentieth century, large multi-purpose dams have served the needs of agriculture, energy and growing cities, and helped protect population from flood hazards. On farm water conservation, particularly the adoption of agricultural practices that reduce runoff to increase the infiltration and storage of water in the soil in rained agriculture is the most relevant local supply enhancement option that farmers have to increase foods production by increasing water availability and decentralized water harvesting conveniently in rural areas for farmers needs. For example, ground water exploitation has grown or in scale. Ground water's capability to provide flexible, on demand water in support of irrigation has been as a major advantage by farmers in rural areas. Thus, farmers need to learn how to reduce water losses increase water productivity and water re-allocation to avoid natural resource of water shortage after 2050 year.

II. Renewable natural resources and foods planting sustainability development

The concept of sustainability has become the current answer to absolving our earth of its environment and economic crises in the 21 ST. century. On the one side,
the pessimists, usually ecologists and other scientists, who are convinced the earth can't forever support the different countries' demand of renewable and non renewable resources. On the other side, are the optimists, the economists, who are equally convinced that the earth, with

market incentives, appropriate public policies, material substitution, recycling and new technology can satisfy the needs and improve the quality of human welfare. Both views are supporting arguments are explored used and sustainable development. Thus, renewable old energy natural resource can keep old energy natural resource to renew to use or research other new energy resource to substitute old natural resource, it will reduce the risk of energy resource shortage if the other new natural resource can be substituted to the old natural energy resource to use in our daily life , such as inventing one kind of new energy resource can be used to substitute gas to drive cars or drive boats or plans or the old gas can be renewed or cycled to use to drive cars or boats or the oil can be renewed or cycled to use to cook. Also, our earth foods, e.g. fruits, vegetables or meats etc. foods if which can be recopied to grow many numbers planting foods from any one kind food or many kinds of foods, such as one meat can be copied to manufacture two to three same kind tasty meats or unlimited same kind tasty meats. I believe the renewable natural resource energy or recopied foods can reduce our foods or energy shortage after 2050 year.

III. The application of sustainable strategy
between local and national and regional
of international countries

A redefined concept is of the society as whole system, made up of three concentric circles: the economy is found within the society, and both the economy and society exist within the environment. Sustainability indicators are therefore said to attempt to measure the extent to which these boundaries are respected.

I think sustainability measure as a whole concept environment, society and economy. At the bottom of the triangle is the environment or the ultimate means which represents natural resources as a precondition for decent human life. The economy (which includes technology, politics and ethics) is on the next, is not independent but serves as a vehicle for achieving ultimate ends. At the top is equity or society or ultimate end which refers to the wellbeing of the human being. According to Daly(1990) who indicated "that the economy therefore succeeds to the extent that it conserves and restores ultimate means the environment, and enables the achievement of ultimate ends society equity. This is the application of sustainable strategies to local, national and regional issues, as well as the role of international agencies in local /national strategies." Our earth occurs issues of overpopulation, diseases and political conflict, developed countries also have to deal with problems, such as pollution and unlimited urban expansion with limited resources. Sustainability is the process suggested to improve the quality of human life within the limitations of global environment. It involves solutions for improving human welfare that doesn't result in regarding the environment. We(human) need to concern living within certain limits of the earth's capacity to maintain life, understanding the interconnections among economy, society and environment and maintaining a fair distribution of foods and vegetables and natural energy resources and opportunity for this generation and the next. Thus, on the one side, our governments need to concern three categories: Social/ political, environmental and economic issues are interconnection. Social issues include poverty, consultation, empowerment and culture. Environmental issues include pollution, natural resources and biodiversity/ resilience and economic issues include efficiency, growth and stability. It seems our governments need to considerate social and environment and economic issues to reduce our natural energy resources and foods and vegetables to allocate to let every country people to use fairly.

IV. Reducing global warming and biodiversity
issue occurrence

It seems that we need to know our society will influence our natural environment good or bad. If our society damaged our natural environment, then it will be possible to influence our foods supply of decreasing numbers. e.g. fishes, pigs, cows, sheep and vegetables and fruits etc. foods . Due to bad climate and air and lands and ocean pollution can influence foods can not be grown easily and successfully in farms or fishes can not be lived healthy in ocean. Then, it will cause our meats, fruits and vegetables etc. foods supply shortage. Even, our gas , oil, water etc., natural resources will cause our oceans and lands pollution if human pollute our oceans and lands. In result, our natural resources used numbers will be reduced due to clean lands and oceans are polluted for long time. Finally, natural resources and meats and vegetables and fruits , rice etc. foods prices will be risen due to which are shortage to supply and developing countries' population numbers are increasing which will cause more demand. Finally, it shall cause many developing countries' poor people who can't eat enough meats, fruits, rice vegetables etc. foods as well as who can't use enough natural resources to attempt to adapt whose past normal daily life, such as lacking enough oil to help them to cook foods to be heat to eat at home or lacked enough water to be boiled to drink. Even, whose health will be poor , then who get diseases to cause die easily when there is no enough oil to buy or enough water to drink. Hence, these developing countries governments need to concern foods and natural resource scarcity problems which will be occurred if who do not find methods to reduce this issue to be occurred after 2050 year.

As Erekson et. al.(1999) concerns about" loss of resources, such as biodiversity or global weather (climate) warming are pacified with the potential of new technology which will lead to greater investments to the future generations for alternative resources and welfare." Hence, I recommend our governments need to concern global warming or biodiversity issue because of our foods and vegetables and natural resources, such as water, air will be possible polluted to be caused shortage quickly if our earth's global warming or biodiversity issue occurrence to cause our earth's large oceans or lands areas to be polluted. Our governments can attempt to control natural resources , such as oil, gas, water supply into the market and not though the political special conditions to keep them, without considering the political and social standings, which rule the control power and the use of those resources. Such as developed countries can be able to minimize the impact of foods or/and natural resources production and consumption over the natural resources, they are only mechanisms built within an economic rationality, which should be possible to control its people's demand of natural resources, e.g. oil, gas, water and supply of natural resources get more balance. Then these natural resources sale price won't be raised more every year. When there developed countries' people , such as American and Britain who can control to reduce to spend to use the excessive natural resources too much in any time and any place habitually. Then , I believe the developing countries' governments e.g. Africa, China, India, which can buy those developed countries governments' excessive natural resources to raise those developed countries' natural resources supply numbers to provide to whose people to use as well as the most important benefit is that developed countries can gain foreign income from excessive natural resources expectation. Then, these governments will raise GDP economic growth. Hence, if developed countries could control whose people consume natural resource numbers and they could also control to produce natural resource supply numbers . Then, they can gain more excessive natural resources export chance to achieve to raise GDP economic growth aim for long term. As Kirkby et al.,

(1995)explained "the complexity of sustainable development our natural environment. If our governments can let our earth natural environment gets creation to maintenance, then our natural environment will be reduced the time to degradation. In the long time result, our society rural and urban economy will be growth , then our different countries' global growth will be caused diversity." Hence, it seems different countries' governments need to concern sustainable development to our natural environment .

V. How to apply agricultural green bio-economy concept to solve control sustainable food consumption and production in a resource-constrained world

Nowadays, challenges for the global food supply have never been so complex. Between now and 2050 year, it has been predicted that growth in the global population and changing diets in developing countries, special in India and China and Africa etc. developing countries which may lead to an increase of around 70% in food demand. At the same time, depletion of fossil hydrocarbons will increase the demand for biomass for biofuels and industrial materials. Hence, developed and developing countries' governments ought need to coordinated to reduce air and water pollution and approached to lands use planning and oceans use planning to supply enough farms to grow potatoes, vegetables, tomatoes, fruits and let cows, pigs, sheep etc. animals can have comfortable and clean farm to live to produce good tasty meats to provide human to eat as well as to reduce pollution to supply fresh and clean water to let fishes to be lived and provides to human to drink clean water. Due to overpopulation will be predicted by scientists after 2050 year, so it will be caused foods and energy shortage possibly. Hence, different countries' governments need have long term perspectives to prepare to have enough foods and energy supply to provide us to eat and use for our earth with resource constraints and environmental limits, and which includes guideline on agricultural research to achieve foods supply aim.

On the one hand, I believe the knowledge-based bio-economy can play in realizing there challenges in particular the balance demand between foods, feed and fuel and the strategic role new technologies can have upon developing a sustainable an green bio-economy. On the other hand, I also think production of the presently high resource dependence and to build more environmentally begin sustainable agriculture system able to feed 9 billion people by 2050 year. I recommend global governments need to concern all aspects of food security including the total food chain and impacts of other land-use and management as well as non food areas, research areas which can be closed to free resources for new priorities, research to manufacture more new unique natural resources, due to gas, oil etc. resources will be used all in one day. On the energy shortage aspect, Substitution of these oil, gas etc. natural resources are needed . For example, nuclear energy is a kind of new natural resource, it can be used to push machines of rockets to be moved in space. In the future, I hope that nuclear energy can be used to drive cars or ships or trains etc. transportation tools in land. Hence, new natural resource research is essential and valid investment to be improved by scientists in the future.

On the global food supply interconnected challenges hand, including climate changes, energy and water supply are further encountered by the financial and economic changes in an increasingly globalized world. As a result, it is unclear how the growing demand for food and bioenergy (both biomass and biofuels) within a wider bio-economy can be met without further compromising ecosystem services on which all economic activities and social depend. I shall emphasizes the interaction of the economic, social and ecological components of our food systems at various levels, with feed backs increasingly the uncertainty and risks relating to future developments.

We need to face the food requirements of a growing world population have to be satisfied and we also need to the face of increasing resource scarcities, such as water, energy and land and foods etc. with the situation further exacerbated by climate change. Thus, we need to focus on our reducing demand through food consumption behavioral changes and structural changes in food systems and food chains change. Due to some developed countries people often to choose to buy these foods to eat excessively e.g. cow meat and pig meat and drink excessive soft drinks, e.g. man-made color juice. So, these developed countries consumers will feel these excessive foods and soft drinks can be rubbish if these developed countries consumers often drink these man-made color juice and eat pig and cow meats often excessively. It seems who ought to change their diet behavior and food consumption to avoid to spend too much money to buy excessive foods and drinks and who often shall not decide to eat and drink them when who feel not hungry habitually . Hence, changing human diet habit is one important psychology factor to reduce water and foods shortage, due to the meats and juices can be reduced to be rubbish if human can learn how to control their diet habit to reduce to consume excessive meats and vegetables and rice and soft drinks etc. kind of foods and drinks. Then, I believe that food and water drinking numbers will be reduced too much in the future. Hence, different countries' governments need to educate whose people to know that why who will face foods and water scarcity possibly and to let who to know how the issue can be avoided to cause by the changing of their diet habit and consumption behavior. Teaching includes, such as let who to learn why resources scarcities are expected to reduce and defining food security concept, the need is for a better understanding of complexity of vegetable systems, the need to improve the diversity and response capacity of food systems to enhance resilience, the need to address both food consumption and production, knowledge generation and innovation through cross-sector approaches is essential and the need for agricultural knowledge and innovation systems that are fit for farming purpose. After developed countries' people are educated to let who to know why who need to reduce to consume excessive foods and soft drinks habitually to aim to avoid the chance of foods and water supply shortage will be occurred after 2050 year. On the other side, in the case of biodiversity, the loss of functional biodiversity destabilizes ecosystems and weakens their ability to deal with natural disasters or human induced stresses, such as pollution and climate change. Hence, scientists need to research how to reduce new diseases to cause foods and water pollution, even new diseases cause to influence human health. Due to unpredictable new diseases will be caused foods, fruits, vegetables etc. can't be grow easily , even cows, pigs, sheep etc. animals are not health to cause diseases to be died easily. Then, those new diseases will be decreases our foods supply numbers seriously.

Resources scarcities are expected to define future food security. The predominant form of agriculture, food processing and retailing relies heavily on cheap inputs and the potential impact on this of long term resource scarcity trends has been largely overlooked. Scarcities are either biophysical limits, such as resource supply and availability or environment limits relating to pollution and its impacts on ecosystems and the global climate system. Hence, every country's government ought to educate to let whose citizen to discuss how to protect future food security topic to avoid resource scarcities occurrence after 2050 year. We need to know we are facing pollution (e.g. land, water, energy) and related to environmental limits e.g. climate change, ocean acidification and biodiversity loss. They represent a real threat, not only to future food supplies, but also to global stability and prosperity, through increasing poverty to developing countries and impacts on international trade, finance and investments. Hence, pollution and environmental limits will have direct relationship to influence every countries' foods supply numbers , then it will influence every country's gross domestic product income if the consumption is reduced by foods inflation.

For example, the combined effect of climate change and bio-diversity which makes the food production systems poorly due to a reduced resilience to shocks and changes over the long term , such as the limited availability of ore resources, soil degradation to loss of biodiversity. Both of these require a long term strategic approach to research and an openness to new research directions. These will need to help provide solutions towards more sustainable food consumption and production, some of which will need to break with current farmers or food manufacturers way of producing food methods. For example, research into ecological approaches: foods nutrient and water clean management and replacement of energy intensive inputs are priorities. Research to support energy efficient technologies for use in the food chain is also needed. Industry should assist in tackling the forthcoming challenges with new business models that can support the decoupling of resource use and changing consumption excessive foods behaviors and improving health foods production methods. For instance, changing the foods supply chains) e.g. more local purchasing) may have huge impacts on costs and also on creating closer links and confidence between producers and consumers.

In conclusion, different countries need find methods to solve foods and energy scarcity problem before 2050 year. I recommend that who can attempt to solve earth warm climate, innovate agricultural production and supply system, change human diet habit and food consumption of behavior, co-operate the trade of foods and energy demand and supply between countries fairly and reasonably, reduce food and natural resource waste, renew and recopy new kind of foods, research new natural resource substitution etc. different methods. However, if every country government can attempt to find any one or more of these methods to solve food scarcity to avoid to occur before 2050 year. I believe that the food scarcity challenge won't be occur after 2050 year in the future.

Environment Economy-Pollution and illness influences oil consumer behavior

How the economic consequences of outdoor air pollution influences consumer behaviors ? Air pollution can increase number of respiratory and cardiovas cular diseases. How they can impact economic growth, e.g. on human health, mortality and morbidity and agriculture aspects ? Whether when this diseases are caused from outdoor air pollution, why it can influence consumer behavior or brings negative consumpton emotion?

The macroeconomic costs of these impacts of outdoor air pollution that are linked to economic activity, and it raises welfare costs related to activity morality and pain and suffering from illness to consumers. For example, market costs are those that are associated with biophysical impacts that directly affect economic activity, e.g. lower crop yields affect agricultural production . Non market costs may also include the monetised welfare costs of morality (premature deaths) , and of the disutility of illness (pain and suffering).

Raising emissions reflect the assumptions on economic growth with increasing GDP and energy demand, especially in fast growing economies, such as the high population countries, India and China. These large changes are due to the increase in the demand for agricultural products and energy (include transport and power generation). For continuousing increase in energy demand to China and India car drivers, when they need to drive their cars to go to anywhere often. The higher emission will bring serious pollution. The environment protecting householders will decrease to use emissions from energy demand for, with reflects technology improvement in energy efficiency, the use of cleaner fuels, and biomass in open fire to cleaner energy sources including LPG, ethanol or enhanced cooking stoves. Hence, when many people get the diseases from air pollution. It will increase the medical (healthcare) cost to governments or when government needs to give welfare assistance to patients.

The three different market impacts of air pollution may include: reduced labor productivity, increased health expenditures and crop yield losses. They may reduce the GDP pollution feedback on the economy. At the global level, the consequences of labor productivity and health expenditure may impact to market cost increases,because increases expenditure to labor productivity, health expenditure and value added generated in agriculture from low productivity changes in crop yields.

What is the welfare costs of mortality and illness ? It is possible to attribute a cost to non-market impacts, such as the premature deaths and the costs of pain and suffering from illness . The welfares cost of the premature deaths caused by air pollution are calculated using the value of a statistical life to any one. Large costs can also associated with the pain and suffering from illness. So, pollution causes diseases to bring welfare cost increases, they include hospital living day to every patient when he is caused illnesses from air pollution. Moreover, it will impact government pollution expenditure to raise welfare cost to assist the low income level pollution illness patients' hospital living welfacre cost when they need to live long days in hospitals.

How does air pollutin impact on consumer automobile choices ? Air pollution levels can bring negatively affect the sales of fuel inefficient cars to China or India car drivers. They will choose to buy electronic cars to drive to replace fuel cars, because electronic cars only need to charge battery and it can reduce air pollution. When China or India their big city people's income level is rising, they will have more money to buy electronic cars to drive to reduce air pollution. Moreover, they believe that electronic cars can have better car quality and reduced air pollution need to charge battery fuel efficiency to compare fuel cars, when they need to often drive cars on roads. Som electronic cars demand will be the preference choice battery fuel efficiency or green driving tools to compare general fuel cars to satisfy China and India car purchasers when they are living in serious air pollution environment cities.

When the high environment protection awareness car buyers number is increasing in the countries, environment protection awareness will influence their car choice decison on which car to buy , when they are living in more heavily polluted cities tend to buy less fuel-inefficient cars. So, the electronic cars number need will increase in China and India both car market, because these two countries have similar characteristics, they have high population and gardens and farms number is less and there are many people are living in cities and many people are high income level , they usually have one car at least. So, they must feel cities are serious polluted by their diving behaviors. So, their environment protection awareness are ususally higher to compare other countries , they have less cities. So high air pollution to cities can excite the environment protection awareness to China and India car purchasers as well as they will prefer to choose to buy electronic cars to replace fuel cars to drive in possible, because they do not hope to live a high car dirty cities to cause their poor health when they have high income level. Also, it implies that it has direct relationship between China and India cities have high income level people number increases and air pollution level increases and electronic car demand number increases and fuel car demand number decreases in China and India car market in micro economic China and India electronic car and fuel car demand and supply market.

I assume that each China and India car consumer makes a relatively fuel or electronic car choice among possible car transmissions, between the option of buying no car and buy car or between the option of buying electronic car and fuel car. However, air pollution will be one major factor to influence China and India car purchase demand number on electronic and fuel car supply number. If china and India's air pollution can reduce, then car purchase number will increase, as well as the fuel car demand number will also increase ,because China and India have many cities are polluted serious. It can influence car purchase buyers how to decide car choice to make car or no car purchase decision, even purchase either fuel car or electronic car decison.

● How consumer decisions are impacted on environment?

Environmental impacts may occur on households, when they need to buy food, mobility, house, household goods and appliances for home use in household consumer behavior view. It can bring direct impacts, that occue because of the use of householder products and services during householders are staying at home. When householders feel need to raise living quality, they will considerate how they use services and related household products. When minimizing the use of natural resources and toxic materials as well as the emissions of waste and pollutants over the life cycle of the service or household product, e.g. using electricity or fuel time at home, cooling time and bathing time at home activities. So, for on householder who has high environment protection awareness and energy protection awareness, he will reduce long time to use electricity or fuel use time for cooking, bathing, watching television, listening radio time activities at homes, because he does not hope energy waste and protect air fresh at homes.

So, consumption is concerned by environment factors, such as demographics, technology, income and prices, psychological, social , cultural environments, e.g. consumers economic behavior is influenced by habt, routines, conventions etc. different environment factors influence. So, economic assumptions of rational and regular behavior is based on long-established principles, such as utility maximization. For example, when one country is encountering serious air or water pollution, then consumers will spend long time to search any data (marketing research activities) when they need to make purchase decision on pollution environment as well as pollution environment is dependent on (e.g. attitude, intention to the consumers).

Because when pollution environment will influence consumption behavior, such as behavioral and experimental economic to consumers. It implies on pollution environment's psychological assumptions on individual consumption motives, such as on the role of mental habits, loss confidence. So, consumers usually feel to spend long time to make purchase choice or decison on pollution environment, exaggerated optimism, expectatons, avoiding miscalculation,short-sightedness more enjoyment etc. psychological factors. When they need to make purchase decision on pollution environment, e.g. when one car consumer will need to make choice to buy one car, when he is living in China city, city is polluted serious. So, he will need to spend long time to gather any car model and brand and quality and fuel quality air polluted level to achieve to choose to buy the most clean fuel and the most least air polluton car to avoid to cause air polluton when he is driving the car in the China's city. So, air pollution way causes the China environment protection awareness car consumers to spend long time to gather any less use fuel car information to avoid to cause air pollution when he needs often to drive the car on the city roads in the China cities.

Hence , air pollution may cause the China car purchasers feel need to spend more time to gather car information in order to decide whether he ought to buy one car or no car purchase choice on the air pollution environment. So, the car must use less fuel to avoid air pollution easily when he drives the car on the China's cities' roads.

Reference

Erekson, O.H., Loucks, O.L. Strafford, N.C. 1999.

The context of sustainability . In: Sustainability

perspectives for resources and business

USA, p. 3-21.

Daly, H.E. 1990, Towards some operational

principles of sustainable development,

ecological economics, 2(1), 1-6.

Kirkby, J; O' Keefe P., Timberlake, L. (eds.) 1995.

The earthscan reader in sustainable development.

Earthscan Publications Ltd., London, 1-14p.

Terrorism attack and fuel price raising influences tourism industry to experience decline life cycle stage

Nowaday, airline industry is entering global competition. So, any some less positive or negative social environment changing which will influence any airlines' passenger behavioral consumption change. For example, air ticket price rises or fuel price rises or the country's season is bad or the global economy is bad or the country has terrible death threat etc. different negative social environment change fastors which will influence any country passenger individual travel consumption desires.

In Special, business class airline transportation demands are also increasing, due to many business travelers need to catch planes to go to any different countries to do business as well as many cargoes need to be carried from planes to transport to different countries to sell. So, business class traveler target group behavioral consumption is difficult to influence travelling consumotion desires from external environmental factors because business class traveler target group concerns to need to catch planes to go to another country to discuss business co-operation with the country's businessmen. So, their business travel desires won't easy to be influenced more than individual entertainment travel consumer's desire.

It seems cargo and business aim of aviation transportation industry has less chance to be influenced to reduce businessmen traveler or cargo transportation numbers to compare to entertainment traveler numbers by external environment change influences, due to the business travelers and cargo transportation travelling desires is difficult to reduce travelling or transportation needs to reduce the " doing businesses to earn profit chance with another country's businessmen". However, ignorance of internal or external market dynamics, catching entertainment travelers business can be detrimental to airline profitability more than carrying cargoes or business travelers business. Because the demands of travelling different countries' travelers' consumption are still more than the demands of businessmen carrying cargoes in any countries every year. So, the global GDP of travelling income sector is still have the important position to any country nowadays.

How can positive or negative social environment change influence any airlines' air ticket prices to be risen or fallen as well as how can these social environment change influence passenger consumption desires ? For example: What is the petroleum price change influence ?In fact, the increase in petroleum price can have chance to affect every airlines passenger has a negative manner to reduce travel consumption because increased oil prices have resulted in the reduction of airline services operations, the number of airline schedules flights, even airline bankruptcies. Whether global economic inflation or deflation, terrorism threats to the country, oil shortage or oil price rising or fallening, bank interest rate increasing or decreasing etc. external factors which have the most influential causes to bring the bad or good effects to cause airline industry share price reducing or increasing or increasing or reducing air ticket price. In result, these external environmental changes will influence the global traveler numbers to be increased or decreased at the time.

To support this hypotheses, this are my research first question, such as : Does a combination of terrorism and price of petroleum significantly influence airline profit changing mostly? The alternative hypothesis was my research second question, such as: Whether a significant relationship exists between terrorism, price of petroleum and airline profitability more than other factors, such as inflation, bank interest rate or air ticket price changing of these factors to influence passenger consumption desires change. I shall indicate that the first assumption was that terrorism has a negative effect on airline profitability and another assumption was that only external factors as oil prices or terrorism affect airline profitability. Finally, the terrorism and oil shortage and oil rising price factors can influence every passenger travel consumption desire to be reduced mainly.

Terrorism attack influences traveller need

However the effects of oil price and terrorism on airline profitability was limited to a regional perspective, so oil price and terrorism external environmental change will only influence some countries' airline traveler numbers to be decreased, e.g. the terrorism attack of plane crash event to USA on 11 Sept. After the terrorism attack happened on USA 11 Sept. incident of terrorism attack was restricted to events of skyjacking, attacks on oil production, refinery and distribution. Then, due oil shortage will be caused due to reducing oil production, refinery and distribution as well as it will influence oil price is risen and airline ticket price is also risen. It will reduce travel consumption desire to some countries if their airlines' ticket prices are also increasing. Other types of terrorist activities, such as attacks on financial targets or senior government officials could have an adverse effect on the petroleum and airline industry. I think the disruption of the production or distribution of petroleum because of incidents of terrorism was costly in terms of loss of business and the inflationary effect on fuel dependent products or services.

In fact, some airlines have adopted more fuel saving technology, so whose fuel consumption would not use more than other non fuel saving technology airlines. It seems fuel price increasing will not be the only factor to influence the airline industry's traveler numbers decreasing due, the owning more fuel saving technologic airlines which air tickets prices won't influence to be risen , due to reducing oil production and shortage influences . However, due to some airlines which have fuel saving technology, so which can avoid to use more fuel to provide planes to use and which fuel costs will be reduced, then which can provide cheaper air ticket fare prices to compare the non fuel saving technology airlines. The result will cause some not owning fuel saving technological airlines which will lose travelling customers in this global airline travelling market, also the not fuel saving technological airlines need to renew their fuel technology if which want to keep their competitive abilities to avoid to close down their businesses. So, what factors will influence the not owning fuel saving technological airlines profitability to be reduce if the oil shortage factor can not influence their planes energy supply to be reduced to cause air ticket prices to be increased? To answer this question, I shall indicate another financial risk factor how it influences airline industry behavioral change.

Also, I shall indicate the financial risk of airline industry evidence from Cathay Pacific airways and China airlines against key determinants of which include interest rate, exchange rate and fuel price risk for the period of January 1996 year to December 2011 year. During this period, these key external factors which were the most serious influence to cause these two airlines choose to change their strategic behaviors. Due to any these financial risks is difficult to predict and it was also changing often, these factors will also affect any airlines stock returns which arise from changing economic conditions, e.g. fuel price movements and fluctuations in exchange rates. These external unpredicted changing factors will attribute to the air tickets cyclical demand, capital investment, fixed costs of labor and landing rights to this global airline industry. Finally, it will cause some airlines need to rise air ticket prices to reduce expenditures increasing.

However, the relationship between fuel price and stock prices varies across economies which will influence travel passenger consumption of desires. For example, the effects of oil price changes in sub-sector indices, such as wood, paper and printing, insurance and electricity. In the past, on global stock exchange market was positively significant in 2011 year. Otherwise, with respect to the U.S.A. aviation industry, some economists suggested that global airlines stock returns were negatively to percentage change in fuel prices related to any airline firm value, e.g. Qantas and Air New Zealand were negatively share price growth to fuel price risk in the short term in the 2011 year. Thus, due to these two airlines share price went down, it will influence investors who loss confidence to buy their shares as well as it will influence travelling passengers who choose to buy other airlines' air tickets to go to travel because they will feel these two airlines have business challenges, e.g. bad service quality and food quality and uncomfortable airline seat environment and poor management style. etc different bad feeling. So, these two airlines' share prices went down, it will influence every travel passenger's confidence to choose to buy their air tickets to sit their planes to go to travel.

Airlines fuel manufacturing supply strategy

However, there are some airlines which are the characteristic of self organization . It means that they are present in that both of oil fuel production and providing flights service in airline industry. So, these self organization airlines can control the oil fuel price by themselves. However, any self supply airline organization is also evident in efforts by businesses acts of terrorism against economic targets by adopting proactive steps, such as airline and airport security. So, it seems any self suply airline organization can reduce the risk to avoid oil price raising and terrorism attacks in airline industry risk management sector because oil shortage won't influence their air ticket prices need to be raised. Beside, these self supply airline organizations which have high technology of fuel efficient aircrafts, the use of one aircraft model, the adoption of direct routes versus customer loyalty programs and other operational cost reductions are strategies for increased profitability.

To solve oil price, terrorism etc. external risk to airline industry. Instead of high technology of fuel efficient aircrafts and self supply airline organization methods can solve terrorism attacks and oil price rising risks. However, I believe that there are other risks will threaten to airline industry. This risks concern traveller individual psychological factors influence, so it means that any airlines can apply psychological methods to predict which airline passengers' travel consumption desires. The risks include such as (1) user factor, such as : the travel country culture and tradition difference will influence the traveler chooses to prefer to go to the country to travel , the traveler's education level is high , who will choose to go to developed countries to travel, e.g. USA, UK. Otherwise, if the traveler's education level is low, who will choose to go to developing countries to travel, e.g. China, India etc. (2) economic factor, such as air tickets and airline fuel costs, (3) human resources and macro economic factor, such as political stability, economic development, educational policy, health policy, environmental policy. However, these risks occurrences are resulting in the relationship of cause and effect events. These events are not directly observable.

Such as, the complexity of relationship between terrorism and airline profitability. Hence, if global airline industry can predict when those risks occur to do protective strategic behavior. It is possible that which can understand why these risk events will occur and their protective strategic behaviors also influence their outcomes to be positive to avoid any external risk threats on the long term. However, I think hierarchy, self supply airline organization efficiency methods which are as possible predictors of user preferences to avoid risk threat events to cause whose airline businesses failure occurrences in airline industry because it can reduce oil shortage factor which causes their air ticket prices need to be rised to keep their planes can have enough fuel supply.

● Why tourism and airline industries have close relationship to influence their profitability between of them.

In my study, I suppose terrorism, profitability and the price of petroleum which had properties of distinct and interrelated close relationship. Moreover, these variables (terrorism, profitability and the price of petroleum) displayed differentiation, self replication, efficiency and hierarchy which can cause risk events to airline industry. However, I also think the other internal and external threat factors of airline industry, such as inflation, bank interest rate, business model, service quality, airline fuel or plane engine technology, air ticket pricing, brand loyalty, airline strategic management, government policy and fuel hedging of these factors which can also raise the risks to threaten any airlines existence in airline industry.

There are two basic business models in airline industry. They are network (full service) and low cost (discount) carriers. The network carrier model employs diversification strategy by increased domestic destinations, serving international routes, providing diverse seating arrangements (business, economy and first class), maintaining a complex system of offering high quality service. Otherwise, low cost (discount) airlines focus on lower air fares. To keep operating costs down, discount airlines offer shorter routes and provide point-to-point destinations rather than through sophisticated flights are primarily in domestic destinations. So, discount airlines operate a common model aircraft fleet, offer a single seating arrangement and cheaper flight services offered to compare network airlines. However, these two basic business models have their unique competitive abilities to provide any airlines existence in airline industry nowadays.

In fact, natural resource of oil is decreasing in our earth. But as the same time, human demand is increasing and oil supply is decreasing, so it also causes the oil fuel price is increasing to supply to airline industry. It influences not only to airline industry, it also impacts of higher oil fuel price to tourism, such as expansion of airports are made based on expected demand increase.

Tourism has been proven to many adverse events, including terrorism, flight disruptions. Beside, the bad natural climate change influences, such as the volcanic ash cloud event occurred in April 2010 year. So, airline industry need to concern climate change because it will cause high fuel prices indirectly. For example, the event occurred the extreme increase in operating costs for airlines in 2008 year, due to unprecedented prices for aviation fuel also meant, that despite the introduction of fuel charges, so this event causes the global airline industry recorded losses seriously. Even if alternative fuels become commercially available for airlines which are still likely to be more expensive than present aviation fuel. Thus, it seems that poor tourism will influence poor travel consumption and low airline tickets sale.

Higher airfares in the future are likely to lead to reduction in travel and cause tourists to shift from more distant to closer destination. When some of the economic responses to higher oil prices are obvious assessing the overall economic impacts on tourism is difficult. However, long term changes in global oil price rises will be similar to global changes in other commodity prices, exchange rates and income. It is therefore important to consider the impact of high oil prices on tourism from a general equilibrium perspective rather than relying only on bottom partial equilibrium. However, I believe tourism and airline industries have close relationship, such as tourism and airline industries are likely to suffer in an environment of high oil prices. Given that tourism destinations receive tourists from a range of origins, it would be useful to understand of some countries are increasing oil prices than others. Such as the net oil importing countries are selling higher oil prices than oil exporting countries generally. For example, New Zealand is an oil import country to provide planes for international visitor arrivals, so its oil fuel price is usually higher to charge to NZ airlines because any NZ airlines need to pay to foreign countries to buy any oil more expensive price. So, NZ airlines usually charge higher airfares to its visitors to compare the other exporting oil countries' airlines.

In economic theory, on income effects indicate negative impacts on tourism demand, the exact effects of higher oil fuel prices for specific destinations are far from clear. However, airline industry's different market segments show different sensitivities to air ticket fares changes. On the first hand, if the visitors are long destinations generally wealthier than average and therefore potentially less affected, as energy costs would be a smaller proportion of their income compared will be those from less wealthy groups. On the second hand, oil prices don't translate into higher transport costs especially not on air routes that are highly competitive and that are maintained for strategic reasons. On the third hand, many other factors shape tourists' decision making, including emotion drivers or those related to images, fashions and perceptions.

Increasing environmental protection awareness of tourists could also be an important factor to influence tourism consumption, instead of oil fuel price raising causes air ticket fares raising factor to reduce traveler numbers. However, oil price raising reason causes also due to high use of cars, vans and domestic air transport in some countries, e.g. Hong Kong, China countries, there are many people like to buy cars to drive. So, the private driver numbers are increasing demand to cause these countries' oil fuel prices raise in the short time suddenly. It will influence HK and China air tickets prices need to be risen , due to there are many cars, vans and domestic air transport tools need to use oil to supply energy to cause oil import numbers will increase to HK and China and HK and China airlines need to pay higher price to buy oil to use. In the result, HK and China airlines air ticket prices will also need to rise and it will influence HK and China travel consumption desire.

Fuel raising price solve methods

● Why oil fuel raising price factor can cause risk to airline.

In long run, implications of changes to supply and demand side conditions of oil fuel energy may differ qualitatively. For example, due to investment responses of producers, consumers and governments in alternative energy sources and more energy efficient plants, vehicles are supplied in order to achieve oil fuel price can't be risen seriously.

However, I believe oil fuel rising charge will be an important factor to influence global airline ticket fares to be also increased. Firstly, on the bank interest changing factor, e.g. bank interest rate rising which only attract more bank saving. But it can not influence the bank savers who choose to reduce relax time to go to other countries travelling. Otherwise, when the bank savers can save more money to earn higher interest in banks, who will prefer to choose to use their saving to consume travelling. Due to who can earn higher interest rate after a period of saving time. So, I believe whose behavioral travelling consumption will be raised when the banks will raise interest rate, then the bank savers won't choose to save more money in banks. So it is possible that who will withdraw more money to consume to go to travelling from their bank saving. It seems bank interest rate changing won't influence bank savers' behavioral travelling consumption to be reduced. Secondly, on the exchange rate changing factor, although any country's exchange changing will cause other countries' money value to be fallen down or risen up. However, it won't influence any travelers' behavioral consumption to be reduced seriously. Although, it is possible that the traveler won't spend too much to go to shopping when who travel to the another country and arrive the country. But, it is not possible to influence the traveler decides to reduce consumption to buy any air ticket to go to travelling. Thirdly, any country inflation also can not reduce travelers' travelling consumption easily because inflation can influence consumers who choose to buy cheaper foods and clothing and reduce entertainments in their every day life. But, one country's inflation can not influence it's citizen do not spend much travelling expenditure because travelers only spend one time or two times of travelling every year usually. So, the travelling expenditure rate of any households is not too much to compare daily essential expenditure. So, it seems that bank interest rate and exchange rate changing and inflation factors won't influence any travelers' travelling consumption of decisions to be reduced easily. Otherwise, if the oil fuel price raises too much, then global airlines' cost will be raised. So, the airlines only choose to increase their air fare prices to aim to avoid loss possibly. It seems that oil fuel price has direct influence airline income.

● Methods to solve rising air fare prices demand.
    I. Why will biofuels energy be demanded ?
I suggest these methods how to avoid the oil raising price factor to cause airline air fare prices to be risen to lead the risk of traveler numbers to be reduced.
The first method: Whether aviation fuel markets will have what benefits from biofuels supply to planes. I shall refer the scope includes trends in jet fuel price, airline response to fuel price, increases and volatility and environmental goals for aviation. The aviation fuel supply industry includes production, distribution and consumption of aviation fuel and it outlines players in the aviation fuel supply chain. For example, at each airport, fuel supply chain organization and fuel sourcing could differ with regard to the role of oil companies, airlines, airport owners and operators and airport service companies. However, major jet fuel purchasers are airlines, general aviation operators, corporate aviation and the military, with most of the jet fuel in global different countries demanders being used for domestic commercial and civilian flights carrying passengers, cargos or both. Commercial aviation fuel efficiency has improved dramatically over time, largely due to aircraft and engine upgrades and operational and air traffic control improvements. So, it seems that fuel supply factor can influence

airline fare prices majorly.

However, jet fuel prices generally correlate with prices of crude oil and other refined petroleum products, such as diesel. So, increasing prices and the persistent price volatility of jet fuel markets import airline industry finances in any countries. However, airlines use various strategies to manage aviation fuel price certainty, including financial hedges, increased vertical integration and adjustments in aircraft utilization and size to avoid the jet fuel raising price risk. Investments in alternative aviation fuel could be a mechanism to diversity expose to the price of petroleum. It seems the use of alternative aviation fuel would serve to diversify the fuel mix to reduce the risk of jet fuel monopoly raising price threat. If a diversified fuel mix were to avoid either fuel raising price in short term or to avoid fuel raising price in long term. Potential benefits include reduced actual fuel costs from only choice of jet fuel supply increased price certainty and lessened fuel costs. This diversify could allow airlines to become more consistently profitable and to make other investments in their businesses.

So, biofuels have potential to meet aviation industry needs, possibly including managing risks of upward fuel price trends and fuel price volatility and avoid risks with greenhouse gas emissions. So, the aviation fuels market could use biofuels to reduce greenhouse gas emission and mitigate long-term upward price trends, fuel price volatility or both.

What are the challenges of high priced oil for aviation? In fact, nowadays not the resources of oil as such, but much more the insecurity of supply, due to geopolitical instability in combination with a tight oil market makes a scenario with much higher oil prices than the world is currently experiencing not unlikely. Aviation is completely dependent upon oil as its fuel source. Since no practical energy substitute is readily available for commercial aviation, a scarcity of petroleum relative to demand will present a major aviation policy. In addition, efficiency gains, due to operational measures and new aircraft medium term. In particular, it has been demonstrated that the annual reduction rate in fuel consumption traffic unit is not a constant, but is itself also falling, in contrast to past estimates.

So, a high-priced oil scenario will have severe consequences for demand, airline revenues, the competitive position of airports and eventually airline networks, strategies and fleet development. In particular, transfer demand, short-haul and leisure traffic can be expected to be heavily affected by high oil prices, due to their relative high price sensitivity. So, different countries' governments or/and airlines are valuable to research another new and potential biofuel energy to substitute oil energy to supply our planes to reduce the threat of oil monopoly supply to influence the cause of air fare raising prices. Because the elasticity is very high to travelers, when the travelers feel air fares are rising high or even low level to influence travelers who will choose not to buy the air tickets to go to travel easily.

Will the fuel (oil based inputs) risk be higher to compare other costs to cause air ticket prices to be increased?, e.g. engineering maintenance, employees salaries, general cleaning, security office expenses etc. expenditures to airlines? If the probability-weighted upside effect on firm value when a risk is resolved favorably is greater the risk than the probability-weighted downside effect if the risk is resolved badly, then expected value work not be enhanced by hedging. So, the risk will be resolved badly to any commercial airlines. Airlines are an interesting case because the direct effect of source of risk resides squarely within the no offset in revenue functions (unlike for oil producers, for example), so value effects from costs feed directly into equity value. Most directly, the risk source is fuel costs to commercial airlines. Jet fuel is of course, a mix product of crude oil, so airlines indirectly face oil price risk. There are reasons to expect that airlines' fuel costs might to convex in oil price (i.e. absent any hedging). For example, oil prices, being generally pro-cyclical in recent times, tend to be highest when airline demand is strong. Airlines are therefore apt to use more high priced fuel than low-priced fuel over time. Airlines can raise air fare benefit is limited by the elasticity of demand. Also, cost functions could be influenced from fuel cost corresponds to upturns in economic activity overall (due to demand pressures on oil related prices), so it causes that airline's capacity delivers their services given their level of fixed capital. The essence of airlines basis risk in the case of jet fuel is essentially the time profile of the refining margin between crude and jet fuel, or the time profile of the price differential between other refined distillates and jet fuel. Thus, it is far from clear that risk management with oil is sure to add value to any airlines. It seems the impact of airline

energy and any countries' domestic or foreign airline passenger travel numbers which have direct close relationship.

II. Whether the relationship between terrorism and oil prices has close relationship.

Whether the relationship between terrorism and oil prices has close relationship. It needs to judge to determine if a combination of terrorism and the price of petroleum significantly predicted airline profitability and which variable whether the further period was the most significant between the terrorism occurrence and the price of petroleum influence. So, different countries' governments or airlines need to collect samples of financial records from which country's any airline commercial passengers and cargo airlines on costs of fuel and any airline profitability. Also, gathering the terrorism data were comparison of terrorist attacks on petroleum in oil-producing nations, and incidents of high jacking aboard any country's aircraft. When any countries' airlines or governments can judge whether the impact of airline energy and terrorism risk level is high or middle or low level. Then, which can use this sample data to measure how to do positive social change to whether to increase or reduce employment in commercial aviation industry, or ought need to invest other higher commercial activity in tourist and other travel related service businesses and when is the most right time to adopt of green technologies by the civil aviation manufacturing industry after the terrorism attacks occurrence to any country. It seems that any countries' governments or airlines which ought concern that the event of when the terrorism attacks will occur and gather past sample data to predict when the next time terrorism attacks event will be occurred and the risk will be high or middle or low level to influence global airline industry development.

III. What factors will influence airline industry's price elasticity of supply and demand?

In fact, the airline industry is largely dependent on the supply of the oil industry. Otherwise, the oil industry is inelastic. However, the increase or decrease of the price of airfare is directly related to the increase or decrease of the oil's price to fuel the aircrafts because there has no any new energy which can be substituted to oil fuel to airline industry. So, it seems oil fuel producers are monopolies to control its sale price to be raised easily.

Another factor that can affect airline industry to be directly targeted by a tragedy brought about by terrorism. The past four years, from 2001 year to 2005 year, there had been at least $40 billion worth of losses in the airline industry because of the September 11 date terrorism attacks in 2000 year. There had been an expected and significant decrease in the demand for the airline industry services because of the attacks that involved planes hijacking and crashing into key locations like the World Trade Center and the Pentagon in USA. Although, terrorism attacks can bring risk to influence fuel price rising in airline industry. However, this risk occurrence to airline industry is only that after the terrorism attacks occurred. It is possible that terrorism attacks won't occur again in the future.

Otherwise, our concerning ought be the greenhouse emissions and how it affects global warming. The air quality would be better once this new regulations are adopted. However, it would affect large airlines. So, it would increase the price of airfares because of economic fees that airline companies have to cover. Air pollution can give a negative impact on the domestic or oversea owned airline companies for long term. If airlines' planes can use clean fuel to fly, e.g. biofuel, then it will bring benefits to global airlines for long term. On the positive side, the environment would be healthier as the earth's temperature would rise, and greenhouse effect would be dramatically reduced. This positive effect can come at a cost that is greater than most people perceive. So, the environment protection travellers who will reduce travelling times to avoid air pollution is caused to influence human health. It seems that airlines need to concern to apply psychological method to predict whose travelling consumption of behavior which is more suitable than behavioral economy method.

On the psychology view point on travelers, who will be more preferable to catch planes to go to different countries to travel, due to the chance of air pollution and global environmental warm issues will be reduced to low risk to influence our health if planes can use biofuel to be energy to fly in the future one day. It seems that spending expenditure to research other non polluted biofuel new energy is one solvable method to global airline industry in the future. To solve, any airlines or countries' governments or oil producers ought choose to spend more time to research new biofuel. Otherwise, the predicting when terrorism attacks event will be occurred, it is more difficult to predict the time more than researching to produce new biofuel energy method in the future.

So, I recommend that researching the new biofuel energy or other kinds of energy to substitute the oil energy and air pollution risk these two factors are the urgent behavioral economy method is used to solve this challenge which the airlines or oil producers or different countries' governments which need to concern nowadays. Because these two negative environment factors are the most influential to cause traveller individual travelling consumption desire to be fallen among of other negative environment factors.

Tourism strategy influences tourism industry reaches growth or mature life cycle stages

The main cost related factors to offline or online travel agents

Nowadays,many online or offline travel agents have interest to find what the main factors that can affect their strategies to reduce airline costs. The main factors include route structure, type and characteristics of the aircracft, cost of labor and management quality, which will influence whether which airline routes are the most suitable to let online travel agents or offline travel agents to help them to sell paper air tickets or electronic air tickets to attract travel consumption more easily.

Thus, a cost-related strategy is the main important factors to influence travel consumption choice between online or offline travel agents. For example, considering that advantages in costs is an important strategy for carriers to remain in travel transportation market.

The deregulation process of travel markets and increasing opportunities for competition have created excess capacity in many markets that causes lower rates, even with its rising costs. Thus, the travel strategic costs management as well as travel consumers that their behavior under different influences can bring competitive advantages over travel players.

Cost reduction in the travel market -based industry is a very important way of being competitive between offline and online travel agents, when facing travel air ticket prices decreasing for every trip. So reduce to total travel cost, e.g. fuel, maintenance, labor etc. is relevant, but the influence of each component on every total trip cost depends on factors that are related or not to airline operation. For example, some airline can adopt the lowest cost model to sell air tickets from offline or online travel agents which compete for travel passengers with traditional modes as self driving road transport trip in large areas of countries domestic travel market, such as US, UK domestic travel market.

However, the decision about the relevance of one cost is not a simple matter. The effectiveness of reduction of each item that comprises the total cost of airline can change over time, depending on both the business model and the scope of the airline company or online /offline travel agent company as well as external factors.

However, there are three types of competition advantage between online and offline travel market: They are such as agility, differentiation cost and the differentiation may be related to a product of superior quality, higher value f the brand or the company's positive reputation. Such as the online travel agent's providing the different airline cheap air ticket price and kind of trips to provide to travel consumer consumer comparison or the offline travel agent's famous brand or positive reputation to let travel consumers feel travel agents can provide many actual trip package to let them to compare by oral clearly. Thus, the online travel agent's weakness is lack of travel agent individual exploration to let every travel consumer to understand every trip package more clearly.

But online travel agent's strength is it can provdide one website to let travel consumer attempt to compare different trip air ticket and/or hotel price to make personal travel pre-booking decision at home. The another advantage is related to techniques that reduce production cost, making it is possible to offer cheaper air ticket, or hotel room rents, or cheap trip package, than the competition. Such as online travel agent can sell more cheap electronic air ticket price to compare traditional offline travel agent's paper air ticket price.

Finally, agility refers to the speed which the company responds to market demands. For example, if the online travel agent can make statistics to analyze how many online travel consumers to choose to buy which airlines' electronic or paper air tickets, e.g. which airline trip destinations and trips and hotels choices are the most popular attraction to them. Then, the online airline has possible to respond to provide to the most popular airline trips choices, electronic air ticket price comparison choices and hotel rooms prices choices to attract many online travel consumers to enter their online travel websites to choose different airline electronic tickets to buy or pre-book hotel rooms from travel agent websites. Also, if the traditional offline travel agents can attempt to gather every travel consumer's destination trips, hotels , airline paper or electronic ticket prices enquires to make statistics to make which travel trip journeys or destinations and airline paper travel ticket prices are the most popular. Then, it is possible that they can respond to every travel consumer individual demand more to attract whose travel agent choice more easily.

Airline travel agency AirAsia in the domestic airline low cost strategy

There are three major characteristics of the airline industry namely is product nature, its expenditure structure and its market entry conditions. Airline agent's product is homogeneous or undifferentiated , causing significant competition in airline domestic travel or foreign travel both markets, which are free from regulations and economic barriers. However, high capital and operating expenditure is another important characteristic of the airline industry. Aircrafts, airlines' major capital expenditure are very costly to acquire . For operating expenditures, aviation fuel and labor make up the two major costs in the industry.

Another important characteristic of the airline industry is the conditions for market entry, which differs between international and domestic airline markets . In the international travel market, airline travel agency entry is very difficult as international flights and routes are the results of regotiations between governments . On the other hand, in the domestic and regional travel market, travel agency entry depends on the level of deregulation or liberalisation.

More and more countries, however are opening up their domestic travel markets for more competition. In addition, government plays an important role to regulate the travel markets and existing players may significant influence over now travel agent entrants.

In fact, the mjor factors influence to international or domestic travel consumption increasing numbers are the global economy and safety issues, instead of other different economic factors, such as travel destination choice, electronic air ticket or paper air ticket price, hotel price , the country's political change, e.g. war occurrence, bad weather , e.g. very cold or very hot etc. different factors infuence. Because generally , the world or any region of it is in an economic crisis or depression , the demand for airline services will fall. The late 1990 year Asian financial crisis for example, resulted in minimal increase in the number of worldwide airline passengers incrased only minimally from 1997 to 1998 year. Another factor of influencing the travel passenger number to be decreased, it concerns safety issues are also an important driver of the travel industry, which is subject to very safety standards to influence travel passengers' travel choice to the country. In addition, they are also unexpected safety related events, such as the 11 Sept. 2001 year tragedy in the US, which caused reduction in passengers . The increasing popularity of low cost airlines is the newest trend in the airline industry if which hope many passengers choose to buy whose electronic air ticket or paper air ticket to catch which planes to fly from online travel agent or offline travel agent channels.

The rise of low cost airlines, such as AmericaWest, JetBlue and Airtran in US, Ryanair and EasyJet in Europe and Vigin Blue in Australia. The share of low cost airline strategy is popular in the US and European airline market. For example, the Southwest airline low cost strategy is the basis of most low cost airlines operations. The key of the strategy is to reduce costs when at the same time offering low prices to passengers. History showed that the low cost airline strategy is easy to replicate , but difficult to implement successfully.

However, I suggest airlines need to know what functions which can attract passengers to chose to catch their planes to fly if they expect to rise passenger numbers. For example, the critical function of the Malaysia airline travel is to connect the major towns and remote interior areas within East Malaysia, which has poor road systems and limited availability of other significant means of transportation . In contrast, West Malaysia has more developed and extensive rod and railway systems.

Therefore, airline travel is not the main mode of long distance transportation. It implies Malaysis airline ought concentrate on focusing short distance transportation strategy for passenger beneficial choice function. For example, a new small Malaysia airline serving one or two routes may enter easily. Otherwise, a larger airline servicing multiple routes may be harder to enter Malaysis airline market. It also means access to capital and labor are the major obstacles for new airline entrants to Malaysia airline market. Thus, small airlines into a larger airline is probably more likely to be successful as in Air Asia's case to Malaysia airline market.

Thus, the airline low cost strategy competition positions include very low or minimal pressive from other airline similar service substitute products, low or medium power of airline similar input suppliers. In conclusion, low cost airline strategy is a god method to be attempted to win competitors in airline market.

How consumers select travel service between online and offline mode in travel industry

Nowadays, the travel industry is operating through two different modes, online and offline respectively. It involves the identification of the competitive strategies adopted by the tour operators. For example, it was found that e-retil travel is platform that is bringing two market forced the demand and supply tour operators and the customers together, and both parties and more inclined towards online mode in near future. Tour operators are gaining by operating at low cost and increasing their business reach when customers get what they desire as per their convenience. For example, many tour operators had promoted tourism destination through website that allow user to use interface for booking transporttion, foreign exchange etc. However, the role of travel operators (agents) should be assisted any airlines to promote their travel package service by internet more easily , such as tourism destination , arrangement of hospitality, restaurants, transportation tools during their trips.

The reasons why consumers choose online travel service include:

Firstly, it is online researching hospitality service. Online travel websites can provide many different accommodation furniture, such as seeking hotel locations, rooms prices comparison, prepaid hotel rooms by visa card payment transaction method, range from luxury five stars deluxe category hotels to small guest houses. The primary need of tourist is to find a place for residing in foreign country or domestic country to ensure whose safety and relaxing needs. Online travel website channel can help whom to find a place , according to his/her needs and paying capacity in the most shorten times.

Secondly, it is online restaurant (food and beverages researching) service. Full service restaurants are divided into two categories, fine dining and casual dining restaurants . Fine dining restaurants are usually located in the premises of luxury hotels, provide high quality food at premium price with good ambience and highly trained professionals. Thus, travel consumers can also compare the different restaurant food price and seek where is the restaurant and find.

What food taste of food supply from the travel agency or travel operator website easily 250 + tour operators are registered with the ministry of tourism (website of tourism ministry) , and the major players in the industry are dealing online and are dominating the travel industry. The major online travel players are Thomas cook, Cox and Kings, make any trips, clear trip, gatra.com and Expedia.

The tour operators whether online or offline offers a large number of services to the tourists including customized package where the customer selects each element of the tour package, specialized tourism package and complete tour guide package.

Nowadays, the tour operational travel (agents) are working through two different modes: offline online . Big brands with luge investment are dealing online and enjoying low cost benefits and huge profit margins. When the small tour operators have their market niche and managing have their market niche and managing their profits by dealing offline.

It is generally prefer offline mode that is the opportunity for small capital investment or employee number for tour operators. But the large scenario is changing as with the usage of internet by the tour operations have given convenience to the customers and now the customers of modern age have started developing preference for online modern. Thus, internet technology change any countries' travel agents or tour operators' air ticket sale method. So, it brings electronic ticket sale method is more popular to compare to traditional travel paper air ticket sale method.

However, online electronic ticket sale method has its disadvantages such as online transaction is unsafe, if the consumer 's name and address and visa card number is stolen to let any internet users to know to be used to buy any products from internet channel easily. Otherwise, traditional walk in offline travel paper ticket sale method is more safe, because the travel consumers can pay cash to the travel agents directly.

However, offline travel agent disadvantages include that the research identified that information communication and technology has very crucial role for tourism industry. Tourist can access any kind of information about tourism destination and tourism products from any part of the world. Tourism comprehends with social media. For example, it was found that (ICT) is bosting up tourism industry. (ICT) helps in searching the location, search for information on tourism products, and e-booking of airline tickets and hotel reservation.

The online travel sale service attraction is that the recent development in the field of information communication and technology and its practical application in tourism and hospitality industry. Generally , online travel sale service must have consumer side and the supplier side.

The decision making prcess of consumer was analyzed and it was found that travel information search and traveller individual electronic ticker pre paid to prebook any plane seat, hotel rooms and restaurants prices comparison to prebook service of traveler individual purchase behavior are corresponding with the usae of (ICT).

What is the online travel sale service strategy?

The two most important things for travel operators (agents) are online travel marketing and strategic management. Former can enhance business operations. Use of (ICT) develops financial capabilities , however, it depends on management choice, financial condition and position. Some researchers recommended that the usage of IT should not be restricted at operational level, however it should be extended up to senior level and should be used for decision making. Social media is regarded as a platform where the tourists and travel operators/agents (suppliers) of tourism industry cross each other. Thus, the role of social media has been directed for future research in tourism industry. Hence, it seems online travel sale service has these features to attract travel consumers to choose to use this online mode to buy electronic air ticket. Such as, airline electronic air ticket price comparison, pre-booking plan seats to avoid full seats flights to delay consumer individual trip plan, pre-booking hotel rooms and prices comparison as well as prebooking restaurant seats and food price and taste comparison, travel destination easy search. Otherwise, these features to attract travel consumers to choose to walk in to travel agents to buy paper air ticket directly. They include: safe cash or visa card payment to avoid personal information is stolen by website payment channel, e.g. via card number, address, name , birth date personal information. Also the travel consumer can enquire any questions from the travel agent and gets individual feedback from the travel agent by oral before who ensure to choose to buy which kind of travel package for whose travel destination. In special, when the travel consumer has much time to spend to enquire any travel trip question, walk in travel agent is the best enquire methods to let the travel consumer to know the trip information clearly.

● Online/offline travel operators (agents) maketing strategies

Offline walk in travel unique segment service strategy

Nowadays, online and offlce travel operators competitions are serious. In fact, tourism marketing , there will be more need for online travel operators in the future, due to online travel sale service is popular to be accepted by online travel consumers. Thus, I recommend walk in offline travel agents need to concentrate on focusing some unique travel service to attract new or old travel consumers if who hope to survive.

I recommend that they can focus on specific specialized services, such as travel consultation (specialization) hypothesizing that systematic differences exist between the usage of travel agents for different travel contexts and travel agents can survive if they focus on specific segments of the market, such as older travelers (segmentation; hypothesizing that systematic differences exist between the usage of travel agents depending on the personal characteristics of travellers). The unique travel needs include: specific services related to package holidays, transport services, beach on city holidays, as well as destinations travellers are not familiar with.

I shall give my opinions to provide insight into alternative strategies for travel agencies in a matured travel market with a high internet penetration as below:

The internet online travel sale service is a reality of popular to let travel consumers to feel convenient to pre-book air seat, hotel rooms , air electronic ticket prices comparison. In order to make final purchase decision very easily in the shortest time. Consequently , it has penetrated the decision making process of travel to attract them to choose to buy electronic air ticket, prebooking hotel rooms or restaurant seats from online travel agent channel more than walk in offline travel agent channel. This is especially true in the tourism business where consumption to consume (booking) and the purchase-related information search (Bieger & Lasesser 2004; Crotts 1998).

In fact , apply website to provide travel sale method has these good consequence. From travel operator (agent) supplier's perspective, the success potential derived from operating a website consist of lower distribution costs, higher revenues and a larger potential market share (due to the ubiquitous access). From traverler's perspective, the internet allows direct communication with tourism suppliers facilitatinf requests for information and allowing services and travel related products, e.g. prebooking hotel rooms, restaurant seats , electronic or paper air tickets, travel trip arrangement package products to be purchased at any time and any place from online travel agents /operators conveniently.

Offline / online travel agency (operator) business depends on earn commissions on behalf of airlines. Thus, offline walk in travel agency (operator) business model that would extend existence as a booking agency (thus focusing on consultation and interpersonal contact) strategy.

As a matter of fact, commission -cutting , which began in the US well ahed of Europe, has had a profound effect specially on business travel agents . Consequently , many of them have re-invented themselves as " travel managers", instead of selling tickets and making arrangements, they charge consultancy fees for reducing the amounts client companies spend on travel (Daneshku, 1999).

● Systematic differences strategy applies to offline walk in travel agent

Thus, I recommend systematic differences strategy can be applied offline walk in travel agent (operator). It means that walk in travel agents could reorient their offline walk in travel agent business to focus on contexts that are less substitutable by other channels and media . Factors hypothetically attributing to the delineation of travel contexts include: helping travellers to choose best travel destinations, helping travellers to attempt to find the number of previous trips (indicating the familiarity with a destination) for their travel reference, helping them to find the cheapest, the most convenient and the most close transportation to ctch during their trips, helping them to find the different types of accommodation and rooms price comparison , nature/type of the trip comparison , arrangement of time of booking (as indicator of spontneous / planned travel) nd helping them to budget overall travel expenditure .

Systematic differences in travel agent use exist in dependence of personal (characteristics with with tourists. Walk in offline travel agents could benefit from a travelling client segmentation strategy and customize and target their services to those travellers that are most likely to be and remain their customers.

Factors hypotheticlly attributing to the traveller segment include: travel expenditure per day, useful travel information as indicator for perceived risk and socio-demographic (age, gender, highest completed and education, professional positions) . Generally, the role of walk in offline travel agent with regard to the travel infrromation search and booking behavior have take an incoming perspective. Such as looking at visitors from different travel markets at a similar destinations. The comparison of central importance in determining whether specialization of travel contexts or market segments is the more promising strategy for walk in offline travel agents.

However, travel package tours strategy must b offline walk in travel attraction . Due to some walk in travellers target segmentation market has still needs. Generally, this travel package tours of travel segmentation consumer who like to enquire the travel agents to concern what the hotel rooms price are the cheapest to provide to them to live, what transportation tools the travel agent can arrange to them to catch anywhere the country destination, the travel agent can provide them to visit during their tour journey. Thus, the travel trip package service is still popular need to offline walk in travel agent (operator). This market is only belonged to offline walk in travel agents (operators) nowadays.

Service fees and commission cuts strategy

The reduction or removal of airline commission continues to challenge travel agencies' profitability It is crucial to understand what trends travel agencies need to be aware of to ensure how to profitability and increase travel agencies' revenues with service-fee models.

Service fees are not only a way to compensate for the loss of airline commission but also a way to generate new revenue sources for travel agencies that guarantee their long term profitability. Many travel agencies are expanding their service fee models, both in terms of the mounts changed and the number of service to airline.

However, if travel agent charge too much service fee to exceed the general airline travel market service fee reasonable or standard level. It will influence many airlines do not choose to find the travel agent to help them to sell air tickets. Travel agents apply fees most often for airline related services. They charge differentiated fees depending on the destination, type of reservation (e.g. frequent flyer), number of tickets sold or type of airline (e.g. full service versus).

However, service fee increases can raise customer loyalty and satisfaction. It won't reduce client numbers or result in a lose in clients.. The reason is that service fees can be tailored to suit individual customer. This helps travel agencies target their clients, with tailored services based on their past purchasing patterns and identity services for which clients' willingness to pay is greater , such as trip planning identity service for which pay , such as hotel only or special promotion.

To revenue mix for travel agencies is increasingly shifting to service fes as airlines have lowered or cut commissions. Successful travel agencies in many European countries are fast adopting, and constantly upgrading , their service fee schemes. Thus, it seems reasonable service fee level is one important factor to influence travel agents and airlines good relationship. In fact, even travel agents raise service fee, it won't influence travel consumer number to be reduced , even they raise air ticket price. It they can provide the informations concerning the reasonable hotel rooms prices and food quality comparison to satisfy travel consumers' living arrangement or helping them to find the reasonable restaurants' food prices and where are their location arrangement or providing the reasonable airlines' electronic air tickets or paper air tickets sale service, even arrangement any high entertainment quality of travel destination trips to let travel consumers to feel satisfactory.

However, I believe the raise air ticket price factor won't influence the travel consumer number to be decreased. Any offline or online travel agents will encounter this crisis. By cutting travel agents' commission. Airlines decreased their dependence on travel agencies as a distribution channel. In fact, three key variable factors will influence travel agents' commission income to be decreased. They include below:

● The unsustainable or no change financial losses by airlines , due to the growth of low cost carriers, leading to an increase in the number of bankruptcies.

● No negative consequences from previous commission cuts: airline had progressively lowed the commission payments.

● No effective resource for travel agencies to satisfy airlines needs.

● The appearance of now airlines and air routes to provide to travel agencies to fall down air ticket price to attract consumers' choices, due to who don't feel to spend much money to go to this new air routes or catch new airline plans , whether these new air routes are excite to entertainment or whether they are safe planes to catch.

● An increase in the number of bankruptcies to cause travel comsumption desire to be reduced.

● New competition forced down air fares.

● The necessity to cut production costs, especially with low cost meaning low production costs and low fares, even if the two are closely linked.

Internet negative influences to travel agents

Although, on the one hand, internet creates offline travel agents to use websites to help them to sell electronic air ticket or travel related products, such as prebooking hotel rooms , restaurants, transportation tools etc. travel service. However, on the other hand, internet also brings travel agencies competitive disadvantage with regad to suppliers' direct websites , when airlines are able to control seat availability and prices. Indeed internet cause the decision is made by the airlines to reduce and/or eliminate travel agency commission has led them to use technology that many of their distrust or are not inclined to use, and to compare prices and travel schedules constantly.

As a result of this travel sale service environment, traditional offline travel agencies are at a competitive disadvantage with regard to online travel agencie and to airline carriers, which have developed their own direct websites where they are able to control seat availability and prices.

Nevertheless, travel agents' pay programmes remain. From some airlines, travel agents receive negotiated incentive commission closely linked to their performance as incentive . However, airlines still need travel agents' assistance to help them to promote air tickets to sell, due to travel agents can provide trip packages, transportation tools, prebooking hotel rooms, restaurants and air tickets arrangement and they can give any enquiries to every individual travel consumer. It is free charge travel professional enquiry service for travel agency's competitive features.

Consequently, how agencies can reduce their reliance on airline commission payments. I recommend these following strategic options to them to apply as below:

● Streamlining operations, controlling staff costs, when ensuring the client feels as little impact as possible.

● Expanding or moving into the leisure business, where commissions on ono-air products remain high (cruise, hotel, railway travel)

● Specializing in geographic areas or becoming niche players for specific leisure products, e.g. destination weddings, student travel group cultural travel, cruises only, cruise and railway travel etc.

● (d) establishing a service fee driven business model.

Concentrating on business travel marketing strategy

The certain characteristics to the business travel market allowed this sector to adapt more easily to the disappearance of commission. Business travel systems have always had different relationship with different customers. They usually have long term buyer relationships, set up long before the commission cap. Some of them quickly renegotiated their contracts to include a transaction or management fee, knowing that the majority of these fee arrangements are specific the need of the client.

The reasons why airlines reduce commission to paid to travel agents. They include petrol costs increasing, e.g. indirect and by pass the established distribution chain by developing airlines' their own websites; reducing or removing commission paid to travel agencies. Consequently, the decision to cut travel agencies' commission clearly shows that airlines wanted to decrease their reliance and dependence on travel agencies as a distribution channel. Thus, the internet appears to be an efficient and cost-effective distribution channel. Also, by creating airlines' own websites and setting directly to their clients, airlines are also to control seat availability to their clients and prices to their websites.

What an e-commerce strategy is used by internet travel websites?

Nowadays, the commercial use of electronic travel ticket travel is common, the most purchased online products include, for example, the name brands in online travel Epedia.travel .com and cheap tickets have been or are being integrated in large online travel firms.

Generally, online travel websites apply these strategies to attract travel consumers as below:

Firstly, shopping mall strategy, means to conduct a comprehensive factors for e-commerce. The online service provider needs to organize catalogs of services, take orders through their websites, accept payments securely, send service or related document, such as airline tickets to consumers and manage client data , such as client profiles.

Secondly, portal strategy, portal websites , such as yahoo give visitors the chance to find almost everything , they are working for in one place. Websites , such as Altavista.com and yahoo.com provide users with a shopping page that links them to many sites carrying a variety of products. Once a client is familiar with a website, who will be more likely to use the online service.

Thirdly, pricing strategy, low price is as a major competitive weapon. It includes a comparison pricing on discount price or price negotiation to let online travel consumers to get the best electronic travel ticket price choice to buy any airline tickets.

Travel agents vs online booking: Tackling the shortcomings and strengths

Consequently, however, one travel consumer who chooses either online booking sale service or traditional walk in offline travel agent to enquire travel service. These both of travel sale methods have shortcomings also. Such as it is possible that online electronic travel ticket purchase has personal data ,e.g. visa card, name, birth data, address, which will be stolen by online crime internet users more easily, who can not enquire any travel questions to get clear travel information concern whose travel destination package service choice or hotel room choice or transportation tool or restaurant choice and airline choice by travel agent. Also, it is possible that walk in travel agent paper travel ticket purchase shortcomings include that the travel consumer can not check any airlines' seat and pre book hotel room or transport tool or restaurant in the shorten time if who needs to fly immediately. Thus, it seems that online travel agent's client group is business travel intention, who does not need to enquire travel agent and has desire to per book airline seat in the short time. Otherwise, the offline walk in agent's client group is entertainment intention , who need to walk in to travel agent to enquire whose travel package and has no desire to pre book airline seat in the short time. Thus, online travel agent ought concentrate on design good travel package for the business travel consumers. Otherwise, offline travel agent ought concentrate on design good travel package for the entertainment travel consumers. Thus, they can have themselves unique travel target package to adopt to their different travel need. Such as business travel consumers need to live cheap and comfortable hotels, catching cheap and fast transportation tools in their business trips, eating in cheap and good taste food in restaurant and spending the less time to catch the airline plan to arrive the destination and cheap and comfortable business class plan seat. Such as entertainment travel consumers need the travel agent can help them to design cheap and enjoyable travel package, includes living comfortable hotel room, exciting and enjoyable trip, good taste food and railway, travel bus, cruise and plane provision in trip.

In conclusion, In fact, tourism is a quite unique area of business in a sense that is a travel sale service product and it can't be observed or manipulated through direct experience prior to purchase . Instead clients have to purely rely on indirect or virtual experience. Thus, every online or offline travel agent ought attempt to design different travel package to attract every business traveler or entertainment traveller trip need because every traveler will have personal unique trip need in this competitive travel sale service market in the future.

Reference

Bieger. Th., and Ch. Laesser (2004). " Information sources for travel decisions: Toward a source process model," Journal of travel reserch, 42(4):

357-371.

Daneshku, S. (1999). " Unwived travel agents unworried bi internet, " Financial Times , London. June 16, 1999:10.

Foucault, B. Lery, N. Rifkin, A. & Silfies , 2000.
" Comparision of textbook prices by retailer and by college" working paper. Cornell University, Ithaca, Ney.

Oil price changes influences tourism industry experiences growth life cycle stage or decline life cycle stage

Why is economic theory, a worthwhile thing to do ? e.g. helping organizations to solve challenges, helping society to solve challanges in macro economic view, part of the attraction and the promise of economics is that it cliams to decribe policies that will improve people's lives. This is unlike most other physical and social sciences. Sociology and political science have a policy component, but for the most part, they are concerned with understanding the function of standards of living, but this is really a by-product of science as an intellectual activity matters, physical science, has the potential to improve people standards of living.

What is the role of theory in a policy science? When my view that economic is a policy science. I mean that however either old or new economic theories one useful in policy. Theory is as a substitute for data. For example, we want to determine how a market price will respond to a tax, we could estimate this effect by running a regression of market price, against tax rates, controlling for as many other variable as possible. This would give us an equation that we could use to product how prices respond to change in taxes of one country has many unemployment people, then if it's government change a little 2 to 3 % import tax to private cars. Then, it may cause the country's car buyers number to import car demand decreases. The elastic to car import tax is high because the country has many people are unemployment. Hence, society is continue changing. So, some economists will research how to apply old economic theories to change other new theories to attempt to solve social and organizational challenges. In new economic theories, they are applied new modelling techniques to old real world problems, they add something to economic knowledge to the extent that we accept formalisation as a source of progress in economic. Some economists focus new economic theory on the dynamic of regional growth and economic activity aspect. When the former foucs on long-run regional growth and later is linked to the " new growth theory". For example, the traditional trade theory is unable to explain the existence of different production structures , e.g. the country's geographical positions in similar regions. Also, trade should lead to conflice face greater market competition and loose incomes. Finally, countries having complementary factors were the best condidates to the formation of trading, so that they will specialize in different commodities. In addition, the traditional trade theory performs poorly when there is high mobility of production factors.

I shall indicate what the difference between new and old economic theories below:

In old economic theories, they may include: Scarcity means that the condition in which our wants and greates than our limited resources. So, we must make choices on how we will use resources. Hence, economic-social concerned with the efficient use of limited resources to achieve maximum satisfaction of economic wants; micro-economic studies such as individuals, firms and industries (competitive markets, labour markets, personal decision making etc.) Otherwise, macro-economics studies the large economy as a whole or in its national economic growth. Government how spends, inflation, unemployment etc. Marginal analysis involves making decisions based on the additional benefits vs. the additional cost.

● Old economic theory

● production possibilities curve

Everyone acts rationally by comapring the marginal costs and marginal benefits of every choice. For example, if you decide to go to college, the opportunity cost of going to college may include work to earn money, production possibilities have four assumptions: Only two goods can be produced, full employment of resources, fixed technology, resources. For example, when one firm produces two products . One is pizza food, another is robots. It produces many robots, then it will produces less pizzas. If it hopes to involve to produce pizzas, but it won't reduce to produce robots. It must need to improve technology in order to improvements in pizza ovens, but robots producing number won't be reduced . If the country has mad cow disease kills 85% of cows, then it will influence the demand for pizza decrease. Then, it may avoid to improve technology to produce many pizza, it can concentrate on applying technology to produce new robot making technology.

In the production possibiliteies curve and efficiency refers this firm can have productive efficiency when robots are being produced in the least costly way, due to pizzas produced number is reduced, this is any point on the production possibilities curve as well as allocative efficiency, when this firm's robots being produced are the ones most desired by society. This optimal point on the ppc depends on the robotic products desires of society.So, the less demand to pizzas, it will influence it applies less technology to produce pizzas, but more technology to be improved to concentrate on producing robotic products.

● Specialization of trade theory

Specialization of trade explains one country can earn comparative advanage when the producer will be lowest opportunity cost to produce. So, countries should trade if they have a relatively lower. For example, US specializes and makes only wheat. Brazil makes only sugar. So, US can export wheat and Brazil can export sugar to earn comparative advantages . When there two countries only concentrate or producing on kind of food in order to earn specialization trade advantages. Free market means little government involvement in the economy, (laissez faire), individuals own resources and the opportunity to make profit gives people incentive to produce items efficiently, wide variety of goods available to consumers and competition and self-interest work together to regulate the economy keep computers and only one company is making them, other making computers to earn profit.

● Invisible hand

This lead to more competition, which means lower prices, better quality, and more product variety. Consequently, most efficient production of the goods, that consumers want, produced at the lowest prices and the highest quality. What does invisible hand mean? It is the concept that society's goals will be met as individuals seek their own self-interest. For example, when society wants fuel efficient cars. Profit seeking producers will make more, then competition between firms results in low prices,high quality and greater efficiency . Consequently, the government does not need to get involved since the needs of society are automatically met. Thus competition and self-interest act as an invisible hand that regulates the free market.

I shall indicate some new economic theories as below:

● Organizational behavioral economic theory

In new economic theories, it may include behavioral economics, it explains how has changes views of consumer theory and finance, hoe to deal climate change and analyze new ways to deal with international environmental problems, farm economy how to raise crop, vegetable, food productivities, how farmers' agriculture growing behavior can achieve crop, raising productivites aim more easily, e.g. predicting climate when is bad change time.

In new miceo economic theory, economists have recommended new economic theory to help organizations to solve problem effectively and efficiently. The problem solving steps include as below:

Identifying the problems, identifying current successes and strengths, analyzing the causes of the problems, identifying the factors that enable our success, envision our desired future, treating the problems, innovating to build more support for those factors that enable success and move us toward the future we desire. For example, whether or not a team is able to sell the big picture and engage in effective strategic planning depends on members' feeling hoping and looking toward a positive future. By appropriate , they mean information that is realistic and timely information that is true and relevant to the situation. Negative information is approriate when it provides the specific boundaries within which a challenge must be met.

In an economic tightening scenario, for example, appropriate negativity might include a target budget reduction amount and time frame. It might also include recognition that staff and elected officials will have to make hard decisions. Hence, in new micro economic theory, it mains to help organizations to find to avoid target budget exceeds to any projects implementations and avoid prolong time to finish any projects for any organizations, less spending and time reducing or raising efficiency and effective achievement will be applied new nicro economic theory to help any organizations to be applied new micro economic theory to help any organizations to achieve benefits (intangible , i.e. reducing time and raising efficiency, tabgible , i.e. less salaries spending and project team members number to any projects).

Hence, new micro economy theory aims to research new organizational behavior can achieve raising efficiency and improving productivities aims. For graphic organizers theory aims to help organizatins to enhance any organizations members' thinking skills by encouraging brainstorming, generating new ideas, connecting parts to the whole, drawing sequence, analyzing causes and effects etc. There are exactly important traits of economic students to make sense out of economic phenomena and to make effective decisions about economic issues. Thus, in new micro economy view to organizations. It explains that every organizational member ought be independent graphic organizer:

They will ought need to be enhanced skills to help that organizations to achieve any aim easily. They may include : organizations show events in chronological orders multiple timeline (sequential organizers), or hierarachy diagram (hierarchical organizers), such as organizers showing the relation between a concept and its subordinate levels of characteristics, ccyclical organizers (organizers showing the sequence of events in a process , e.g. circle organizer), conceptual organizers . (organizers showing how a mian concept is supported by facts, evidence and characteristics, e.g. concept definition map).

So, new micro economic thoery explains that every organizational memeber may explain that every organizational memeber may have different organizer role when they need to cooperate with other members in themselves organizations any time. When they know whether what their organizer role is in the time. They can make thinking strategy skill more easily in short time , it will bring any organizations much intangible economic benefits, such as reducing meeting time, avoiding over-spending and prolonging time to finish any projects for the organization efficiently.

● Division of labor theory

The another new micro economy theory is divison of labor, organizational coordination and market mechanisms in collect time, problem solving skills. It is a view of economic organizations as problem-solving driven by trial -and error learning and collective selection. It assumes any one economic organization ought produce " well constructed" goods and services, achieves productivity among workers and solving problems by technological search and economic production activities raising skills, the most cheap and the most useful function in order to raising the product productivities and quality improvement.

● Logical process theory

For logical process theory , it implies that most technologies and industries and born with a highly vertically-integrated structure, undergo a distintegration process as the industry grows in the expansion phase, and then re-integrate in the maturity phase, but often along integration proles that differ signicantly from those of the original infant industry. Thus, the degree of vertical integration of an industry undergoes major changes along its life cycle. For IBM computer company example, its needs to find any new product to make new market share, such as IBM electronic book publish will be on new technological product market. Due to ecommerce is popular, many readers began to accept to apply internet technological tool to read any books. So, IBM had attempted to sell electronic books in this new ecommerce e-book publishing market. So, IBM needs to expand its traditional computer sale market to (AI) artificial intelligent mobile and electronic book publish both markets. IBM's computer products has reached maturity phase, it needs to change its another new technological products market. It ought not follow its old logical process to continue research how to invent new computers. It ought change to research how to invent new (AI) mobiles and innovate its electornic book reading platforms to attract many electronic books attractively as well as invent new (AI) mobiles to attract many (AI) mobile users. If it still hopes to continue to win its computer competitions in technological product industry.

● Managerial economics

Another new economic theory is managerial economics, it means tha application of economic methods to the managerial decision making process. It is a fundamental part of any business. It is more attention in business as mergers become more aware of its potential as an aid to decision making, and this potential is increasing all the time. For example, global warming challenge will riase cost to our socity, how governments assess the possible scale of cuture green-house gas emissions, and hence of man-made global warming, involves economic forecasts and economic calculations. Those forecasts and calcualtions will provide the basic for poicy on environment pollution issue how to avoid future social cost raises in possible.

Hence, managerial economics may mean how managers find the most efficient way of allocating scarce resources ans reaching their objectives. It aims to predict and compare the cost and benefit may occur when the manager chooses to do the action. In a neoclassical framework, it treats the individual elements within the economy (consumers, firms , workers) as rational agents with objectives that can be expressed as quantitative functions (utilities and profits) that are to be optimized, subject to certain quantitative constraints.

What is the relevance of the managerial economic theory? For example, protesting against global capitalism that economics is of no use in answering the fundamental questions involving value judgements, like reducing pollution, indeed, economists themselves often admit that their science can only make positive impression of the limitations of economics. Hence, in managerial economic view, government should make use of market forces in order to achieve a more efficient solution.

In the terms of reducing pollution, would governments aim to reduce pollution by 90% in the next ten years? But rich and poor countries would suffer overall from a policy of reducing pollution by 90% and that future generations might not benefit either. So, managerial economic theory aims to let policy maker how to make the more reasonable analysis to conclude and to solve any issue for organization leader or government leader, even individual consumer.

● Social entrepreneurship theory

The final new economic theory is social entrepreneurship for each country, regardless of its socio and economic development, one of the main key indicators of success is the social stability of society. Impossibilty of market and government, are the factors that contribute to the need of social enterprise that provides partical and dynamic solution for local social problems. This social innovation form an environment that promotes scientific, technical , technological and informational innovations increase efficiency of new techniques and technologies reduce innovation costs. So, the new economic theory explains society needs to change. So, social entrepreneurship is needed because society is needed to innovate that serves to adopt social changes and development.

Some economists believe that social enterprise is a new way to solve social and economic problems and focus of social innovation and brings positive change to society. In any one social entrepreneurship, it needs coordinational strategy for the development of social entrepreneurship .So, every one is stakeholder to the social entreprenership. Thus, today a significant theoretical basis for this new economic theory , " social entrepreneurship" concept in the new economic model is formed . Consequently, social entrepreneurship is an innovative form of business, which successfully combines social aims and commercial practice .

Consequently, social entrepreneurship is a innovative form of business, which successfully combines socail aims and commercial practice. Social entrepreneurship ought may solve these social challenges, such as unemployment, poverty, skillful workers number shorten . However, socail entrepreneurship works where the government can not work , due to the lack of funding, and the business does not want to become of low profit ability.

Hence, social entreprensurship is a charity and business approaches to solving social problems. Also unlike traditional business that works for the seeking profit only , social enterprise, performs social functions and works where the government can not work , due to the lack of funding , and the business does not want to become of low profitability. Social enterprise changes the traditional economy model, it does not depend on external sources (donors, grants and donations) , the necessary start up capital , receives income from its own activities. It carries on non-profit activities. It includes socio-oriented structure, the goal of activity is to mitigate or solve the specific social problems. Consequently, profits are reinvested in activity expansion or for social purposes in case of charity organization there is no profit and in traditional business the profits share between shareholders.

New economic development in Tourism and oil industries

● How to develop new economic tourism industry

How to develop tourism industry in new economic environment? Any examination of the new economic development of travel and tourism requires definitions of the subject and its components, which are suitable for economic analysis. However, in new economic development to tourism industry, it is also important to look at tourism conceptually, in order to set the scene for a deeper understanding of the future new tourism industry development.

Tourism is neither a phenomenon nor a simple set if industries, however, in new or old economic development environment. It is a human activity which encompasses human behavior, use of resources, and interaction with other people, economies and leisure enjoyment environment. It is also involved physical movement of tourists to locales other than their normal living places.

In future new economic environment, traditional travel needs to include these element in order to satisfy traveler enjoyment and leisure feeling: They may include: Tourist needs and motivations, tourism selection and behavior and constraints , travel away from home , market interactions between tourists and those supplying products to satisfy tourist needs and impacts on tourists , hosts, economies and environments.

In new economic environment, the tourism products may include: carriers, in any forms of transport for tourist travel accommodation, man-made attractions, which could also include the managed areas of natural attractions, private sector and public sector support services, middlemen, such as tour wholesalers and travel agents.

The tourism resources may also include: Natural resources, lands , minerals, water and biological; labor resources, human work, and enterprise; capital resources, manmade enhancement and other resources. The travel and tourism resources problems may include: As there is frequently a mismatch between producer and consumer perception of what constitutes the tourism product , there may be conflict in ideas of which resources are properly involved as well as many of the resources likely to be in demand for tourism are public goods , or even free resources.

In new economic development to tourism industry view, we need to consider that tourism and travel has the reputation of being a relatively clean and pleasant industry in which to work or invest in order to attract a greater number of resource suppliers than as less well-perceived industry, which therefore keeps rewards prices down by competition, how to attract those retiring from or travel business for example, if their finances are already sound, income from travel is not expected to be optimal , travel and tourism is frequently highly seasonal , offering rewards that are competitive with other industries only some of the time, destination products are often in locations which are of little use to other industries, so that competition for resource use if minimal and hence rewards are low.

In general, tourist purpose may include: recreational purpose : holiday, health and sport and religion as well as business purpose: company business , e.g. conventions and sales trips. So, in new economic tourism development aim, tourism industry need consider hoe to achieve incentive trips to let these both tourists to feel. For example, the overall type of tourism required, destination arrangement, travel mode, accommodation and attraction visiting and purchasing method or distribution channel. The purchasing method choices may include: whether to buy an inclusive package or separate service, whether to buy direct from suppliers, such as airlines or hotels or use an agent , which tour wholesaler or operate or agent to use.

I predict the tourism development in new economic view, it may have these characteristics: Few enterprises in travel and tourism are large, highly cashed-up and have a large asset base, enterprises within travel and tourism that are not in a financial position to diversify, and those do well success to the above –average growth obtainable in travel and tourism compared with many other industries, they would therefore tend to expand within the sector. The result of individual enterprise growth and integration within travel and tourism is an increase in the concentration of that industry. The degree to which output is produced of fewer and fewer enterprises. This can be only be accounted for realistically with the context of an individual economy, Levels of concentration in any part of travel and tourism in the future are likely to depend on two opposing factors: The constant demand by many tourist market segments for new experiences and products, which encourages the development and survival of more and diverse enterprises, and therefore leads to the reduction of concentration as well as technology, which in travel and tourism frequently calls for large capital outlays and requires mass markets for efficient use, promotes integrations and large scale enterprise, especially in air travel and non-personal services (marketing and information communication, travel insurance , tourism payment methods). IN these areas, concentration will undoubtedly increase in future new economic development environment.

● How new economic development in oil industry

The future global economic growth, it will influence personal incomes and GDP rise. They would carry different weight in different countries at different times. Starting from low levels of incomer and economic development. Household consumption will change from being dominated by basic heat to rapidly rising energy use for higher levels of comfort in space heating and cooling (and large dwellings), and greater use of electrical appliances, finally to a degree of saturation influenced by the income distribution patterns of the country concerned. Income distribution typically changes very slowly, so that the technical market for heart will never be saturated because there will always be a proportion of poor people living in small spaces less comfortably than the average. Industrial energy consumption will be influenced by technical efficiency within each sector, and by changes in the structures of the economy, e.g. changing proportions of agriculture, heavy and light industry, and services. One may eventually see evidence of diminishing marginal returns to additional energy inputs compared to other inputs. Energy consumption in the energy transformation sector may be influenced by income, which drives the demand for electricity to influenced by income, which drives the demand for electricity to grow faster than the demand for heat, but is also subject to the chosen technology of transformation, which is influenced by the cost and availability of primary energy inputs (fuels) in new economic development environment.

IN new economic development environment, it will influences that fuels do not compete in all sectors; for example, the transport sector is dominated by oil. Nuclear and hydroelectric power (and most renewables) reach the user through electricity; electricity itself competes with the direct burning of fossil fuels. Electricity provides the means by which other fuels can compete with oil and gas in sectors, such as space heating and process heat. It also is the only means of powering applications such as motors, computers and lighting: these subsectors are difficult to analyze. However, there is strong evidence that higher incomes do not weaken the demand for electricity so much as the demand for energy in total (in contrast to the effect on the demand for non-electric energy forms).

Econometricians look at the historical record of change in fuel prices and quantities to distinguish several factors between the new economic development and old economic development to oil industry in the future. An income effect. Increasing (reducing) fuel prices reduces (increases) the purchasing power of consumers' income: higher incomes caused by lower prices will increase energy consumption; the consumers' allocation of the increased income to energy purchases may reduce as income rises. Thus income may be heading in a different direction from fuel prices that the effect of fuel price changes when incomes are rising means simply that rising incomes have increased demand. Reducing the cost of using energy through win-win efficiency measures causes a similar problem . On the consequence, in future new economic development environment, it may influence in both cases demand will be less than if the future oil price or efficiency has not changed. The other effect is that an efficiency or substitution effect. An increase in fuel prices may cause consumers to spend more on new equipment, building materials and management operations, which will reduce the amount of fuel required to give the same energy result to the user. The extent of the efficiency effect depends on what happens to the price of the new equipment or building: if those price s rise in line with the fuel price, changes in the balances between fuel and capital or management will not occur. A new user technology , such as the development of the combined cycle gas turbine generator may increase efficiency and thus greatly reduce the quantity of primary fuel needed to produce the required output in this case electricity. If electricity prices had remained sticky, and the electricity and gas markets were not competitive, some of this advantages could have accrued to the gas suppliers in the form of an increase in price, because th4 unit of gas produces more output of electricity, it would have a higher value. In reality, the development of new economic competitive environment in both gas and electricity has tended to ensure that the benefits of such technical advanced accrue to the consumer through lower final prices. The same many apply in the case of improved efficiency in future non-manual driving auto vehicle development: the consumer's cost of motoring is reduced in new economic non-manual driven auto vehicle (Artificial intelligent vehicle) can replace manual driven vehicle , even electricity battery can replace oil energy to be used in vehicles. So, oil price may be influenced to reduce in future new economic development environment.

In fact, the past oil price occurrence history of the dramatic structural had changed a high price imposed on airlines, travelers, and destination countries, all of which will have to navigate through times of shifting or even declining travel demand. I assume that a high oil price scenario is assumed in the long term in order to highlight the changes , such a senario would mean for consumer behavior and the competitiveness of several destinations.

Low oil price in the 1970 and early 1980 did not bring significant growth of international air travel, but its growth has been strongest between 1980 and 2004, a period with stable and relatively moderate oil prices. Also, the rapid development of the low-cost carrier business model in the 1990s further fueled air travel growth by capturing tourism leisure demand , such as weekend leisure travel to cities using mostly secondary airports in any big area countries, such as UK, US . However, the tourism growth is whole influenced by high oil prices, due to oil price had been continue rising in possible.

Basis of oil is shortage supply product, oil is assumed to be the main energy source for the aviation sector for the nest 30 years. Although, second-generation biofuels seem to be on the horizon, the economics as well as the production scalability and aviation biofuel shortage will be a main challenge to airline industry. So, I assume that oil price will continue rise up, if there have none any aviation biofuel can be reflected to oil to use for air plane energy.

Until 2004, the only factors to have affected air travel growth, negatively were in external shocks , such as 9/11, causes catching air plane crisis or US regional geopolitical conflicts. It brings some travelers feel fear to go to US travel, as well as until recently 2019, human mouth disease can influence air to have disease to anyone from mouth. So, global travelers number had been continue decreasing, because they are fear to get disease by air when many themselves every stranger travelers are sitting on the without windows air planes. Although, mouth human and air disease and US 9/11 air attack both matters may influence oil price falls effect, because air planes flying times will reduce. They won't need frequent to fly, to cause aviation oil energy need reduce. Consequently, oil price will decrease, due to travelers number reduces and air planes flying times are also influenced to reduce. (oil demand decreases cause oil price decrease). Although, air lines ' cost will also be influenced reduce, but oil price decrease can not bring travelers number increase , when air ticket price reduce because global many leisure and business trip travelers feel fear to catch air planes frequently when human mouth air disease occured in 2019. So, oil price decreases can not grow up tourism industry growth or rise tourism income.

However, the obvious impact of a high oil price is an increase in the operating costs of airline. Moreover, fuel cost as a percentage of airline operating costs vary significantly based on the length of the flight. The longer the flight, the higher the fuel costs as a percentage of the airline operating cost. So, from an online's perspective, long -hauel flights represent the most criticial challenge to profitable operation because the share of fuel on these flights, compared with other cost items, is largest, because of the unfacorable fuel economics, due to fuel costs even at high-load factors. For example, Thai airways dropped its non-stop Bongkok to US flights in the summer of 2008 for commercial reasons, because fuel reached operating cost levels of 55 percent on this route, a cost burden that could not be passed on to their customers. So, the estimated price elacticity of passengers demand at this Bongkok to US flights route is high, if Thai Airways rises less air ticket price, it will influence many travelers to choose other airlines to catch air plan to fly. Hence, due to Thai Airways can not make decision to rise air ticket price, because it believes that it will lose many travelers, so it only chooses to drop this non-stop Bongkok to US flights to avoid fuel cost rising economic loss.

However, although micro and macro economic theories may also that oil price variable or change, it may influence global tourism income. But, recently, on 2019, human mouth and air diseases, it can influence global individual leisure and business trip travelers feel fear to catch air plans to avoid their bodies get this kind of death sickness when they sit in the no fresh air supplying air planes. They feel that they reduce leisure travelling flying times or business trip flying times with strange travelers to sit in crowd air planes together. Then, they must many avoid human moth and air disease to avoid death crisis. Hence, in this global human mouth and air diseases threat environment occurrence, even oil price sudden reduces to low price, it brings airline's cost reduces and air ticke price reduces. However, when air ticket price reduce to be very cheaper, it can not still attract global many leisure or business trip travelers to buy air tickets to fly frequently. Why does air ticket reduction, it can not attract many leisure or businee trip travelers to buy air ticket to fly ? The main reason is because human mouth and air disease influences global many travelers feel fear to catch air planes frequently. In psychological view, this kind of human mouth and air sickness will bring long time negative influence to global traveles do not want to catch air planes for business trips or travelling leisure frequently. So, it implies that oil price changing to influence air ticket price reduction factor ought not main factor to influence tourism income. It may include traveler individual negative emotion psychological factor, such as human mouth and air disease or 2019 9/11 attack both cases, they can influence global travelers feel fear to catch air planes to fly to avoid death threat. So, oil changing price ought not be only one absolute main factor to influence global tourism income significantly.

On conclusion, in economic view, it seems that oil chang price may have indirect or direct relationship to influence tourism income, instead of some unpredicted external environment factors influence, such as US 9/11 attack crisis and human mouth and air disease factors, they may be main factors to influence travellers number to reduce in non-economic external unpredicted environment view.

Tourism industry life cycle stage strategy

Our global tourism development had been developed from birth cycle stage to decline life cycle stage nowadays. From 1960 beginning, when airplanes were popular to be increased need to global travelers. Hence, from 1960 to 1970 is whole global tourism industry birth cycle stage. Till to 1971 beginning, many Asia, e.g. Singapore, Japan, China and Western, e.g. UK,

UK etc. countries people, they have jobs to do ,and they have more extra money to prepare to choose any leisure activities. From 1971 to 1980, it is growth life cycle stage to global tourism industry. Many airplane manufacturers had been beginning to manufacturer many airplanes because they felt global traveler number would increase. In fact, in this ten years, global traveler number had been increasing every year. Then, from 1981 to 2019 this fourty years, it is global tourism industry nature life cycle stage. It means that every year travel number had been increasing more significantly to compare past. Also, many travelers feel need to travel every year. So, global travel tourism industry may reach the most top travel clients level in this fourty years. However, till to 2020 , due to COVD19 human mouth and disease occurrence, it influences global travelers feel fear to catch air planes to travel because this kind COVD 19 human mouth disease may cause lung disease from air. When many travelers are sitting in the close window air plane, if one person has ths kind COVD19 human mouth disease. The sick person may contact air to let the persons to breath to cause lung disease in possible in airplane. So, global travelers number is decreasing after 2019 . Also, it implies that tourism industry is facing decline life cysle stage.

It brings these questions: IS it right time to develop space tourism? Can space tourism help future tourism industry to re-grow its life cycle stage from nowadays decline life cycle stage? Can space tourism develop to nature stage from birth life cycle stage ? I shall attempt to give evidence to explain whether space tourism may be developed to let human has more one kind tourism . It may be future leisure new trend for travelers, instead of earth travel. Because one day earth tourism destination may not bring leisure interesting to global traveler, then space tourism may be attempted to replace this kind of travelling activity . So, space tourism is birth life cycle stage. However, our earth tourism may define moral tourism, nature tourism, green tourism, responsible tourism in future new travelling leisure trend.

It bring these questions: Can our future tourism industry meet the expectations with the terms " ecological tourist"? Which factors affect the product life cycle of eco tourism? Nature and green tourism may be our earth new kind of travel activities, when many young and old age travelers like to climb mountains, they feel life nature scene more than non-man made) nature scene in their journeys, they do not like to visit cities to travel. It is possible that they often work in offices, this office working factor may influence many travelers like green tourism in the future. So, green or nature tourism will be our future popular tourism leisure activities. It may influence nowadays our tourism decline life stage to re-grown to nature life cycle stage in possible in this COVD19 people mouth disease influential environment.

New economic development in Tourism and oil industries

● How to develop new economic tourism industry

How to develop tourism industry in new economic environment? Any examination of the new economic development of travel and tourism requires definitions of the subject and its components, which are suitable for economic analysis. However, in new economic development to tourism industry, it is also important to look at tourism conceptually, in order to set the scene for a deeper understanding of the future new tourism industry development.

Tourism is neither a phenomenon nor a simple set if industries, however, in new or old economic development environment. It is a human activity which encompasses human behavior, use of resources, and interaction with other people, economies and leisure enjoyment environment. It is also involved physical movement of tourists to locales other than their normal living places.

In future new economic environment, traditional travel needs to include these element in order to satisfy traveler enjoyment and leisure feeling: They may include: Tourist needs and motivations, tourism selection and behavior and constraints , travel away from home , market interactions between tourists and those supplying products to satisfy tourist needs and impacts on tourists , hosts, economies and environments.

In new economic environment, the tourism products may include: carriers, in any forms of transport for tourist travel accommodation, man-made attractions, which could also include the managed areas of natural attractions, private sector and public sector support services, middlemen, such as tour wholesalers and travel agents.

The tourism resources may also include: Natural resources, lands , minerals, water and biological; labor resources, human work, and enterprise; capital resources, manmade enhancement and other resources. The travel and tourism resources problems may include: As there is frequently a mismatch between producer and consumer perception of what constitutes the tourism product , there may be conflict in ideas of which resources are properly involved as well as many of the resources likely to be in demand for tourism are public goods , or even free resources.

In new economic development to tourism industry view, we need to consider that tourism and travel has the reputation of being a relatively clean and pleasant industry in which to work or invest in order to attract a greater number of resource suppliers than as less well-perceived industry, which therefore keeps rewards prices down by competition, how to attract those retiring from or travel business for example, if their finances are already sound, income from travel is not expected to be optimal , travel and tourism is frequently highly seasonal , offering rewards that are competitive with other industries only some of the time, destination products are often in locations which are of little use to other industries, so that competition for resource use if minimal and hence rewards are low.

In general, tourist purpose may include: recreational purpose : holiday, health and sport and religion as well as business purpose: company business , e.g. conventions and sales trips. So, in new economic tourism development aim, tourism industry need consider hoe to achieve incentive trips to let these both tourists to feel. For example, the overall type of tourism required, destination arrangement, travel mode, accommodation and attraction visiting and purchasing method or distribution channel. The purchasing method choices may include: whether to buy an inclusive package or separate service, whether to buy direct from suppliers, such as airlines or hotels or use an agent , which tour wholesaler or operate or agent to use.

I predict the tourism development in new economic view, it may have these characteristics: Few enterprises in travel and tourism are large, highly cashed-up and have a large asset base, enterprises within travel and tourism that are not in a financial position to diversify, and those do well success to the above –average growth obtainable in travel and tourism compared with many other industries, they would therefore tend to expand within the sector. The result of individual enterprise growth and integration within travel and tourism is an increase in the concentration of that industry. The degree to which output is produced of fewer and fewer enterprises. This can be only be accounted for realistically with the context of an individual economy, Levels of concentration in any part of travel and tourism in the future are likely to depend on two opposing factors: The constant demand by many tourist market segments for new experiences and products, which encourages the development and survival of more and diverse enterprises, and therefore leads to the reduction of concentration as well as technology, which in travel and tourism frequently calls for large capital outlays and requires mass markets for efficient use, promotes integrations and large scale enterprise, especially in air travel and non-personal services (marketing and information communication, travel insurance , tourism payment methods). IN these areas, concentration will undoubtedly increase in future new economic development environment.

HOW TO PROLONG TOURISM LEISURE MATURE LIFE CYCLE STAGE AS WELL AS AVOID DECLINE AND DEATH LIFE CYCLE STAGE OCCURENCE FROM COVID 19 HUMAN DISEASE

Any businesses expect to reach the mature life service cycle stage and they also hope to prolong to stay in this stage and avoid to have chance experience decline life service cycle stage, even death stage in future whole business life cycle stages. However, in fact, there are many businesses need to spend long time to have effort to reach mature life cycle stage from birth and growth both stages, even when they have effort to experience this the topest level stage, many can not stay to prolong time in this stage, then they will reach next stage, such as decline life cycle stage, even final death life cycle stage possibly. Hence , research whether how can reach the mature life cycle stage in short time and prolong to say in this stage. It is one common researching value question to any businesses. Such as COVID 19 human disease had been occurrence in 2019 end , it bring global tourism industry traveller number began to reduce. I shall attempt to explain how airline organizations implement strategies to avoid to enter decline service life cycle stage as below:

● How to avoid to reach the decline service life stage rapidly to global airlines tourism service industry due to COVID 19 human disease occurred Strategies for growing and maturity a product or raise service performance, and increasing profit margins and prolonging to stay on the mature service life stage. I believe that it is any service businesses final aim. However, in any service life cycle stages, when the service , e.g. airline tourism leisure service industry will experience the decline service life stage , due to the COVID19 human disease influences to global travelers began to feel fear to catch airplanes to avoid air contact to give this kind of disease from 2020. So, nowadays, airlines ought have the suitable or right strategies to help them to solve travelers reducing number to influence their profit growth to encounter decline life service cycle stage later.

Life cycle strategy is based on product or service life cycle thinking from marketing, the factors may influence when the business can reach the mature life cycle stage, but some unpredicted factors may influence their clients number reduce, such as this airlines organizations traveler number reduces is due to COVID 19 human disease influences they feel fear to catch airplanes to travel case, their strategies may include: market growth rate, market growth potential, breach of service lines, number of competitor, distribution of market, share among competitors, customer loyalty , barriers to entry and technology improvement etc. factors to influence the global airlines tourism service industry can continue develop or expand to future overseas tourism market, when COVID 19 human disease may be killed by new medicine later.

Such as this COVID 19 human disease influences travelers feel fear to catch airplanes to avoid get this kind of disease and it influences global travelers number is decreasing in 2020 case, when the airline organization reaches the growth life service cycle stage from the birth stage, if it expects to spend short time to reach the mature life service cycle stage. Before COVID 19 human disease had not been killed by new medicine, if they hope to attract many travelers to choose to catch their airplanes to fly , the extension strategies that any airline organization can attempt to achieve, they may include, rebranding, establishing airline service in order to differentiate the other airline competitors tourism service , ticket price discounting and seeking new marketers, rebranding is the creation od a new look and feel for an established airline tourism service from the airline's competitors.

The airline service life cycle extension strategies also may include these methods to help the airline organization to grow or grow up or develop its airline tourism market rapidly, e.g. repackaging and new sizes, the appearance of airline tourism service can be crucial gaining a passenger's attention and developing tourism interest , new formulas or additional airline tourism features to the tourism country, lower ticket prices to maintain interest or liquidate surplus stock new airline tourism service advertising campaign, altering the new airline channel of destination, such as online ticket purchase.

Hence, after COVID 19 human disease had been skilled by new medicine , any airline organizations need to consider how to choose the most suitable strategy from different kinds of key strategies to expand their airline new tourism channels throughout the different airline tourism service life stages, in these four distinct stages: introduction, growth, maturity and decline or possible death stage, when this COVID 19 human disease had occurred from 2019 end, it may influence global travelers number had significant been reducing to bring any airline organizations may enter the decline life service cycle stage rapidly, even death life service cycle stage comes consequently.

Any airline organizations can use various marketing strategies in each stage to try to prolong the life cycle or attempt to reach the mature life cycle stage in short time. Avoiding to experience decline life service cycle stage, such as the COVID 19 human disease occurrence causes global travelers number began to reduce. It is ensure that any airline organizations do not expect to experience or reach the decline service life stage due to this COVID 19 human disease influences. The question is that how the airline organizations can maintain a strategy in the decline stage , such as COVID19 human disease influences global travelers number reduced and it brings many airlines income began to reduce, for example, reducing the airline promotional expenditure in this COVID 19 human disease occurrence period, reducing the number of airline distribution outlets , e.g. Hong Kong to New York airline flight channel reduces implementing ticket price cuts to get passengers to but the maintaining the airline tourism service and waiting for airline competitors to withdraw from the global airline tourism market.

Thus, following the initial growth, in this COVID human disease occurrence period, when the new airline organization enterprise enters the expansion stage during which the routing operation succeeds. The new airline organization can either reach the mature life service cycle stage either it can prolong to stay in this stage or it can not prolong to stay and enters to decline service life cycle stage , even death service life cycle stage. So , how to avoid the decline service life cycle stage comes to the new airline organization in this COVID 19 human disease occurrence period. It is any airline organizations concerning question when they are experiencing in the mature life cycle stage, but when COVID 19 human disease occurs to influence global travelers number began to reduce. May the airline organization experience the decline service life cycle stage rapidly when the COVID 19 human disease occurs ? It depends on whether it's strategies implementation are effective , its' strategies are effective, it may avoid to reach the decline life service cycle stage in short time easily due to COVID 19 human disease influences.

For this COVID 19 human mouth disease case , since 2019 had occurred, it brought serious tourism industry economic loss to any countries, many people loss jobs, many people feel fear to enter any shops when they are in crowd shop environment, e.g. restaurants can not permit to allow many people to sit closely, because when one person has COVID 19 human mouth disease, he can bring this disease to another person from air. So, many restaurants lose many clients in morning, lunch and night busy eating time, even ships also can not permit many people to enter their ships, because they avoid many people may contact, if one or some people has/have COVID 19 mouth disease, when he/she talks to the salespeople in the shop. It has high chance to cause many people get COVID human disease by mouth. So, any shops can not allow crowd in themselves shops to avoid any people have COVID 19 human disease occurrence. So, this COVID 19 human mouth disease may influence many businesses are experiencing decline life cycle stage, because clients number is continue decreasing, unless drug invention succeeds to fill this kind human mouth disease. Otherwise, on the consequence, many businesses will face death life cycle stage in short time possible. So, it is good example to explain unpredicted external environmental factor to bring global businesses will face decline life cycle in 2020 or next year, even after two years latter. So, COVID -19 human mouth disease may also influence any businesses had been experiencing long time in the mature life cycle to change to decline life cycle stage in possible.

Instead of the businesses are experiencing in either birth or growth life cycle stage. for example, UK Cathay airline had been experiencing long time in the mature life cycle stage from 2000, when its clients number had been increasing, but when the end of 2019, COVID-19 human mouth and air contact disease had occurred in global to influence any people feel fear to catch airplanes to travel or business travel frequently, due to airplanes have none windows, its none window environment will bring COVID-19 disease to any passengers when the airplane has many passengers are sitting together closely, if anyone has COVID-19 disease, he will cause any one airplane service waiter, passenger , even pilot to have COVID-19 disease easily.

So, global airline industry is experiencing decline life cycle stage. even Cathay airline is one big UK developed airline , it's passengers number is large in the past, but when COVID-19 disease occurs to cause travelers number had been decreasing. Hence, Cathay airline is experiencing decline life cycle stage from mature life cycle stage. It needs to implement dismissing staffs to keep salaries expenditure reducing strategy in global, e.g. HK will have 4,000 front line airline service staffs or airport check in service staffs , they will be dismisses in HK Cathay airline market. Although, HK government had given money to support it to continue to alive in order to avoid dismissing employees decision . But, Cathay airline had made decision that it will dismiss many airline service staffs in different countries. In fact, if Cathay airline expects it would not reach to the decline life cycle stage later, this dismissing employees strategy aims to avoid spending much salaries expenditure , it may be one good method to avoid decline , even death life cycle stage occurs in this year or latter.

On conclusion, it is difficult to predict what factors may cause the business itself will face decline life cycle stage occurrence in any time. Hence, any businesses ought to spend time to research whether which methods or strategies can help them to continue to expand their market or fight any kinds of threats in those four identified business life cycle stages. To avoid business can not continue develop or die, when the business is experiencing in the decline life cycle stage, the strategy is that , the organization needs to spend time to observe or learn how and why its market environment is changing in order to make the most accurate or effective strategies decisions to solve any challenges in any one of these four life cycle stages successfully.

● How new economic development in oil industry

The future global economic growth, it will influence personal incomes and GDP rise. They would carry different weight in different countries at different times. Starting from low levels of incomer and economic development. Household consumption will change from being dominated by basic heat to rapidly rising energy use for higher levels of comfort in space heating and cooling (and large dwellings), and greater use of electrical appliances, finally to a degree of saturation influenced by the income distribution patterns of the country concerned. Income distribution typically changes very slowly, so that the technical market for heart will never be saturated because there will always be a proportion of poor people living in small spaces less comfortably than the average. Industrial energy consumption will be influenced by technical efficiency within each sector, and by changes in the structures of the economy, e.g. changing proportions of agriculture, heavy and light industry, and services. One may eventually see evidence of diminishing marginal returns to additional energy inputs compared to other inputs. Energy consumption in the energy transformation sector may be influenced by income, which drives the demand for electricity to influenced by income, which drives the demand for electricity to grow faster than the demand for heat, but is also subject to the chosen technology of transformation, which is influenced by the cost and availability of primary energy inputs (fuels) in new economic development environment.

IN new economic development environment, it will influences that fuels do not compete in all sectors; for example, the transport sector is dominated by oil. Nuclear and hydroelectric power (and most renewables) reach the user through electricity; electricity itself competes with the direct burning of fossil fuels. Electricity provides the means by which other fuels can compete with oil and gas in sectors, such as space heating and process heat. It also is the only means of powering applications such as motors, computers and lighting: these subsectors are difficult to analyze. However, there is strong evidence that higher incomes do not weaken the demand for electricity so much as the demand for energy in total (in contrast to the effect on the demand for non-electric energy forms).

Econometricians look at the historical record of change in fuel prices and quantities to distinguish several factors between the new economic development and old economic development to oil industry in the future. An income effect. Increasing (reducing) fuel prices reduces (increases) the purchasing power of consumers' income: higher incomes caused by lower prices will increase energy consumption; the consumers' allocation of the increased income to energy purchases may reduce as income rises. Thus income may be heading in a different direction from fuel prices that the effect of fuel price changes when incomes are rising means simply that rising incomes have increased demand. Reducing the cost of using energy through win-win efficiency measures causes a similar problem . On the consequence, in future new economic development environment, it may influence in both cases demand will be less than if the future oil price or efficiency has not changed. The other effect is that an efficiency or substitution effect. An increase in fuel prices may cause consumers to spend more on new equipment, building materials and management operations, which will reduce the amount of fuel required to give the same energy result to the user. The extent of the efficiency effect depends on what happens to the price of the new equipment or building: if those price s rise in line with the fuel price, changes in the balances between fuel and capital or management will not occur. A new user technology , such as the development of the combined cycle gas turbine generator may increase efficiency and thus greatly reduce the quantity of primary fuel needed to produce the required output in this case electricity. If electricity prices had remained sticky, and the electricity and gas markets were not competitive, some of this advantages could have accrued to the gas suppliers in the form of an increase in price, because th4 unit of gas produces more output of electricity, it would have a higher value. In reality, the development of new economic competitive environment in both gas and electricity has tended to ensure that the benefits of such technical advanced accrue to the consumer through lower final prices. The same many apply in the case of improved efficiency in future non-manual driving auto vehicle development: the consumer's cost of motoring is reduced in new economic non-manual driven auto vehicle (Artificial intelligent vehicle) can replace manual driven vehicle , even electricity battery can replace oil energy to be used in vehicles. So, oil price may be influenced to reduce in future new economic development environment.

New and old economic theories explain oil is not main factor to influence tourism income

● Can economic theory explain old price change to influence tourism income?

I shall attempt to apply old and new economic theory to explain whether oil changing price has direct relationship to influence global tourism indusry development or tourism income as below:

Is oil changing price the main to influence tourism income or tourism development or economic growth ? If oil price rises ar falls, it will or won't cause tourism income decreases or increases? If they have cause and effect relationship, what are the main factors to influence tourism income changes by oil price rises or falls ?

I aim to investigate how any why among oil price shocks will influence tourism income variables. We may distinguish between these oil price shocks: Supply-side , aggregate demand and oil specific demand shocks. I assume that oil specific demand shocks affect inflation and the tourism sector equity index. By constrast, I also believe that aggregate demand oil price shock exercisr an effect, either directly and indirectly tourism generated income and economic growth. So, in old economic theory, supply-side , aggregate demand view to oil specific demand shocks will influence tourism income varies. So, governments ought implement strategies against future oil price movements or plan for economic policy development.

In fact, instead of oil price changes will influence tourism income, it could also harm economic growth and tourism activities, due to the effect they expert on transporation, production cost, economic uncertainty.Because tourism activities is one important sector to influence any country's leisure consumption GDP income source. So, sudden fluctations in oil prices may also influence economic growth. It is based a hyphthesis known as the tourism led economic growth. So, it seems that they have direct or indirect relationship to case effect between oil price and tourism activities and development. So, increase on tourism income, the called " economic-driven tourism growth". In addition, high oil prices are affecting certain tourism industry segments , e.g. airlines, cruises lines, hotel, rent travelling car services etc. for oil, importing countries example, with reference to macro economic effects, higher oil prices generally lead to higher inflation, when they negatively influence to country's income.

Hence, from a micro-economic perspective, positive oil price shocks lead to a decline in disposable income. for low income people, it will bring an immediate and negative impact on tourism, mainly due to they feel tourism leisure is regarded as a luxury good, when oil price shocks to rise suddenly . It influences any airline or cruise entertainment service providers' costs are influenced to raise. Then, they need to increase air ticket or cruise ticket price. It will bring on negative tourism leisure demands-side the oil price increases low income group, potential tourism leisure consumers. Hence, it seems that oil price may have indirect relationship to influence tourism leisure consumers' needs.

● How the price of oil changes influences global tourism industry growth or recession?

In macro-economic view, sudden mid and long term oil price shock can influence global torusim industry growth or recession. For example, a oil price of US$180 per barrel was considered only a few years ago, now this has a realistic scenario to which all plaers in the T&T sector have to adapt. At such a high level, the price of oil will become even more critical to almost every part of the tourism value chain. Although, weak global demand, caused by global economic recesson, resulted in a steep oil price decline to US$45 per barrel by the fourth quarter of 2008 in the past low oil price occurrence history, this won't change the mid to long -term oil forecast.

In fact, the past oil price occurrence history of the dramatic structural had changed a high price imposed on airlines, travelers, and destination countries, all of which will have to navigate through times of shifting or even declining travel demand. I assume that a high oil price scenario is assumed in the long term in order to highlight the changes , such a senario would mean for consumer behavior and the competitiveness of several destinations.

Low oil price in the 1970 and early 1980 did not bring significant growth of international air travel, but its growth has been strongest between 1980 and 2004, a period with stable and relatively moderate oil prices. Also, the rapid development of the low-cost carrier business model in the 1990s further fueled air travel growth by capturing tourism leisure demand , such as weekend leisure travel to cities using mostly secondary airports in any big area countries, such as UK, US . However, the tourism growth is whole influenced by high oil prices, due to oil price had been continue rising in possible.

Basis of oil is shortage supply product, oil is assumed to be the main energy source for the aviation sector for the nest 30 years. Although, second-generation biofuels seem to be on the horizon, the economics as well as the production scalability and aviation biofuel shortage will be a main challenge to airline industry. So, I assume that oil price will continue rise up, if there have none any aviation biofuel can be reflected to oil to use for air plane energy.

Until 2004, the only factors to have affected air travel growth, negatively were in external shocks , such as 9/11, causes catching air plane crisis or US regional geopolitical conflicts. It brings some travelers feel fear to go to US travel, as well as until recently 2019, human mouth disease can influence air to have disease to anyone from mouth. So, global travelers number had been continue decreasing, because they are fear to get disease by air when many themselves every stranger travelers are sitting on the without windows air planes. Although, mouth human and air disease and US 9/11 air attack both matters may influence oil price falls effect, because air planes flying times will reduce. They won't need frequent to fly, to cause aviation oil energy need reduce. Consequently, oil price will decrease, due to travelers number reduces and air planes flying times are also influenced to reduce. (oil demand decreases cause oil price decrease). Although, air lines ' cost will also be influenced reduce, but oil price decrease can not bring travelers number increase , when air ticket price reduce because global many leisure and business trip travelers feel fear to catch air planes frequently when human mouth air disease occured in 2019. So, oil price decreases can not grow up tourism industry growth or rise tourism income.

However, the obvious impact of a high oil price is an increase in the operating costs of airline. Moreover, fuel cost as a percentage of airline operating costs vary significantly based on the length of the flight. The longer the flight, the higher the fuel costs as a percentage of the airline operating cost. So, from an online's perspective, long -hauel flights represent the most criticial challenge to profitable operation because the share of fuel on these flights, compared with other cost items, is largest, because of the unfacorable fuel economics, due to fuel costs even at high-load factors. For example, Thai airways dropped its non-stop Bongkok to US flights in the summer of 2008 for commercial reasons, because fuel reached operating cost levels of 55 percent on this route, a cost burden that could not be passed on to their customers. So, the estimated price elacticity of passengers demand at this Bongkok to US flights route is high, if Thai Airways rises less air ticket price, it will influence many travelers to choose other airlines to catch air plan to fly. Hence, due to Thai Airways can not make decision to rise air ticket price, because it believes that it will lose many travelers, so it only chooses to drop this non-stop Bongkok to US flights to avoid fuel cost rising economic loss.

However, although micro and macro economic theories may also that oil price variable or change, it may influence global tourism income. But, recently, on 2019, human mouth and air diseases, it can influence global individual leisure and business trip travelers feel fear to catch air plans to avoid their bodies get this kind of death sickness when they sit in the no fresh air supplying air planes. They feel that they reduce leisure travelling flying times or business trip flying times with strange travelers to sit in crowd air planes together. Then, they must many avoid human moth and air disease to avoid death crisis. Hence, in this global human mouth and air diseases threat environment occurrence, even oil price sudden reduces to low price, it brings airline's cost reduces and air ticke price reduces. However, when air ticket price reduce to be very cheaper, it can not still attract global many leisure or business trip travelers to buy air tickets to fly frequently. Why does air ticket reduction, it can not attract many leisure or businee trip travelers to buy air ticket to fly ? The main reason is because human mouth and air disease influences global many travelers feel fear to catch air planes frequently. In psychological view, this kind of human mouth and air sickness will bring long time negative influence to global traveles do not want to catch air planes for business trips or travelling leisure frequently. So, it implies that oil price changing to influence air ticket price reduction factor ought not main factor to influence tourism income. It may include traveler individual negative emotion psychological factor, such as human mouth and air disease or 2019 9/11 attack both cases, they can influence global travelers feel fear to catch air planes to fly to avoid death threat. So, oil changing price ought not be only one absolute main factor to influence global tourism income significantly.

On conclusion, in economic view, it seems that oil chang price may have indirect or direct relationship to influence tourism income, instead of some unpredicted external environment factors influence, such as US 9/11 attack crisis and human mouth and air disease factors, they may be main factors to influence travellers number to reduce in non-economic external unpredicted environment view.

Bibliography

Backman, K., Backman, S., Uysal, M. And Sunshine, K. (1995). Event Tourism : An Examination Of Motivations And Activities. Festival Management And Event Tourism, 3(1), 15-24.

Fishbein, M., & Ajzen, Z. (1975). Belief, Attitude, Intention And Behaviour: An Introduction To Theory And Research, Boston: Addison Wesley.

Hsu, C.H.C., Cai , L.A., Li, M(2010). Expectation, Motivation And Attitude: A Tourist Behavioral Model. Journal Of Travel Research, 49(3), 282-296. http://dx.doi, org/10.1177/004728750 9349266.

ICT Information And Communication Technology Switzerland, 2005. ICT Fakten (ICT facts). Available from http://www.ictswitzerland.ch/de/ict%2fakten/factsfigures.asp(retrieved Dec.12, 2005) in German.

Lind, (2001): Befolkningen, Familjen, Livscykeln- Och Ekonomisk Tillvaxt. Institutet For Tillvaxtpo-litiska studier/Vinnova/Nutek.

Lohmann, Martin (2001): The 31 st. Reiseanalyse-RA 2001. Tourism: vol. 49, no.1/2001;pp.65-67, Zagreb.

United Nations Population Division (2001). World Population Prospects: The 2000 year Revision, New York.

Weber E.U., & W, P.Bottom (1989). "Axiomatic

Measures Of Perceived Risk: Some Tests And extensions." journal of behavioral decision making, 2 (2): 113-31.

However, green or nature tourism strategy may include these elements : Quality, tourism should have an impact on the quality of life for all members of the tourist process, exploitation of nature resources should be optimal and ensure their generation, balance, distribution of benefits among participants in the tourist process must be fair. So, future any kinds of green or nature tourism will need have these features in order to attract many travelers to visit any countries' green lands, e.g. they may rent cars to travel to green lands. So, developing attractive green lands will be one kind new travelling trend for green tourism in global future travel market.

There are two types of models that contribute to the better understanding of future tourism industry development, explanatory model refer to factors that cause development growth. For example, whether the travelers feel necessary to travel to different destinations, very often nice landscapes and sightseeing, pescriptive modes (e.g. life clcle explanations, physical models) examines tourism from what appears on ground e.g. large hotels facilities etc. Hence, any kinds of tourism leisure must need build these both models in order to attract travelers to choose to buy the tourism package from the travel agent more easily. It is important tourism leisure element to any one travel agent's tourism service package if it hopes to develop its tourism service success. So, the expansion of the tourist region over the natural boundaries of the city centre that occured in the first place as a result of the growth of tourism demand, is the end causing this very expansion to continue.

Butler (1980) involves a six stage evoluation of tourism, namely explanation, involvement, development, consolidation, stagnation, and post-stagnation. The last stage is further characterized by a period of decline, rejuvenation or stabilization. The applicability of the model to a given area has been assessed and judged of a tourist destination's development matched the six phases conceptually described by Butler reference

Butler, R.W. (1980). the concept of a tourist area cycle of evolution: Implications for management of resources. Canadian Geographer, 24, 5-12.

Hence, our tourism industry is facing decline life cycle stage because COVD 19 human mouth disease has influenced many travelers feel fear to catch airplanes to travel, even they also feel to contact the potential COVD 19 human mouth disease people when they arrive the country , they feel that they may contact these sick people, instead of airplanes. So, this kind disease had influenced many travel agents reduce tourism service package number , due to many travelers' tourism leisure activities will reduce, due to travelers number reduces, they only carry cargos to transport to replace travelers COVD 19 disease influence our tourism industry is experiencing decline life cycle stage nowadays. Unless, COVD 19 human mouth attacking to lung disease can be treated by new medicine invention . Otherwise, tourism industry can not re-grow to mature life cycle stage easily.

The most used framework for examing stagnation and possible decline in tourism destinations has been tourist area life cycle model (Butler, 1980). The model has been operationalized frequently in the tourism lierature. It includes series of stages in tourism development, leadning eventually to the stagnation and post-stagnation stages. When a nature destination can either decline, however, it does not offer a systematic explanation of hoe tourism destination might avoid decline . Such as COVD 19 human mouth disease may influence travelers feel fear to catch air planes. So, even the country has beautiful nature scene to attract people to travel, althoug it is a nature attractive destination, but due to COVD19 disease occurs, it may influence this country's this nature attractive destination to enter decline life cycle stage at this moment.

Hence, tourism industry's life cycle stage , sometime it can be influenced by non predicted factor, such as COVD19 disease factor, it can influence travelers' travelling desire to be reduced suddenly from 2019 , due to they feel afraid to catch air planes to avoid to get this kind COVD 19 human mouth disease to bring lung disease when they are sitting in closed window inside air plane environment. So, COVD 19 human counth disease causes global tourism industry is facing serious decline life cycle stage. The question is that any one does not know when this kind COVD 19 disease will be treated by new medicine invention, so if this kind COVD 19 disease still can not be killed by new medicine invention, then it will continue to influence global tourism development to be improved , even any nature attractive scenes, they can not persuade any travelers to catch air planes to visit any countries to travel easily. But, however, we still need to keep our natural environment to prepare future COVD 19 diease disappears , e.g. parks are important places for the protection of ecological systems and natural resources as well as for the provision ot recreational and tourism opportunities for the public. Then, nature or green tourism can be continue to develop to attract many travelers to travel after COVD 19 disease disappears in the future.

● What are the characteristics of birth life cycle stage to tourism industry ? Butler , R.W. (1980)'s model begins with a discovery and exploration or birth stage in which a location is discovered by a small, select group of people as a place with desirable assets often, this discovery is nature population who may see the perceived assets. As just ordinary aspects of their environment or local culture. The early tourists have very little support in the form of amenities, and typically, this is preferred and is part of a location's of being undiscovered. The early tourists, therefore rely heavily on and interact frequently with the residents of the region. This small group of early tourists is largely in dependent and shares information about a destination by word of mouth or by select affinity groups. Over time, as more people are introduced to the destination, the number of visitors begins to increase. So " word of mouth" will be traveler information to persuade them to make travelling destination choices in the tourism industry beginning. It is tourism industry's birth life cycle stage characteristics . However, internet invention can let any one see any countries' scene photos, so it is one kind of good advertisement method to introduce any countries' scene, instead of travelling magazine in tourism growth and maturity life cucle both stages.

Moreover, space tourism is at the birth life cycle stage. It needs travelers feel interest to travel space, if this kind space tourism service providers hope to implement their any space journeys in success. These factors may influence its development succeeds. Nowadays, its target market is wealthy travelers group, wealthy individual are needed, as they serve as the main consumers for space tourism . For space tourism to succeed there must be enough demand from those who are able to afford to expensive ticket. To date there have only been seven commercial space travelers, or space tourists, although they prefer to be called space flight participant, as they see themselves as pioneers and adventers as opposed to ordinary tourists. So, any future space tourism that price must need to reduce to general public, e.g. ordinary income level people, they can spend, if space tourism hopes to reach from stage stage rapidly. So, space tourism is still far to mature stage.It depends on whether how long time its any space journey ticket price can be reduced to any one can pay. So, when its customer target is not only wealthy travelers, many ordinary or common income level people, they can pay to any one space jounrney. It may mean to reach growth life cycle stage.

● What characteristics to space tourism growth stage?

When human space tourism of commericalization of activities in outer space can bring these feeling to let any one space traveler feels then, it may mean that it can reach growth stage, such as they may feel their any space journeys may bring positive impacts that outer. Space recreation can produce, in order to come up with space tourism, exploring and untravelling the hidden anystories of the space are needed. Also they can feel need drastically broadens and enrichs human's technical awareness and constructive knowledge need from any one space tourism journey package. When space tourism reachs mature life cycle stage? What its characteristics are? When any one space travelers can feel that not only earth based attractions that simulate the space experience , they must need to catch airships to experience this different tourism experience, such as space theme parks, space training camps, virtual reality facilities , space hotels (skotel), multimedia interactive games and tele robotic moon rovers controlled from earth, but also parabolic flights, lasting up to three days or week long stay at floating space hotel, including participatory educational ,as well as sports competitions (i.e. space olympics). Hence, above these will be nay space tourism development. It can reach mature life cycle stage characteristics when any one can feel the real travelling mouth to compare to travel our earth anywhere, they can not find that they feel space tourism may be same to our earth's holiday (need to rela) or cultural (know different places or specialized tourism, e.g. expectations of adventures , even space scientists discover new experiences to expectations of adventure or get more information, scientific interest feeling. Then, at this moment, we can call space tourism has reached the mature stage. However, I believe that to develop space tourism in success. We must need to control space tourism ticket price to be reduced to general low income people. They may spend budget level. So, ticket price may be one major factor to influence future space tourism growth when it can reach mature stage. Also, it mean that whether space tourism may become another kind of popular tourism lesiure activities to use. It depends on ticket price factor, instead of its any space tourism trip arrangement factor. So, any one space tourism service provider must need long time to spend in order to implement its different strategies, e.g. ticket price, space trip arrangemet to achieve its their space tourism to achieve its their space tourism different destination package in success if they hope their future space tourism business can grow up in short time.

Airport service life cycle stage improvement strategy
Any organizations will have life cycle stage from birth, growth , mature to decline. In airport service organizations have theis life cycle stages in service aspect. Airports organizatins aim to provide safe, comfortable , even shopping environment to let passengers to stay and to wait to transfer another air planes to visit another destination or arrive the country's airport to check out or check in to enter the airport to leave. If airports have life cycle stages, what the characteristics to every stage? How to improve airport service in order to reach mature life cycle stage rapidly? How to implement airport service strategy in order to reach mature life cycle stage to the aorport organization rapidly?I shall explain as below:

Any airports need to be planned in order to raise excellent service to let passengers to let any travelers choose to travel the country whether the country can provide excellent service and facilities. It will bring indirect emotion impact to influence the travelers chooce to revisit the country to travel again. However, soft or hard element or) staff service performance or airport facility), they will influence whether the different countries travelers to choose to travel to re-visit the country again. So, learning how to keep the mature or airport service life cycle stage to stay long time, it will be one important factor to influence any airport business in success.

In the birth life style stage to airport, airport organizations must maintain the capability to provide expert advice to airport owners an matters including operational safety, during construction, environmental compatibility, and airport development standards. No other private or public organization can be expected maintain this level of proficiency. These value-added services enhance public trust when assuring consistant application of standards for the nation's airport system. So, it seems that when the new airport is built if it hopes its passenger customers can consider themselves emotion need. So, it ought concentrate on nowadays airplane landing cunways or airport transfer free service transport etc. facilities can let them to feel safe when they were walking in any airport places. If they feel anywhere are dangerous when they are walking or staying in the ne sirport, then new airport non safe or dangerous factor may influence travelers to choose the country to travel again.

Any new airports will need have good new national airport plan in order to it might operate in the near future with respect to safety areas. The plan elements may include as below:

Achieving zero accidents aim, establish standard safety areas at all commercial service airports , achieving the most minimum 85% of all passenger flights operate on runways with safe feeling, increase measure to 100% of all passenger flight operating on runways with standard safety areas after three months. Within 5 years, 95% of all passenger flights begin and end on runways with standard safety areas.

On benefits aspect, aims to mobilize work force to improve safety area performance describes realistic investment benefits. So, in any new airports birth life cycle stage, they must need to consider safety and expenditure for repair aspect in order to keep its service performance to avoid passengers have dissatisfactory feeling when they are staying in their new airports.

When the country has many travelers travel to the country , then the country's new airport passengers number must increase. It is its the new airport growth life cycle stage. These are critical success factors influence the airport, whether it can improve service performance in order to excite different countries travelers visiting the country's airport desire or grow up the visitors number successfully. The critical success factors may include: Having necessary support from internal and externa stakeholders to implement and willing to share information and identify anywhere the total airport facilities of repair needs that are both reliable and feasible projections to let passengers to feel more safe feeling when they are staying in the airport, understand its future service vision and mission, set strategic direction and goals to process/product specific objectives and decision-making across and doen the organization, define, model and prioritize planning prcesses critical for mission performance, practice hand-on sernior management ownership of planning process and allow field, personnel flexiblity in performing jobs, adjust organizational structures , an essessment program to evaluate planning process and product management , e.g. national airport system performance, create organizational understanding of the value management to customer and stakeholder current and future expectations developing human resources management strategies to support new process that solves needs planners and engineers, building information resources strategies change, especially for entering data at the source and maintains data integrity and timeliness.,establish central support group to support reengineering efforts, outreach and training efforts across the organization, phase in short-and long-term results that achieve set goals and objectives over the next two years.

Thus, when one new airport begins to feel passengers number is increasing.

It ought experience the growth life cycle stage to the new airport , if it hopes that it can reach mature life cycle stage rapidly as well as keeps its mature life cycle stage to stay in this stage long time or reachs the airport service performance to the most satisfactory level in this mature life cycle stage. It must need to attempt to plan these strategies to implement in order to avoid decline life cycle stage occurs in short time. So, it explains why some new airport can experience the development to mature life cycle stage from grow life cycle stage in short time,even when it reachs mature life cycle stage. It can keep to stay in this stage long time. The reason is that it had prepared effective strategies to achieve how to improve its airport service performance aim in order to satisfy passenger needs. When they are staying in the country's airport any time. Hence, every year revising service performance is needed to any airports.

Any airports must have development processes. The question is that whether the airport needs how long time to reach growth or mature life cycle stage from birth stage or decline life cycle stage will be delayed how long to occur. The development processes may mean that the airport development life cycle stages changes that had toard a particular result or even as a series of continuous actions or operations coducting to an end (Merriam-Webster, 2013).

reference

Merriam-webster (2013). On line dictionary. Available at:

https://www.merriam-webster. com/(last accessed July , 8 2013).

Hence, any airport organizations with experience development pricess. When the new airport is built, it must be in the birth life cycle stage. Its passengers number can not increase rapidly. It needs time to grow their number. But, when the new airport operates a period, many different countries begin feel this new airport is existence in the country. They will attempt to catch airplance to visit this country airport to catch airplane to visit tis country airport to travel. If they feel this country airport service performance can satisfy their short time staying feeling or its passengers or airports visitors number may increase rapidly. It meand that this airport is experiencing growth life cycle stage. So, if the airport can attract many visitors in short time. It will reduce time to growth life cycle stage from birth life cycke stage.

So , service performance may be one important factor to inflow the airport grows. When the airport develops to the period, passengers number can not increase rapidly, it may be the airport's mature life cycle stage. Due to it's passengers number can not grow rapidly, its passengers number also may reduce. When its passengers number has significant decrease, if its reduction number is increasing more. It implies that the airport is experiencing decline life cycle stage. All any country's airport may experience whole life cycle stages. If the country's airport can not implement successful strategies, it may experience birht life cycle stage in long time because it can not grow its passengers number significantly. So, any airports need to learn how to help them to change growth life cycle stage, even mature life cycle stage can stay in long time easily. If they hope to attract many different countries passengers to visit their airports or travel themselves countries or enjoy to stay short time in themselves airports in order to grow themselves airline industry development.

● How can processes improvement management strategy influence airport service performance?

Overall processes in an airport may involve passengers, luggage, cargo, aircraft movements, ground handling, and crews . All of these operations can be systematised into processes at airport terminal. Three main types of processes can be established departing , arrival and transfer . Departure consists in catching a flight to a final or intermediate destination, arrival consists in landing and leaving the airport, and transfer consists in landing at the airport only to catch another flight to a final or an intermediate destination. Airports also deal with cargo. It involves in the movement of cargo by air, cargo fies from the shopper to the consignee through one or more airlines. However, when the airport can let them freight forwarder, being familiar with the necessary procedures how permits the airline to concentrate on the provision of air transport and to avoid time consuming details of the facilitation and landside distribution system. It will raise efficiency and improve service performance. The services product by the ground handling are crucial to the success and efficiency of the airport operations.

These services are usually provided by specialised companies. Briefly, it includes the luggage treatment, passengers carrying from plan to terminal when needed and aircraft assistance. Also, focusing on crew, there are two majoe processes, one for departures and the other for arrivals. The crew members also have to pass the security and passport controls. However, they have special channels for this. Once they reach the aircraft, the similarities with the passengers' procedure stop. Hence, they have to perform a set of activities , such as check the aircraft load sheets and help passengers to name a few. Also airport terminal operations processes for passengers and luggage, typically for departures , passengers do the check on the airline area, pass security controls, proceed to the general lounge and lastly to the gate holding area. arriving passengers are able to immediately go from the luggage claim area, but the non-passengers have to pass the passport control at first. After this passengers have to decide if they need to declare goods or not as the paths are different . Hence, if the airport can reduce all of this service processes are less complex as immigration check in-out service, liggage claim can be efficient to carry when passengers need to find themselves luggage. Then, it will reduce waste time and let they satisfy airport service absolutely. So, reducing service process time amy also help the airport to increase customers number significantly. When airport role is the middleman between airlines , cargo transport service providers and passengers, e.g. short time transport cargo service and reducing passengers check in or check out service time. then, it will let them to feel more satisfactory service to the airport.

Hence, airport capacity is as a multifactor function leaves open the exact relationship between the factors but stresses that all factors are relevant to assess airport capacity . So , understanding airport capacity and what drives the capacity usage at airports may provide an insight in the set of instructments available to optimise the use of capacity. All of these factors may influence any capacity of an airport, they may include as below:

For example, technical constraints, e.g. ATM per hour service in a runway in a combined arrival and departure fashion, when many passengers are staying at the airport, they can withdraw money from ATM easily. So, ATM number facilities service supply number and location choice to the airport factors will infuence passengers ' satisfactory level, another factor is environmental constraints, it can directly offer the wellbeing of the communities surrounding the negative emotion to passengers and communities surrounding the airprt. For this factor, the change in technology and/or operational procedures can provide more capacity in the system.

Airline business models factor, it can affect the capacity spoke model when other under a point-point one ,these models directly affect the peak hour operational capacity, particularly in big international hubs. Airlines often compete with high frequencies between destinations, thus increasing the number of movements. In addition, conncectivity also has downsides for this model: the delays in one airport might be exported and sometimes in another, due to the connectivity influencing the real capacity. This factor has been setting economic incentives or pricing models. Furthermore, expanding information systems, from one airport to multiple airports gate-to-gate concept, and the use of larger airport to redcuce frequencies.

Hence, above these factors may influence whether the airport needs how long time to reach maturiry life cycle stage when it is staying the growth life cycle stage. It depends on how its strategies implementation and how environment influence its implementation , if it hopes to achieve to reach the maturity life cycle stage in success in short time.

Finally, I shall explain life cycle cst analysis to any country pavement strategy will bring what significant influential benefits to any airports continue to develop in order to avoid to reach decline life cycle stage time in short time easily , when they are staying in the mature life cycle stage. In the construction or rehabilitation investments of highway's pavements, it is already common to perform a life-cycle analysis or life cycle cost analysis for different alternatives to airport pavements. Becauae when any airport pavements are using for a long time, every day has many airplanes need to fly to land on the pavement. It can bring significant repace influence when thc airport has many airplanes are needed to land on the pavements every day in the maturity life cycle stages.

Hence, how to evaluate the repair cost expenditure budget in order to satisfy every day air planes land on the airport pavement need. In the calculations are different cost factors (including direct and indirect cost)to any airport itself pavement. Direct costs are related to the critical construction cost landing on pavement activities and are calculated with information from the airport agency and constructors that work for them. The indirect costs are related with the loss of daily revenue of the airport during work activities, such as landing on the airport pavement.

Runways are the most critical pavements area of airport , so it is critical to ensure the quality of these pavement to let airplanes to land on the airport safety, e.g. they need to be constructed with sufficient strength to carry the moving airport and have a high resistance to skidding and aquaplaining. It is most of the time accomplished with reconstructions or deep rehabilitation. Hence, predicting how much will spend on airport pavement facilities expenditure must need in every day.

However, the life cycle assessment (LCA) is a mult step procedure for calculating the life time environmental impact of a product or service is needed to any airport organizations, when they reachs maturity life cycelt stage . The complex process includes goal and cope definition in inventory analysis impact assessment. The process is vaturally iterative as quality and completeness of information is constantly being testes. When the definition of the aim and scope of the study is done the next step is the development of an inventory, in which all significant environmental burdens during the lifetime of the product,, such as airport pavements or process , such as airplanes landing on the pavement or airplanes leaving from the pavement in the airport.

(Araujo, Oliveria & Silve) 2014 explained that life cycle snslysis of pavements are focused on the activities of extraction, production, transportation application of materials, concisely the construction of the road. Because its difficult to obtain other relevant data knowing that the use phase of the pavement is predominant with repect to energy consumption and also to gas emissions related to the atmosphere. One of the main factors for the use phase is the rolling resistance, this depends on the surface and structural characteristics of the different pavements.

Hence, , if the airport can have good repairment or renew skills to help its pavement to improve. Then, it may bring long time benefit, such as reducing airplanes energy consumption and also to avoid gas emissions or reduce gas emissions accident occurrene, even air plane landing on pavement accident occurrence chance can reduce to the zero. so, defining the expected pavement performance time improvement strategy can influence whether the airport pavement can satisfy all airplane users how long time landing on or leaving on the airport pavement. Also it is the major factor to influence airport main function success for any airplanes arriving to the country's airport pavement or leaving from the country's airport pavement. Hence, calculating any airport pavement life cycle costs factor. It is necessary to analysis and interpret carefully the results to identfy the most economic pavement strategy in any airport's whole life cycle development stages.

reference

Araujo, J.P.C. Oliveria, J.R.M. & Silva H.M.R.D. (2011) . the importance of the use phase on the LCA of environmentally friendly solutions for asphalt road pavements. transportation research part D: trasport and environment, 32(0), 97-110. Retrieved in March 2015 from://
dx. doi.org/10.1016/j.trd.2014.07.006.

CHAPTER FIVE

Factors influence oil industry life cycle stage

● How new economic development in oil industry

The future global economic growth, it will influence personal incomes and GDP rise. They would carry different weight in different countries at different times. Starting from low levels of incomer and economic development. Household consumption will change from being dominated by basic heat to rapidly rising energy use for higher levels of comfort in space heating and cooling (and large dwellings), and greater use of electrical appliances, finally to a degree of saturation influenced by the income distribution patterns of the country concerned. Income distribution typically changes very slowly, so that the technical market for heart will never be saturated because there will always be a proportion of poor people living in small spaces less comfortably than the average. Industrial energy consumption will be influenced by technical efficiency within each sector, and by changes in the structures of the economy, e.g. changing proportions of agriculture, heavy and light industry, and services. One may eventually see evidence of diminishing marginal returns to additional energy inputs compared to other inputs. Energy consumption in the energy transformation sector may be influenced by income, which drives the demand for electricity to influenced by income, which drives the demand for electricity to grow faster than the demand for heat, but is also subject to the chosen technology of transformation, which is influenced by the cost and availability of primary energy inputs (fuels) in new economic development environment.

IN new economic development environment, it will influences that fuels do not compete in all sectors; for example, the transport sector is dominated by oil. Nuclear and hydroelectric power (and most renewables) reach the user through electricity; electricity itself competes with the direct burning of fossil fuels. Electricity provides the means by which other fuels can compete with oil and gas in sectors, such as space heating and process heat. It also is the only means of powering applications such as motors, computers and lighting: these subsectors are difficult to analyze. However, there is strong evidence that higher incomes do not weaken the demand for electricity so much as the demand for energy in total (in contrast to the effect on the demand for non-electric energy forms).

Econometricians look at the historical record of change in fuel prices and quantities to distinguish several factors between the new economic development and old economic development to oil industry in the future. An income effect. Increasing (reducing) fuel prices reduces (increases) the purchasing power of consumers' income: higher incomes caused by lower prices will increase energy consumption; the consumers' allocation of the increased income to energy purchases may reduce as income rises. Thus income may be heading in a different direction from fuel prices that the effect of fuel price changes when incomes are rising means simply that rising incomes have increased demand. Reducing the cost of using energy through win-win efficiency measures causes a similar problem . On the consequence, in future new economic development environment, it may influence in both cases demand will be less than if the future oil price or efficiency has not changed. The other effect is that an efficiency or substitution effect. An increase in fuel prices may cause consumers to spend more on new equipment, building materials and management operations, which will reduce the amount of fuel required to give the same energy result to the user. The extent of the efficiency effect depends on what happens to the price of the new equipment or building: if those price s rise in line with the fuel price, changes in the balances between fuel and capital or management will not occur. A new user technology , such as the development of the combined cycle gas turbine generator may increase efficiency and thus greatly reduce the quantity of primary fuel needed to produce the required output in this case electricity. If electricity prices had remained sticky, and the electricity and gas markets were not competitive, some of this advantages could have accrued to the gas suppliers in the form of an increase in price, because th4 unit of gas produces more output of electricity, it would have a higher value. In reality, the development of new economic competitive environment in both gas and electricity has tended to ensure that the benefits of such technical advanced accrue to the consumer through lower final prices. The same many apply in the case of improved efficiency in future non-manual driving auto vehicle development: the consumer's cost of motoring is reduced in new economic non-manual driven auto vehicle (Artificial intelligent vehicle) can replace manual driven vehicle , even electricity battery can replace oil energy to be used in vehicles. So, oil price may be influenced to reduce in future new economic development environment.

New and old economic theories explain oil is not main factor to influence tourism income

● Can economic theory explain old price change to influence tourism income?

I shall attempt to apply old and new economic theory to explain whether oil changing price has direct relationship to influence global tourism indusry development or tourism income as below:

Is oil changing price the main to influence tourism income or tourism development or economic growth ? If oil price rises ar falls, it will or won't cause tourism income decreases or increases? If they have cause and effect relationship, what are the main factors to influence tourism income changes by oil price rises or falls ?

I aim to investigate how any why among oil price shocks will influence tourism income variables. We may distinguish between these oil price shocks: Supply-side , aggregate demand and oil specific demand shocks. I assume that oil specific demand shocks affect inflation and the tourism sector equity index. By constrast, I also believe that aggregate demand oil price shock exercisr an effect, either directly and indirectly tourism generated income and economic growth. So, in old economic theory, supply-side , aggregate demand view to oil specific demand shocks will influence tourism income varies. So, governments ought implement strategies against future oil price movements or plan for economic policy development.

In fact, instead of oil price changes will influence tourism income, it could also harm economic growth and tourism activities, due to the effect they expert on transporation, production cost, economic uncertainty.Because tourism activities is one important sector to influence any country's leisure consumption GDP income source. So, sudden fluctuations in oil prices may also influence economic growth. It is based a hyphthesis known as the tourism led economic growth. So, it seems that they have direct or indirect relationship to case effect between oil price and tourism activities and development. So, increase on tourism income, the called " economic-driven tourism growth". In addition, high oil prices are affecting certain tourism industry segments , e.g. airlines, cruises lines, hotel, rent travelling car services etc. for oil, importing countries example, with reference to macro economic effects, higher oil prices generally lead to higher inflation, when they negatively influence to country's income.

Hence, from a micro-economic perspective, positive oil price shocks lead to a decline in disposable income. for low income people, it will bring an immediate and negative impact on tourism, mainly due to they feel tourism leisure is regarded as a luxury good, when oil price shocks to rise suddenly . It influences any airline or cruise entertainment service providers' costs are influenced to raise. Then, they need to increase air ticket or cruise ticket price. It will bring on negative tourism leisure demands-side the oil price increases low income group, potential tourism leisure consumers. Hence, it seems that oil price may have indirect relationship to influence tourism leisure consumers' needs.

● How the price of oil changes influences global tourism industry growth or recession?

In macro-economic view, sudden mid and long term oil price shock can influence global torusim industry growth or recession. For example, a oil price of US$180 per barrel was considered only a few years ago, now this has a realistic scenario to which all plaers in the T&T sector have to adapt. At such a high level, the price of oil will become even more critical to almost every part of the tourism value chain. Although, weak global demand, caused by global economic recesson, resulted in a steep oil price decline to US$45 per barrel by the fourth quarter of 2008 in the past low oil price occurrence history, this won't change the mid to long -term oil forecast.

In fact, the past oil price occurrence history of the dramatic structural had changed a high price imposed on airlines, travelers, and destination countries, all of which will have to navigate through times of shifting or even declining travel demand. I assume that a high oil price scenario is assumed in the long term in order to highlight the changes , such a senario would mean for consumer behavior and the competitiveness of several destinations.

Low oil price in the 1970 and early 1980 did not bring significant growth of international air travel, but its growth has been strongest between 1980 and 2004, a period with stable and relatively moderate oil prices. Also, the rapid development of the low-cost carrier business model in the 1990s further fueled air travel growth by capturing tourism leisure demand , such as weekend leisure travel to cities using mostly secondary airports in any big area countries, such as UK, US . However, the tourism growth is whole influenced by high oil prices, due to oil price had been continue rising in possible.

Basis of oil is shortage supply product, oil is assumed to be the main energy source for the aviation sector for the nest 30 years. Although, second-generation biofuels seem to be on the horizon, the economics as well as the production scalability and aviation biofuel shortage will be a main challenge to airline industry. So, I assume that oil price will continue rise up, if there have none any aviation biofuel can be reflected to oil to use for air plane energy.

Until 2004, the only factors to have affected air travel growth, negatively were in external shocks , such as 9/11, causes catching air plane crisis or US regional geopolitical conflicts. It brings some travelers feel fear to go to US travel, as well as until recently 2019, human mouth disease can influence air to have disease to anyone from mouth. So, global travelers number had been continue decreasing, because they are fear to get disease by air when many themselves every stranger travelers are sitting on the without windows air planes. Although, mouth human and air disease and US 9/11 air attack both matters may influence oil price falls effect, because air planes flying times will reduce. They won't need frequent to fly, to cause aviation oil energy need reduce. Consequently, oil price will decrease, due to travelers number reduces and air planes flying times are also influenced to reduce. (oil demand decreases cause oil price decrease). Although, air lines ' cost will also be influenced reduce, but oil price decrease can not bring travelers number increase , when air ticket price reduce because global many leisure and business trip travelers feel fear to catch air planes frequently when human mouth air disease occured in 2019. So, oil price decreases can not grow up tourism industry growth or rise tourism income.

However, the obvious impact of a high oil price is an increase in the operating costs of airline. Moreover, fuel cost as a percentage of airline operating costs vary significantly based on the length of the flight. The longer the flight, the higher the fuel costs as a percentage of the airline operating cost. So, from an online's perspective, long -hauel flights represent the most criticial challenge to profitable operation because the share of fuel on these flights, compared with other cost items, is largest, because of the unfacorable fuel economics, due to fuel costs even at high-load factors. For example, Thai airways dropped its non-stop Bongkok to US flights in the summer of 2008 for commercial reasons, because fuel reached operating cost levels of 55 percent on this route, a cost burden that could not be passed on to their customers. So, the estimated price elacticity of passengers demand at this Bongkok to US flights route is high, if Thai Airways rises less air ticket price, it will influence many travelers to choose other airlines to catch air plan to fly. Hence, due to Thai Airways can not make decision to rise air ticket price, because it believes that it will lose many travelers, so it only chooses to drop this non-stop Bongkok to US flights to avoid fuel cost rising economic loss.

However, although micro and macro economic theories may also that oil price variable or change, it may influence global tourism income. But, recently, on 2019, human mouth and air diseases, it can influence global individual leisure and business trip travelers feel fear to catch air plans to avoid their bodies get this kind of death sickness when they sit in the no fresh air supplying air planes. They feel that they reduce leisure travelling flying times or business trip flying times with strange travelers to sit in crowd air planes together. Then, they must many avoid human moth and air disease to avoid death crisis. Hence, in this global human mouth and air diseases threat environment occurrence, even oil price sudden reduces to low price, it brings airline's cost reduces and air ticke price reduces. However, when air ticket price reduce to be very cheaper, it can not still attract global many leisure or business trip travelers to buy air tickets to fly frequently. Why does air ticket reduction, it can not attract many leisure or businee trip travelers to buy air ticket to fly ? The main reason is because human mouth and air disease influences global many travelers feel fear to catch air planes frequently. In psychological view, this kind of human mouth and air sickness will bring long time negative influence to global traveles do not want to catch air planes for business trips or travelling leisure frequently. So, it implies that oil price changing to influence air ticket price reduction factor ought not main factor to influence tourism income. It may include traveler individual negative emotion psychological factor, such as human mouth and air disease or 2019 9/11 attack both cases, they can influence global travelers feel fear to catch air planes to fly to avoid death threat. So, oil changing price ought not be only one absolute main factor to influence global tourism income significantly.

On conclusion, in economic view, it seems that oil chang price may have indirect or direct relationship to influence tourism income, instead of some unpredicted external environment factors influence, such as US 9/11 attack crisis and human mouth and air disease factors, they may be main factors to influence travellers number to reduce in non-economic external unpredicted environment view.

COVID 19 human disease how influences global airline fuel manufacturers to rapid reach decline life cycle stage

Recently, since 2019 end, COVID 19 human disease confirms that any one can be gotten this kind disease by the COVID 19 patient individual mouth or air, hand, even things contact. This kind disease may hurt the heath person individual lung to let him/her to feel difficult to breathe, even death. So, this kind disease had influenced many people feel fear to catch airplanes, because when many passengers are sitting in the airplane, if one or more is/are COV19 human disease patient, then the patient has possible to bring this disease to let the health passengers to get his/her COVID 19 human disease in the none window airplanes environment easily. SO, when this kind of human disease is threatening global travellers to avoid to catch air airplanes to fly to travel frequently. Then, airplanes won't need to fly often. When airplanes do not need often fly in sky. Then gas fuel demand will be influenced to reduce to airlines because airplanes won't need often catch many travellers to go to different countries, due to travellers number reduces as well as many different countries' travellers had begun to reduce travelling times frequently and their airports restrict any high body temperature people to enter their countries, because they will have possible to bring COVID 19 human disease when they arrive any airports. Consequently, airplanes do not need to buy and use any more gas fuel to provide them to fly any more since COVID 19 human disease occurs.

How COVID 19 human disease influences global gas fuel sale number? Because travellers number had been decreasing, airlines do not any airplanes often catch many passengers to fly to any countries again. Surely, gas fuel demand to airplanes may be also influenced to reduce and it can also influence whole tourism leisure industry development will experience to the decline cycle life stage absolutely. Before , due to global has many travellers feel need to travel leisure activity. So, global travellers increasing number impacted to global needs to have many airplanes to be provide to fly every day frequently. Before average per day had above 10,000 times of airplane flying times in our earth every day, so it implied that gas fuel need must be influenced to increase to airlines, because airlines must need to buy a lot gas fuel to provide their airplanes to fly to different countries every day , when any countries have many travellers need to fly to different countries to travel. It is sure that airline gas fuel product must reach the maturity life cycle stage in this airplane gas fuel manufacturing industry, because travelling leisure activities are accepted to be on kind of popular habit leisure to global travellers, when air ticket price had been decreasing, it can also attract many travellers accept to spend money to buy air tickets to go to different countries to travel frequently.

So, cheap air ticket price and popular tourism leisure activity factors may influence global travellers number increases. When global travellers number increases, it impacts to global airplanes need to increase flying times to fly frequently and air tickets also increases purchase number. Consequently, airlines also are influenced to need to buy a lot gas fuel to provide to airplanes to fly. SO, due to gas fuel demand increases, but gas fuel supply number is not enough, then gas price can be influenced to raise, when airlines demand gas fuel number is more than gas fuel supply number. It is based on economic theory, when demand to the product increases in the market, but the product has shortage to supply, then price may be influenced to bring sale price increasing chance. So, in this airline gas fuel demand and supply case, due to airplanes need to fly frequently, so global flying numbers had been influenced to rise and global airplanes need to buy many airplanes to catch passengers or travellers to fly to different countries. So, airlines must need to buy a lot gas fuel to provide airplanes to fly to different countries every day in this airline industry mature life stage. Thus, before 1029, it is gas fuel manufacturing industry and airlines travelling transport industry and tourism industry their maturity cycle stage period. Every day, global gas manufacturers need to attempt to find any lands have gas and explore any gas lands, than using technology to manufacture gas fuel in order to supply and satisfy any airlines' gas fuel needs every day. But, since COVID 19 human disease occurred in 2019 end, it influenced many airlines lose confidence the travellers number will increase, due to travellers number had been beginning to reduce every day and airplanes' flying times are also influenced to reduce , these both factors must influence gas fuel need reduces to any airlines their airplanes needs.

Hence, after 2019 end, it may be global tourism leisure industry decline life cycle stage, moreover, it may also be global airline transport flying service industry decline life stage both. So, global gas fuel need on airline sector must be influenced to reduce, when global airplanes did not often fly and global airplanes flying times had been influencing to reduce to per day 500 flying times, even less from the top level per day 10,000 flying times. SO, it can prove that they have relationship between tourism leisure industry and airlines' airplanes transport flying service industry and airline gas fuel product manufacturing industry. It means that when any unpredicted factors influence tourism leisure industry's life cycle stage changes, then the unpredicted factors may influence airline transport flying service industry and airline gas fuel product manufacturing industry life cycle service or gas fuel product stage change suddenly , such as this unpredicted COVID 19 human mouth disease, it can influence global tourism leisure industry and airline airplanes transport flying service industry and airline gas fuel product manufacturing industry had been beginning to experience the decline life cycle stage nowadays.

What COVID-19 human mouth disease can let airlines transport service providers and gas fuel manufacturers and tourism leisure service providers to learn? Airlines clearly have a lot on their airplanes at the moment, but since COVID-19 human mouth disease occurred in 2019 end. Many airlines had brought many airlines to prepare to catch global different countries travellers to go to different countries to travel, but nowadays, they do not need to be driven to fly to countries per day. These airplanes are staying on any countries' airports, but per day airlines need to pay high rent to the countries' airports when they are staying on the countries' airports. SO, their airport airplanes rent expenditure must be high, but their airplanes do not need to fly to different countries every day again , because COVID -19 human mouth disease influenced global travellers number had been reducing continue. With unpredicted consequences, many airlines will choose to sell their airplanes later, it none any one medicine can be invented to kill this kind of human mouth disease later, because if some airlines did not make decision to sell their airplanes, then they may nor regrow to growth life cycle stage from decline life cycle stage easily, due to passengers number reduces and it can influence their income reduces. But airline staffs still need to pay , e.g. pilots, airplane front line staffs and airports front line check in service staffs. Hence, sale of airplanes their assets may be the final strategic decision, when any airplanes can not continue to fly every day after 2020 year. Due to COVID 19 human disease can not be killed by any new medicine. If this kind of disease can not be filled for two or more years, then I believe that there are many airlines will experience to death life cycle stage from decline life cycle stage rapidly, otherwise if they can choose to sell some airplanes , they may keep cash available to prepare to reduce expenditure more easily. Although, some airlines made decisions to dismiss some airline service staffs, even pilots to achieve reducing salary expenditure in this decline life cycle stage. But, it will raise unemployment rate to bring social negative challenge. If later airlines choose to sell airplanes their assets to raise cash available strategy. However, it implies that gas fuel need must be influenced to reduce, due to COVID-19 human disease will continue to occur. So, it is the right time, gas fuel manufacturers ought not only concern how to manufacture more airplane gas fuel product to satisfy airlines airplanes transport flying need in this COVID-19 human disease occurrence stage. They ought find any new gas fuel users in this gas fuel market, if these airplanes gas fuel manufacturers expect to re-grow their gas fuel manufacturing and sale business to reach the growing life cycle stage from decline life cycle stage again in the future. Otherwise, many of gas fuel manufacturers will experience the death life cycle stage from decline life cycle stage within one to two years soon as possible.

Hence, if the gas fuel manufacturers can attempt to find other new kinds of gas fuel users in this gas energy market , instead of airline airplane gas fuel market and vehicle gas market main both markets. I believe that they can re-grow to growth life cycle stage from decline life cycle stage again in possible. Although, gas price must be influenced to reduce, because excess of gas supply to airline markets before 2019 end, but when airplanes do not need to fly frequently in this COVID -19 human disease occurrence environment. The COVID-19 pandemic human disease had had a significant impact on the aviation industry, due to travel restrictions and a significant full in demand among travellers. Significant reductions in passengers number have results in airplanes do not need to fly , airplanes feel price must drop, due to oil price war occurred. Hence, due to airline fuel price falls down, it causes many gas manufacturers' gas sale number also reduces to airline market. So, it is right time , any gas fuel manufacturers ought attempt to seek other new gas users, instead of airplanes users or cars users basic both gas users market. If they expect that they can change to experience regrowth life cycle stage from decline life cycle stage again and avoid to reach the final death life cycle stage within one to two years, due to COVID-19 pandemic human disease external environment factor influence.

In fact, on early assessment of the impact of COVID-19 on airline industry, it seems to have a more serve and more rapid impact on air traffic of fuel (oil price plummeted during the first quarter of 2020). It implies that global airline fuel price had been falling down due to COVID-19 human disease influences to global airplanes' flying times reduce. Moreover, COVID-19 impact on Asia-Pacific Aviation worsens, we have seen that first airline casually in the region, such as China , Singapore, Japan, Taiwan aviation fuel need has been influenced to reduce much significantly. Consequently, Asia-Pacific Aviation fuel price had been influenced to reduce much significantly. Then, it also influences Western Aviation, e.g. US, UK etc. Their flying times are also influenced to reduce, then fuel price sale to western Pacific Aviation can also influenced to fall down. Hence, it seems that COVID-19 human disease may also influence global aviation fuel price falls down. If the fuel manufacturers still only depend on sale aviation fuel income. I believe that the fuel manufacturers may reach to the death life cycle stage rapidly in short time. So, seeking new fuel users market is real need to any one fuel manufacturers , because global medicine scientists still can not guarantee when the kind of new medicine can be invented to kill COVID-19 human disease successfully. So, In this COVID-19 human disease threat environment, many experiencing mature life cycle stage airlines, such as US airline, Cathy airlines , UK airlines , Australia airline etc. they may be influenced to experience decline life cycle stage , even death life cycle stage within two year rapidly. Also, this kind of disease can also influence many travel agents' travelling leisure business development to experience decline stage cycle stage as well as it can also influence any airplanes fuel manufacturers to experience decline life cycle stage from mature life cycle stage in possible. Hence, it is right time , they need to change any new market users or service strategies in order to keep their businesses can continue regrow to the growth life cycle stage again.

● Electronic vehicle invention factor how influences future gas vehicle market life cycle stage experience changes

Nowadays, since electronic vehicle invention, it brought competition to fight traditional gas vehicle martet. Electronic vehicle is only needed to be charged battery, then battery will bring energy to push the electornic car to be driven fastly. So traditional vehicle market is experiencing decline life cycle stage. When, electronic vehicle is popular to be accepted to every drivers. In fact, when we drive cars on the roads, our cars will have gas emission to polluate our sir. Earth warmth is dramatically increasing. The main reason is that global air is polluted, e.g. frequent driving activities will bring air pollution when gas emission is caused. Hecnce, environment vehicle is only needed to charged battery. Every time battery charged can bring one day driving time power or enerty to let drivers to drive . So, basing on environmental protection and battery long time driving both reasons, it brings strengths to electronic vehicle to persuade global any drivers to choose to buy electronic vehicle more than traditional gas vehicle. I shall research these questions: These questions may concern: Will the gas vehicle be influenced to experience the decline life cycle stage rapidly when the electronic vehicle is accepted to be popular to drive ? Can traditional gas vehicle avoid decline life cycle stage comes as well as if traditional gas vehicle real prepares to experience decline life cycle stage ? Can it re-grow to change to enter growth life cycle stage again? Can new electronic vehicle market influence traditional gas vehicle market to shorten time to experience decline life cycle age rapidly?

In our driving history, cars invention had helped us do not need to spend long walking time to go to anywhere conveniently. In fact, due to technological limit, e.g. bus, taxi, tram, train must use gas to be energy to push them to be driven on the roads. When car invention period, or it may call car market birth life cycle stage period. In the 1800 year beginning , human does not know what car function or why we need car. When cars had been invented, it is global whole car industry borth life cycle stage period. This period its characteristics are: In societies , people accepted car tools to drive on the roads. Many people feel to spend money to buy cars, it is waste money, because they may choose to catch any kinds of public transport tools, e.g. bus, train, tram, taxi, ferry, undergroundtrain to arrive any destinations conveniently. So, from 1800 year to 1900 year, global whole car industy had been still keeping in the growth life cycle stage. Because in global society, many people hasd been general accepting public tranposrt tools, their fee are vey cheap and passengers can spend short time to catch them to go to anywhere, they can provide long transport service time for office working people, student from morning to evening time. Hence, this 100 years period, global car sale number could not significant increase, because public transport tools could bring convenience to any one when they needed to leave homes to arrive far away destination in short time.

Hence, global car industry ought not develop rapidly, because many peoplecould not accept to spend money to buy cars to replace to catch any public transport tools. But after 1900 year, global whole gas vehicle industry began to experience growth life cycle stage. Because global many people had jobs to do, unemployment ratio begain to reduce. In society, rich people number began to increase. It based on theseboth factors: families began to consider to attempt to buy any kinds of cars in order to attempt to buy any kinds of cars in order to let them to feel enjoyable to drive to go to anywhere. So, from 1901 year to 2000 year, it may be global whole gas vehicle market growth life cycle stage . In this period, global car buyers number had been increasing significantly . In average, global every family may own at least one car, even more. It depends on whether how many members number, the family has and whether the family has how many member(s), he/she has own one car licence. Moreover, in society, many people began to accept second hand cars, because second hand cars must be chaper to compare new cars as well as it is real one good choice for the low income car buyer social consumer groups in society. So, in this global vehicle market growth life cycle stage, instead of new car buyers number had been increasing significantly, the second hand car buyers number had also been increasing significantly in the same time. So, global new cars and secod hand car buyers number had increased rapidly every year, because global population is increasing. It also caused many working people did not like to spend long time to queue to wait public transport tools, it is another factor to persuade people chooce to buy cars to drive to go to offices or schools or anywhere in their relax time, e.g. holiday, sunday. So, this 100 year, may be global whole car industry growth life car cycle stage.

After 2000, it may be global car industy mature life cycle ctage , many car manufacturers begun to innovate any kinds of traditional cars to change to advanced engine function, auto-window, auto dooe functions , navigation road locaion search function, even non-manual driven artificial intelligent car invention. So, after 2000 year, due to global car buyers begun to pursue comfortable drivin feeling. They need to pursue comfortable driving feeling. They need to buy unique design of cars, or more functions of cars to drive on the road . Hence, global different unique function and styles of cars purchase needs had been significant increasing. Moreover, car prices had also been increasing more, due to more different unique functional and styles of car purchase needs had been increasing in order to satisfy the rich or high income car buyers group. So, after 2000, it may be global car market 's mature life cycle stage.

But, I believe that global car market's mature life cycle stage can not keep long time. The main reason is because the electronic car invention. After 2000 year, since one kind of new transport tool of electronic car invention, it influences many gas car owners or non car owners feel interesting to learn how to drive electronic cars and feel whether what advantages that electronic cars can satisfy their driving needs. IN special, environmental protection awareness drivers must believe electornic cars can reduce air pollution when they choose to drive them on the roads , due to none gas emission effect to pollute our earth air. When they choose to drive electronic cars, due to they only need to charge battery, then their electronic cars can be driven on the roads in short time rapidly. Even, report also indicated driving electronic cars accident occurrence chance may be also influenced to reduce to compare driving gas cars usually. So, electronic vehicle market may be future main competitor to global traditional gas vehicle market.

May electronic vehicle invention influence future gas vehicle shorten time to experience to decline life cycle stage rapidly? How gas vehicle market may avoid the shorten time to experience decline life cycle stage if electronic vehicle market may influence its development in global car manufacture industry? I shall attempt to solve these challenges as below:

IN fact, electronic vehicle innovation is not long time , so the global electronic vehicle manufacturing and sale market is experiencing birth life cycle stage. Can electronic vehicle market reduce to shorten time to experience growth, even mature life cycle stages. It depends on these factors:

The factors may affect battery electronic vehicle energy consumption and driving behavior impact. They may include whether environment protection awareness will increase or decrease to global nay one gas car owners or non car owners. Because if global environment protection awareness increase, it will influence gas car owners or non car owners (potential either battery electronic vehicle energy or gas vehicle energy car choice buyers), begun to feel their frequent driving gas vehicle behaviors may bring air pollution or global warming, temperature rises weather disaster occurrence in the future. They alsoknow battery electronic vehicle energy consumption price may be cheap to same to gas vehicle energy consumption. Moreover, they may feel that if they change to drive battery electronic vehicles, it may help them to minimize environmental air pollution impacts of the end of life stage and brings positive impacts on improving climate change and air quality for our future. So, if many car owners or non car owners feel that they have responsibility to protect our climate environment pollution. Then, battery electronic vehicle buyers number will have possible to increase rapidly in short time. Due to the significant impact of gas vehicle and battery electronic vehicle their life cycle analysis can be utilized to analyze the advantages and disadvantages to cause car buyers make comparison between them and gas vehcile and battery electronic vehcile both kinds vehicles are highly complex supply chain choice in the automobile industry nowadays. Moreover, due to carbon intensity of this stage was calculated from emission factors at the global car manufacture industry. Hence, emission factor may be one important influential factor to influence any one makes car purchase decision or either gas or battery electronic car purchase decison.

For example , in our societies, if many peopl own environment protection awareness, then global gas vehicle buyers number may be influenced to reduce, even the owning gas vehicle families may be influenced to choose to buy battery electronic cars to replace their gas cars. They may sell their gas vehicles to any one, even to steel manufacturers easily. Hence, gas vehicle on steel existence number may also reduce ot they can disappear in our road in short time rapidly. If batttery electronic vehcile can be popular to accept to drive on the road to any one driver in our societies. Then, battery electronic cars may be influenced to increase driving needs to any one driver. it's sale number may also influenced to increase rapidly. Consequently, it may have chance to experience to growth life cycle stage from birth life cycle stage in short time rapidly in global whole electronic car manufacturer and sale market.

Then another influential factor concerns how owning car consumers feel the charge of the battery energy use of resources in comparison to conventional gas energy use of resources to driving cars. In combination with the regional electricity mix these factors influence the energy materials for a specific car market. For these first life cycle phases a range of values is possible to battery electronic car market. If in our societies, there are many people choose to use battery charge energy resource to drive electronic cars, their prices are very reasonable to compare gas vehicles or they feel gas will face rapid shortage challenge, if global any one only likes to drive gas vehicle. Then, they may be influenced to choose to buy the battery electronic vehicles to replace gas vehicles. Hence, enery resource used to car my also be one main factor to influence any one car buyer individual either battery electronic car or gas vehicle purchase choice.

Hence, it implies that the life style environmental impacts and energy resource used both impacts of battery electronic cars are a topic of increasing relative importance of the vehicle production stage and the maximum impact on climate change (ingc02/km) that is observed by many climate scientists, their observation to climate change good or bad change effect may influence global battery electronic vehicle needs. So, how clean are battery electric cars, it will be one popular topic for environmental scientists to environmental protection awareness car owners and non car owners. T o analysis hoe to cause electric car life cycle changes. The arrival of the electric car has brought with it an array of life cycle factors that influence the carbon emission level to any one country's environment.

Influence of national electricity grid over the use phase, so it implies that if the country feels carbon emission level is high , due to gas vehicle may bring carbon emission to pollute air to the country. Although, factory's carbon emission or airplane carbon emisson may be one factor to influence the country's air pollution level to be increase. The year has high carbon emission level, it considers gas vehicle air carbon emission level whether it is high or low in the year. So, if the country's gas vehicle car owners number is sudden increasing rapidly. Consequently, it will evaluate that the car increasing number may influence the country itself carbon emission level to be high and it may cause air pollution seriously.

Hence, battery electric car industry life cycle whether when it can experience growth life cycle stage or mature life cycle stage from birth life cycle stage, it depends on what carbon emisson level to any one country. If this year has many countries believe their high carbon emissin level is due to gas vehicle 's carbon emission causes. Then, this high carbon emission level report factor may raise many car owners or non car owners consider environment protection awareness and it may also influence many car buyers choose to buy battery electric cars to replace gas cars to drive on the road frequently in this year.

Also in order to avoid themselves countries' air pollution is more serious. Hence, global carbon emission rise or fall level and any one environmental protection awareness psychological both factors may influence future battery electric car market development. They may have close relationship to influence any one traditional gas vehicle owner to buy one new battery vehicle vehicle to replace it to drive on the road, or any one potential car purchaser makes final battery electric car or gas vehicle decision absolutely. On conclusion, above these factors may explain whether it is possible that battery electronic vehicle invention may influence future gas vehicle market changes to decline life cysle stage from mature life cycle stage. It depends on whether environmental protection awareness to car owners increasing or decreasing number , carbon emission level whether it is high or low, gas energy resource facing shortage factors to influence future electronic vehicle need.

MTR transport electric energy need factor

Nowadays, transportation and economic development have close relationship. Economic development stimulates transportation demand by increasing the numbers of workers commuting to and from work, customers traveling to and from services areas, and products being moving by lorries on the roads between products and customers. According to Bailey, Mokhtarian and Little (2008) indicated "transportation route is past of distinct development pattern or road network and mostly described by regular street patterns as an important factor of human existence, development and civilization. The route network combined with increased road transportation investment result in changed levels of conveniently reflected through cost benefit analysis, savings in travel time, and other benefits. " These benefits are noticeable in increased catchment areas for services and facilities , shops, schools, offices, banks and leisure activities.

What are the crisis of neglection to care transporation system ? Why do any countries need to design road transportation system? Can MTR transport be popular to be accepted to cause transport electric energy need increases? For example, the Japan country lacks design road trsnaportation system effectively. So, the crisis of road traffic fatalities will raise and the econominc influence will be changed. The crisis indicates more than 7,000 people die annually as a result of motor vehicle crashes in Japan. Driving when under the influence of alcohol is the leading cause of motor vehicle crash fatalities in both developed and developing countries. So, alcohol is the most serious factor to raise personal risk when drivers are driving in Japan. However, a number of studies have shown that deterring drink driving is an important way to cause fatalities. There is a demonstrative need for social change in Japan.

Japan has recently strengthened its already strict laws in order to reduce the number of alcohol related road fatalities. Those deforms lowered the legal blood alochol contant limit increased, the penalties for offenders. The Japan road traffic legal needs. Any driving a motor with a alcohol limit of 0.03 or higher Japan's maximum sentence is up to 3 years imprisonment or a fine not exceeding 500,000 yen dollars. Is law impact to reduce drinking alcohol to drive in Japan? What are economic influence of the crisis of road traffic fatalities in Japan?

The rational choice theory of offending suggests that offenders are active decision makers who influence a large number of variables into decision whether or not to commit an offence. On the cost-benefit analysis, it is the punishment a possible jail, large fines worth is the reward the convenience of driving home without the expause of a taxi and innovenience to the alcohol drivers in Japan. Instead of law reforms when it detects alcohol in the air exhaled from the alcohol and other offenders and it educates children about the dangers of drinking and it also explains why alcohol driving can also threaten drivers' life when who are drinking alcohol and driving behaviour in the same time in Japan.

On the economic influence hand, implementation of the policy deregulating alcohol sales and alcohol production did not appear to increase traffic fatalities among adult or teenage males or females in Japan. We found that male adult fatalities demonstrated a statistically significant decline following enactment of the deregulation policy in 1994 year. So, Japan implement law to threaten alcohol drinking behaviour is useful. It can influence the alcohol availability and consumption, alcohol production and sales, the 24 hours operated convenience stores or liquor discount stores incomes to be reduced. Even, Japan overall GDP is also reduced from the deduction of liquor alcohol production and sale, also the occurrence of traffic accident fatalities chances will be also reduced.

The Japanese economy has entered a rapid process of liberalization since the mid-1990 year. Many sectors previously under direct government control are now regulated by the competitive market place. The Japanese alcohol beverage market has changed. The entry of cheaper import alcohol products resulted in a encouragement of alcohol consumption to Japan drinking drivers and an raising of increasing of more import alcohol products supply to Japan. Although, it is beneficial to Japan GDP growth. But it also raise the occurrence of chance to traffic accidents rate to cause alcohol drinkers to be death or hurt when who choose drinking alcohol to drive at the same time in Japan. So, alcohol import can bring more consumption, but it can also raise many traffic accidents occurrence in Japan in the same time.

In conclusion, alcohol is not good for health to drink when the consumer often buys alcohol at drink habitually. So, if many Japanese, including the alcohol driving consumers and the alcohol non drinking consumers both who often buy different countries alcohol to drink daily. It will cause their bodies to be unhealth for long term in Japan. It is possible to increase Japan's government's medical expenses to assist the low income or poor people in the future. So, although alcohol import can raise Japan GDP growth in the short term, but it also raise Japan government's medical expenditure to the low income or poor Japanese long term in the future, So it's economic benefit will not good in the future if Japan still import much alcohol to sell in its country.

Many commercial users depend on road transport facilities, with movement of products and services from place to place on the roads, aspect of global and urban economic survival. Hence, developments of various transportation modes have become important to physical and economic developments. For example, urban locations with such relative advantages are found where different transport routes with high degree of connectivity, within the intra and inter urban road networks. On similarly, commercial activities like banking, retail/wholesale businesses and professional services can take advantage of nearness to concentration of activities attracted consumers service providers. This partly caused increase in demand for commercial space and its effects on commercial property values along commercial roads can be rose. However, some countries' roads need to provide pedestrian movements more than the businesses activities, e.g. shorten the time of lorries parking on the road to let pedestrian movements on the narrow road. If the country government did not consider the roads need to let more pedestrian movements or shorten the time of lorries parking on the road. It will cause traffic jam or traffic density of the individual roads. Hence, governments need to concern the locations of commercial property buildings and the relationship between the explanatory variables of the design road networks.

What are construction of roads design networks benefits? In fact, construction of roads increased substantially with the opening up of residential environments that also is getting much benefits from increasing demand for spaces in commercial properties. Many private companies, retail stores, commercial banks aggregate in the main roads of cities, which get advantage of opportunities afforded by locations near central of cities to attract many pedestrians concerning their businesses existence. This led to high concentration of vehicular and pedestrian movements. Specially along the access main roads in the central of cities. The main roads exhibits linkages to form networks of minor routes along which commercial properties locate. If commercial users are displaced residential users, causing sites to be at the highest and best uses with increases in the values of commercial properties. However, it seems road network development is affected by the compact nature of various routes that sometimes causes volume of traffic jam. Thus, demand for transport can't be treated solely as a derived demand road. Improved main and minor roads access an city or rural areas is a necessary (but not sufficient). Precondition for increased productivity, the UK Standing Advisory committee On Trunk Road Assessment (SACTRA, 1999) noted "various ways in which transport can affect economic growth, for example benefits include through reorganization and rationalization of production, distribution and land use: reducing labor costs by expanding catchment areas etc."

What is land use and road transport design system relationship? Land use refers to the whole range of human activity and of the built environment, and to some aspects of the natural environment. This is a way relationship between land use and road transport. Governments need to design how to use land and how to design road transportation systems. e.g. where are built the main roads and/or where are built the minor roads are the most suitable locations in the cities or rural areas ? If the main roads is located in the not suitable locations at the centers of the cities or rural, it will case the increasing traffic volumes and levels of congestion, including air pollution, noise, ground water pollution from run-off , loss of soil functions and loss of bio-diversity to natural environment. By influencing the spatial structure of locations in the urban environment, so land use planning can help to mitigate any negative effects resulting from land use changes.

Modelling and land use transportation interactions has become an important aspect of road design transport planning. On the one side, for example, design roads in urban centers, it can increase land use and it can also reduce employees or students catching buses or driving cars' time spending to go to workplaces or schools users. Hence, the land use and roads designing transportation can give benefits to residents and employment people to reduce time to wait buses or taxies etc. public transportations to go to workplaces or schools or shopping centers etc.

anywhere. It seems to assist bus companies or taxi drivers to earn more income, On the other side, designing urban transport systems is also important . Increased densities mean more destinations become within convenient walking and cycling distances and consequently the use of these modes tends to be higher. Also in dese cities public transport systems are able to offer higher levels of service and operate more economically, when the provision of sufficient road space to meet potential demand becomes impractical. It aims to reduce the danger of driving or walking in urban areas. The transport modes (that is walking, cycling, public transport) and the extent of car dependence is less, due to driving users dependency is less on rural roads. Hence, building main roads can concentrate on designing convenience to pedestrian walking to close to their houses on the streets. However, poor transport design and land use can cause to spend too expenditure not only transport costs on governments and transport users both and also the costs of providing other services. These include the usual utilities and also education and health services as well as negative externalities , such as greenhouse gas emissions. Most such studies concluded that there are significant financial and economics cost advantage of inner city redevelopment compared with fringe development.

However, such policies won't necessarily be successfully, in particular because of the two ways road problem, they may result in additional private investments and employment opportunities flowing into the region, buy may equally result in population and employment opportunities flowing out of the target region because of the improved access to other centers. Hence governments need to analyze how to arrange the land use to assist the property developers to choose where are the suitable locations to build offices or factories or shopping centers or houses at capital or urban cities to adapt to whose the growth of living population. For example, to judge where the land use whether where main roads or junior roads are built where are the suitable locations to satisfy the lorry drivers to park their lorries are the safe locations ; to design the minor roads to let the pedestrians to feel no danger to walk on the streets when the cars are driven to near to the streets on the minor roads. Thus, the factor of choosing where the land use to design the main or minor roads areas, sizes and lengths and of the minor or major roads can influence the drivers and pedestrians feel safe or dangerous when who are driving whose cars on the roads or who are walking on the streets to arrive the offices, schools, cinemas, church, houses etc. destination.

Designing road transportation networks how to assist economic growth ? I feel it is not all transport investments will be equally effective in enhancing economic growth. Designing road transport investment is a necessary, but on its own not sufficient requirement to earn significant economic growth at either a national or regional level. There are conditions under three categories: economic conditions, investment conditions and political conditions. In fact, although in some circumstances, transport investment may be a necessary condition for enhancing economic growth, it is rarely on its own a sufficient condition. Other factors including the broader policy environment, need to be present if the investment is going to be successful in addressing regional economic objectives. My some suggestions the following key aspects as being most relevant including:

a. Scale economies for example, where these dominate, lower transportation costs through improved accessibility may encourage increased concentration of firms in core regions, until the point that diseconomies set in.

b. Size of the local market.

c. Local land and labor conditions.

d. The nature and scale of transport improvements.

e. The nature of backward and forward linkages

in the country 's local economy.

In any countries, road transportation improvements don't guarantee increased economic development. To increase economic development, an improvement needs to assist any lorry drivers to drive in short trips to reduce transportation costs and shorten time driving on the road or to make transportation more reliable, e.g. reducing the numbers of traffic jams on any roads. A proper economic climate must also exist as well as other support services. With these factors to influence transportation improvements can become catalysts for economic expansion. However, road transportation improvement that intends to induce job creation, when employers need many lorry drivers to help them to transport products and to move products on the roads often. So, the employers need to employ many transportation workers and lorry drivers to help who to transport their products to send to clients, due to the transportation time is shorten and work efficiency is rasied, so the transportation times are also increasing every day when the road transportation roles are improved. On the other side, improving transportation can raise productivity when many customers need to buy many products and the lorry drivers may drive whose lorries to transport many products between factory and office or between factory to the client's home or between the shop and the client's on the road in the short time fast.'

I recommend one model links in an overall road transportation network includes these four modes.

I. Maximizing use of the existing road highway system.

II. Extending or improving the multi-lane divides system local roads and connectors.

III. Continually improving the entire road highway network in response to business activities demand.

The improvement of modern road transportation successful factors include:

● How to improve the highway network

modernization includes obsolete interchanges and other segments of the road, transport network of new designs to improve the life and service of pedestrian walking streets, rebuilding certain in main or minor roads. To the extent that labor markets operate more efficiently and more jobs are created to raise economic expansion if our governments can improve road transportation system to design to satisfy business users demand when lorry drivers need to move or transport whose products on the streets, but who will not influence pedestrian are walking on the streets. Hence, excellent transportation design network can subsequent plan efforts, it can also rise economic efficiency, community and social effects, it can also encourage transportation users to attempt to drive lorries to transport products a lot of times in one day fast and who can also avoid traffic jams occurrence on the road easily. On the one side, economic development is a concept referring to the material aspects of community welfare. There are numerous factors need of development: growth in income and wealth, equitable distribution of income, decreased infant mortality rates, increased literacy rates. On the other side, economic growth means which is sustainable increase in community income and /or wealth. (wealth is the net of resources that generate income). It seems the link between transportation facilities and economic growth has close relationship. Good transportation facilities support economic growth by lowing the transportation costs of users of the transportation network, such as roads. Direct users benefits are reductions in travel, times and fuel consumption, increased reliability and increased safety in the movement of people and products, users' transportation costs are reduced, resources are used for other purpose.

The relationship between transport and economic development occur in two directions, in the sense that (i) land use and economic development are major drivers' of demand for transport (in terms of quantity , type, location and mode); and (ii) transportation investments and other initiatives (such as regulations, pricing) can influence levels, patterns and locations of economic development. The principal role of road transportation is to provide access between spatially separated locations for the business and household sectors, for both commodity (lands transportation) and person movements. For the business sector, this involves connections businesses and their input sources between business factories and other business shops and between business and their markets. For the households sector, it provides people with access to workplaces and education facilities, shops and social recreation, community and medical facilities etc. on the roads. I feel different countries' road transportation system can be self funded in the sense that the majority of the costs of transportation system investment operation and maintenance are either paid directly by users (for example, through car operating costs) are funded initially by governments and recovered from transport users (for example, through petrol duties and road user charges). Governments' road transportation system and their use also give rise to some external costs(externalities). These include global environmental impacts (greenhouse gas emissions) and local environmental and health impacts (for example, noise partial pollution and road accident costs). The direct effects of transportation investments are to reduce road transportation time and costs through reducing travel time, decreasing the operating costs of transportation and enhancing access to destinations within the road network. A good road transportation network also needs to reduce any economic disbenefits, for example where projects reduce congestion or the risk of injury. These incremental benefits of transportation investments may be measured through commercial cost benefit analysis. Other indirect consequences of road transportation network should also be considered when evaluating effects on productivity and the spatial pattern of economic development. Good road transportation design network benefits can include lower costs and enhanced accessibility, due to better transportation links and services expand markets for individual transportation using business and improved access to input.

The economic contribution of road transportation policy can be assessed from various perspectives. These include:

● Effects on aggregate economic welfare (e.g. the sum of consumer and which is the times of cost benefit analysis, as linking to transportation productivity effect.

● Micro economic, for example, enterprise or household level productivity effects.

● Macro economics, for example, contributions to GDP investment or employment and the spatial patterns of economic activity.

One key characteristics of road transportation is split between infrastructure and operations. Infrastructure refers to the right of way on which vehicles operate, which may include ancillary facilities to ensure efficient and effective operations (for example, traffic signals, railway stations). In developed countries, are in most transportation is operated by the private cars, road trucks, the majority of bus and coach services. In long term , overall purpose, to ensure transportation system helps to develop that maximizes the economic and social benefits and minimizes harm. Hence, governments need to concern who are their main target users to use every road. Such as the road is used to near to park and leisure, or local and national economic conditions, keep clean natural environment etc. facilities to provide different benefits to different target users to enjoy to use. It seems that good transportation networks designing can influence economic activities, shopping convenience or business convenience etc. activities to cause whether the country's economic behavior to achieve close relationship successfully. Possible relationship between road networks, location attribute, demand and supply and accessibility and commercial property values of these factors which will influence different countries' concerning to choose where to build main roads and sub minor roads in different cities and rural locations. However, I shall suppose hypotheses how governments to find the most suitable places to build main roads and sub minor roads to whose cities and rural. There is no significant relationship between commercial property values and individual contributions of explanatory variables to variability in commercial property values in whose countries.

In conclusion, I suggest methods how to design suitable transportation networks to governments to build, such as it is essential to establish a technique that may be useful for determining relative accessibility of locations in the network of main roads and sub minor roads. Even, when relative advantages are determined, there is need to develop models that will be useful for predicting commercial properly values. The model may become tool for professional estate surveyors and values to change their practice of using intuition to determine relative access of locations in a road network. Similarly, there is the need to predict the supply of, demand for, and fair market values of commercial properties by developers. Hence if the cities or rural locations can attract many businesses to build commercial properties, governments can build the main roads in the locations. Otherwise, if the cities or rural locations can not attract many businesses to build commercial properties, governments can build the sub minor roads in these locations. Hence, the main roads must have high transportation valuation to let big lorries to drive and park in these main roads easily and conveniently. It seems capital cities may not influence to build the main road factors. Natural environment, commercial properties values, the lands areas size and shape and pedestrian walking numbers on the streets and lorries available numbers on the areas will be other factors to influence where to build main roads in any cities or rural in the country.

In road concept, the route network consists of primary and secondary roads, known as main roads and minor roads respectively. Main roads are usually moderate or high capacity roads that are below highway level of service, carrying large volumes of traffic between areas in urban centers and designed for traffic between neighbors. They have intersections with collector and local streets and commercial areas, such as shopping centers, petrol stations and other businesses are located along such roads. In additions, main roads link up to expressways and freeways with inter-changes in cities or rural. Road network constitutes an important element in urban development , due to urban areas have many farms, gardens, forests , so roads and building needed to provide accessibility required by different land uses and the proper functioning of such urban areas depends an efficient transport network existence. In computing des, the network indicator are used to partition road network into different parts in reasonable way. The results in number of connection to describe density differences in road networks. The parameter records how many roads connect to each road in a network. For two roads with the same length, the ones in the dense area will connect to more roads than that in a sparse area and the connection differences will indicate the density differences to some extent, so road density can also be calculated as the total length of all known roads divided by the total land area in a road divided by the total land area in a road network. Hence, governments need to consider road length to decide how to build main or minor roads to design its transportation systems for businesses activities , such as driving lorries and parking lorries and products are been moving on the streets from roads easily and conveniently. As Wikipedia Contributors (2008) indicate that "transport networks are spatial structures designed to channel flows from the points of demand to points of supply and to link the points together in a transportation system. They are useful for transport network analysis to determine the flow of people, products, services and vehicles." Hence, governments need to research whether where the shopping centers, cinemas, houses, hospitals, schools, offices, factories etc. are located, then, which need to follow these location datas to predict the cars, lorries, taxies, buses etc. of the demand numbers of transportation users to design the lengths, width and distances and the construction of main and minor roads locations and their supply numbers in different capital cities or country roads. It aims to reduce traffic jams and shorten time and air pollution as well as increasing the available spaces to let the lorry drivers to move their logistc on the road easily and reducing the accidents occurrence when the pedestrians are walking on the streets. If the vehicles can be moved on the roads easily. It will also increase time efficiency and productivity to any businessmen. Hence, how to design of the main roads and/or minor roads in any capital or country cities. It will influence any country's economic growth long time in the future.

● Underground train transportation tool is popular needed to influence transport electric energy need trend incrseases more than transport gas energy need

Understanding individual passenger behaviour is essential for the design MTR transportation, because who can choose to catch bus, taxi, tram, train ferry etc. different kinds of public transportation tools. Individual traveler who decides to catch which kinds of public transportation tools, it depends on whether the public transportation tool can provide real time travel information, liking link travel time schedule. So, MTR underground train needs to understand where it has terminal to give convenience to the local living areas of time travelers to choose to catch MTR easily. Although, MTR ticket fare is one factor to influence any passengers choice. But, those other factors can also influence them to choice. e.g. MTR any terminal location of convenience, short time travelling, none crowding in busy (peak) time, MTR platform waiting arrival time, none sudden MTR engineering machines broken accident events occurrence frequently etc. different factors, any one of these factors which can influence passengers who choose to catch MTR or other kinds of transportation tools.

Why route choice can influence passenger behavioural choice ? Usually, the busy time passengers will regard the route choice as a coordination problem to influence them to choose to catch which kinds of transportation tools. The route choice is as an opportunity costs to influence any busy time passengers to decide to choose to catch which kind of transportation tool which is the best right choice in the right time among of them. In the short time, for example, it seems any busy time passengers will choose to catch bus to substitute MTR underground train transportation tool, due to who feels the bus can arrive any destinations to compare other kinds of transportation tools in the most short time. However even if the MTR can either charge cheaper ticket fare to sell full day or charge discount ticket fare to sell in the busy (peak) time to compare to bus fare. It is possible that the busy time passengers will still choose to catch bus, if between the bus terminal and the another bus terminal that distance is the shorter time route to spend time to arrive destination to compare between the MTR terminal to the another MTR terminal arrival time . Also, although the busy time passengers will feel to enounter traffic jam to influence sitting or waiting bus time to be longer time in possible and who also feel MTR can avoid traffic jam problem. However, usually any busy (peak) time passengers will feel the chance of traffic jam occurrence will be less. So, the short bus route choice is more potential factor to influence the busy (peak) time passengers still to choose bus to catch.

However, if anyone wants to investigate results of day-to-day route choice which can be transferred to more realistic environment. It is necessary to explore individual behaviour in an interactive experimental set up to ensure busy (peak) time passenger transportation behavioural choice. For example, a passenger has a choice between a main road (M) and a side road (S) for travelling from (A) to (B). (M) is faster if (M) and (S) are chose by the same number of passengers. So, this method can be researched whether MTR terminal station is located at the main road (M) or the side road (S) where is more suitable to accept to passengers generally.

Why trip time reliability and crowding factors can influence MTR passenger choice? Other problem is MTR busy (peak) time's crowding in public transportation occurrence of MTR underground train transportation tool is becoming a growth to concern as MTR demand growth at a busy (peak) time. To capture the MTR passengers benefits with reduced crowding from improved MTR public transport service and image. It is necessary a identify the relevant dimensions of crowding that are meaningful measures of what crowding means to MTR passengers. Two main influences on MTR model choice that are growing in relevance are trip time reliability and crowding. It represents a benefit-cost framework. In fact, MTR passengers can be willing to pay more expensive ticket fare, it MTR can avoid crowding and short and the accurate arrival trip time between terminals is reliable to occur. How to measure of MTR crowding, e.g. weighting the gap between the busy time, the standard (i.e. objective) and the perceived (i.e. subjective) metrics. We are not in a position to definitely map the two dimensions, which is a crucial requirement for translating objective improvements into equivalent subjective gains that then can be applied, willingness to pay estimates MTR ticket fares to obtain the additional MTR passenger benefits of MTR public transportation investment to any terminal stations. Because MTR crowding has a negative impact on passengers in terms of psychological on emotional distress. MTR passengers are willing to stand for up to 20 minutes of the service is fast and reliable. However crowding outweighed these benefits from a MTR passenger's perpective, experienced crowding leads a increased dissatisfaction. e.g. stress and less privacy during who needs to stand up in MTR. Due to there are no enough places to supply to them to stand up in MTR. If the MTR trip time was longer time between the passenger's terminals, who will feel more dissatisfaction and it will cause who feels whether who ought need to choose to catch other transportation tools to substitute MTR next time. e.g. bus, train, tram, ferry, taxi etc. So, from an operator's perspective, the MTR service frequency or MTR size is significantly influenced by the level of ridership, which sends a signal to respond if the monitored crowding level exceeds the benchmark standard in the busy time. e.g. in the morning time or at the night time, the students or employment people who need to go to schools or offices (working places). The locations of different places between MTR terminals and crowding are regarded as a key service attribute for MTR pubic transportation along with other factors, such as travelling time and reliability, e.g. service quality, none engineering machines are broken to cause MTR stops suddenly.

Given the increasing importance of crowding on both the disutility to existing MTR public transportation users and the influence to it. MTR passenger can choose to use either the MTR public public transportation or other public transportation. It is timely to review the MTR current measures of crowding defined by transportation authorities. MTR operators ought evaluate whether they apporpriately reflect MTR each traveler experiences and perceptions of crowding in busy (peak) time. I suggest that MTR needs to buy other underground trains to supply to the busy (peak) time passengers to let them have enough seats to sit down, so who do not need to stand up in any MTR underground trains when they catch MTR underground trains in busy time. It aims to let who are willingness to pay the estimation of reasonable ticket fares to compare the other kinds of transportation tools in the busy (peak) time.

What is the crowding difference between train and MTR underground train? In fact, crowding won't be happened to brother these transportation tools easily in the busy time and non busy time both. e.g. bus, taxi, train, tram, ferry. Because passengers can not choose to stand up in these transportation tools easily, due to these transportation tools have no enough areas (spaces) to let them to stand up easily . So, the crowding will be avoided to occur in these tranportation tools usually. Otherwise, MTR will have many passengers who can choose to stand up because MTR design of length is very long and it has enough areas (places) to let passengers to choose to stand up, even there have none any seats are provided to let them to sit down. So, MTR passengers will feel more dissatisfaction and crowding easily, especial in any peak (busy) time every day.

Comparing to bus, much more diverse crowding measures are defined in the passenger rail industry. For passenger, different specifications for measuring crowding are found across countries and even within a country. For example, rail crowding measures in the UK, the passengers in excess of capacity is crowding measure that applies to all London and South east operators weekday train services at a London terminus during the morning peak from 0700 to 09: 59 , and those departing during the afternoon peak from 16:00 to 18:59 (office of rail regulation 2011 year). The overall PIXC figure is considered the planned standard class capacity of each train service as well as the actual number of standard class passengers on the service at the critical point. i.e. the location on a trains of standard class passengers that surpass the planned capacity as the difference between the number of actual passengers and the capacity of the train divided by the number of passenger is within the capacity . So, it seems train and MTR underground public transportaton tools had been encountering the crowding problems in peak time, the difference in train passengers need to wait next train or more train arrival is who doesn't plan to enter the train, when who discovers the current train has no seats to provide to them to sit down in whose trip. Otherwise, MTR passengers can choose either to stand up within the large areas (places) if who discovered there are no any seats to provide to them to sit down or who can wait the next MTR arrival in order to who can sit down. It seems MTR transportation tool crowding environment includes in waiting platform and inside of the MTR underground train. Otherwise, train transportation tool crowding environment only includes the waiting platform and the passengers will not have crowding feeling inside of the train, due to none of passengers choose to stand up inside any trains because any train inside has no enough places to let them to stand up. How MTR can attract many passengers. On the commuter departure time choice of any reference point researching hand, the departure time decisions of commuters are of fundamental importance of peak period MTR traffic congestion. However, whether on the demand side, MTR underground train congestion relief measures, such as MTR ticket fare to every terminal station needs to be charged cheaper fare or discount fare in the peak (busy) time every day. To aim to attract many passengers to choose to catch MTR Underground train public transportation tools, substitute to choose other public transportation tools in the peak time.

Over the past decades, there have been very active research efforts in the departure time problem, both in econometric modeling and dynamic user equilibrium fields. Although, these works provide valuable insights into dynamic commuter decision making, they do not identify the commuters' response to gains and losses related to whole actual arrival time to reference points who may have relative. The appliability of the reference point hypothesis of prospect theory to the commuter's departure time decision making to obtain a better understanding of how departure time choice in MTR platform during their waiting underground train arrival time. However, every MTR underground train actual arrival time and deviation variables related to reference points (gains and losses) are the key factors in the departure time choice model. How the MTR underground train of every commuter's daily departure time decision can be modelled when the reference point hypothesis of prospect theory. The MTR underground train's schedule delay is defined as the difference between the preferred arrival time (PAT) and the actual arrival time (AT) for a given MTR commuter. In a daily MTR commute, a commuter in the indifference band actual arrival time is an essential feature of MTR schedule study. Two reference points are the earliest acceptable arrival time and the work starting time for a given MTR platform waiting passengers. In psychological view point, prospect theory proposes that the displeasure of a loss is perceived or greater than the pleasure of a gain of the same attitude and therefore, the value function is stronger for losses than gains.

To conclude, it seems that if MTR waiting passengers need not spend long time to wait underground train arrival in platform and it can provide seats to let them to sit down in the busy (peak) crowding time. It will make them to feel pleasure, even the MTR ticket fare is not fair and reasonable to charge higher fare to compare other kinds of public transportation tools fares. So the peak waiting time factor can influence the passengers to choose other kind of transportation tools to catch easily. Moreover, MTR's two reference points are the earliest role. Similarly a loss is observed when the MTR platform waiting commuter experiences or actual arrival time which is beyond that the MTR schedule time. Due to that a MTR waiting commuter is as an early side arrival of whose actual arrival time is earlier than whose preferred arrival time.

Reference

Bailey, L., Mokhtarian, P.L. Little, A. (2008). The broader Connection Between Public Transportation, Energy Conservation And Greenhouse Gas Reduction, Report Prepared As Part Of TCRP Project J-11/Tasks Transit Cooperative Research Program, Transportation Research Board Submitted To American Public Transportation Association in http://www.apta.com/research/into/online/land_use.cfmi, accessed 17 April 2008.

The UK Standing Advisory Committee On Trunk Road Assessment (SACTRA) (1999). Transport And The Economy (Report To UK DETR). Retrieved From: http://webarchive.nationalarchives.gov.uk/20050301192906 ; http://dft.gov.uk/stellent/groups/dft-econappr/documents/pdf/dft_econappr_pdf_022512.pdf

Wikipedia Contributors (2008). Arterial Roads In Wikipedia, The Free Encyclopeda, http://en.wikipedia.org/w/index.php?title=Arterial_road&oldid=212832640(accessed May30,2008).

● Why electric transport tool service increasing causes gas enery to transport needs decrease

Any countries must need road, sea and air transport to assist businessmen to transport products in local or overseas. If the country's road , sea or air transport system service quality is poor. It will influence any products transport time, speed, inefficient transport to anywhere.

How to raise the country's transport system in order to improve efficiencies to let any businessmen can deliver their products to anywhere easily,e.g.

warehouses, client homes, supermarkets destination in the most short time to avoid delay occurrence to let clients feel unsatisfactory or complaint their perform their delivery services poorly. I shall discuss the factors how to improve any countrues' transport systems to achieve the most efficient way as below:

Any countries' transport systems will create economic value, e.g. demonstrate value for money, economic worth, viable commercial worth, financial affordable worth, achieveable worth. Any countries' transport systems can bring welfare value by economics. It has direct relationship to take the form of measured economic activity, i.e. GDP. The form of measured economic activity can impact on any countries' economic economic geography, locally , regionally and nationally's local GDP impacts. The welfare impacts may include: leisure time savings, e.g. the local people drive cars or catch any public transportation tools to go to any geogrpahical location's shopping centers, big gardens, swimming pools, cinemas etc. places to carry on any kinds of leisure activities.

Environmental impacts may include avoiding noise, air pollution on road transportation aspect , when the main road is only on on focus on the main city,
but the city lacks other roads to let any drivers can choose them to drive, instead of the main road in the city. Then, when many cars are driven on the busy transport
time, e.g. morning working time or night busy time between 6:00 and 9:00 AM, between 6:00 and 9:00 PM. When either many working people need to catch public transport or drive themselves cars to go to offices to work or they need to catch pubic transport tools or drive themselves cars to home. Then, the only one main road problem will need them to stay themselves cars on roads, due to traffic jam or traffic accidence occurrence problem causes when many cars are driven on the road in the busy transport time. It will influence they can not go to offices or homes easily daily, even in the busy transport time, their cars' gas need to be used much to cause air pollution and traffic noise is easily caused easily in the busy transport time on the road. When the city has only one main road for drivers in the busy transport time. So, poor road transport system can bring poor impact on economic welfare benefits arising from proved labour supply from commuting, time savings, including exchequer benefits. Consequently, the county's GDP will be fallen down, due to labour market effects which do not add to welfare value.

Whether can poor transport system impact indirectly on GDP or not on local, regional , or national economic geography impacts? Does transport lead to greater economic activity i.e. higher GDP? DO they lead to change in economic activity location? Does transport impact the existence of business location and new economic activity opportunities? The measurement on every country's transport how impacts on economic change, facilitating geographic division of labour and specialization. It can be analyzed on these general aspects:

Costs and speed of travel time (Economic value of travel time savings) . Travel time savings to users from improved transport is a key of economic value, but it has only less influence,journey time reliability is more important to business frieght as well as business travellers, network connectivity enhancements as well as business travellers, network connectivity enhancement can help people and goods travel more quickly (i.e. linked to jounrey time and journey time reliability, as well as opening new destinations and new journeys, comfort and quality service provision is relevant to public transport, e.g. detering jounreys at particular times or by certain modes (e.g. overcrowding), impact on productivity at work for commuters, safety and security , due to loss of output from workers, transport accidents occur easily. All of these issues will impact any countries' standard of living to local people (geography) , even GDP income.

Why does the direct and indirect effects of transportation have a positive impact on the economic growth and development of a country? Does it influence acccess to goods, services and
employment opportunities in any regions? Underdeveloped countries must need to consider how transport system influences their economic growth. For example, the costs of transportation and production are reduced through timely delivery and enhancing the economies of scale in the production process, when the road is often traffic joam, gas cost, time waste , air pollution cost, noise has many roads, but if one lorry drivers needs drive more than one day to day to deliver goods to another city's warehouse every day. It will bring psychological pressure in terrible, when they need long time to drive on the road. They can not sleep easily because road accident will occur easily when they need to spend long time to drive lorries on the road.

So, how to solve the long driving time on road transport problem will be one issue concerns human life welfare benefit aspect, instead of economic benefit aspect. The transport system welfare worth needs to include human life worth. It is a valuable insight into the causality (ot lack of causality) between transport and economic growth and will serve to compare to any countries' national level and local geographical location level both.

In special, underdeveloped countries' public transport time whether it is long or short factor, it will influence workers their going to offices to work time. If they often need spend long time to catch buses, due to traffic jam,then it will influence their efficiences to be reduced, productive number is influenced to reduce also, because traffic jam causes they often go to offices too lately.It can influence workers' bad emotion to work every day. So, traffic jam will bring negative relationship between low efficiency and bad emotion to the workers, because they need to spend long time to wait, public transportation tools and traffic jam also influence their working emotion. Consequently, service and working performance will be influenced to poor, because long time traffic jam problem causes their bad emotion to work. It is one critical factor in the path of more widely spread economic growth and urbanization for traffic jam problem to underdeveloped countries.

However, transport system can also influence developed countries' economy. How does it influence on environmental impacts aspect from mature stage. Its business activities must raise, dramastic expansion during this period, such as underdeveloped country, US, UK. In order to acheive long term sustainable development , new demands are being placed on transport sector, such as underground mass transit rail transport , ferry, local air frieght transport, train , e.g. Japan, Fance, US high speed prior rail. Because their developed countries , business and entertainment activities needs increase, it influences high time efficient and rapid speed public transportation tools needs are also needed in societies. These new technological public transport tools invention will impact on climate, noise, human health, land use and damage to ozene layer, acidification aspects, instead of economic beneficial aspect.

For long -term sustainable development to be achieved, the various activities within developed and underdeveloped societies must be adapted to what can be tolerated by humans and by the natural environment. Transport is an activity which affects humans and the natural environment for both the development of society as a whole as well as for the mobility for the individual. For Swedish underdeveloped country example, air pollution in Swedish urban areas has beed reduced, but in many places concentrations of certain substances deiving from transport activities are still at unacceptable levels and much more has to be done. Carbon dioxide emissions and noise are examples of environmental problems demanding further efforts. Measures to limit the exploitation of valuable natural and cultural environments to protect biological diviersity are also needed. So, if Swedish still hopes to develop its tourism industry to attract many travellers to choose to travel itself country. It needs to solve environmental problems from different modes of transport are of different dimensions, such as improving its air transport to avoid cause different problems and rail transport differs in turn from road transport.

The transport problem to Swedish may include poor technological communication information to its public and purchasers of transportation and communication services as to the environmental effects of different solutions is significant in creating the demand for environmentally sound public transport service concepts. It is therefore important that such lacking high technological communication and information system is presented in as completem accurate and clear way as a method for non-monetary comparison of the environmental public transport service system aspect.

In real, it's public tranport service system is needed to be improved and upgraded in order to let travellers feel Swedish's any rail, underground train, ferry, bus , taxi etc. different public transport travelling service can provide excellent performance to serve their travelling passengers, when they need to catch any kinds of public transport tools to go to travel. They can feel convenient and comfortable to attract them to visit Swedish to travel again. Then, its tourism industry GDP income will be raised, if Swedish government can innovate any new kinds of purchase ticket equipment to install in and public transport stations to let travelling passengers feel that they do not need to spend long time to queue to buy tickets to catch ferry, train, underground mass transit rail on stations conveniently. Because long time purchase ticket queue waiting will cause travellers feel its public service performance dissatisfaction and they will complain , even they won't choose to catch the kind of public transport, even the travellers won't choose to travel Swedish again, if they feel Swedish is one developed country, but it neglects to take care about travellers' catching public transport travelling service needs.

It is one poor or bad feeing to let travellers choose to Swedish again. Hence, Swedish needs to improve its public transport service performance in order to achieve to raise their comfortable and satisfactory catching public transport tools needs to let travellers to feel. They may include efficient land use for transportation tools, comprising issues concerning natural and cultural environment, natural resources, biological diversity and aesthetics, noise reducing, public transportation energy consumption and time consumption reducing, raising public transport service facilities performance functions and other issues concerning the model. For example, Swedish government can facilitate the public transport price conparison and journey time spending comparison information gathering enquiring machines public transportation selection method of public transportation services to let every travellers can evaluate different modes of public transport when they are staying in ferry, bus, train, underground mass transit rail, taxi stations.

A travelling family can seek its sustainable transport selection system for passenger transport tool. When they touch the enquiry machine, they can compare busm ferry, train, underground train, taxi price and journey spending time from their transportation stations to another destinations. Then, travelling passengers can compare these public transport tools ticket prices, journey spending time immediately when they touch the public transport enquiring machines in stations any time. Then, they can make the most righ choice to decide whether they ought catch which kind of public transport tool to arrive the another journey destination. It is one every attractive high technological enquiry method to help any travelling passegners to choose which kind of public transport tool, it can be the most cheap transport tool at the moment in any public transport stations. So , for developed countries innovative its public transport service performance will need future passengers' journey needs daily. Hence, they can not neglect how to improve public transport service needs to satisfy passengers to feel satisfaction, if Sweden government hopes its tourism industry can raise GDP income in long time.

● How underground train MTR can let passengers to feel catching time reducing

It has close relationship between globalization and global tranport development. How globalisation impacts on the environment via changes taking place in the transport sectors. In fact, it is not clear how the relative price changes that result from openness will affect the environental composition of economic activity. For example, some countries will produce more environmentally intensive goods, others will produce fewer.

On the other hand, liberalisation will raise incomes, perhaps increasing the willingness to pay for environmental improvement. These potential income effects increased outweigh the negative scale effects with increased economic activities. When combined with the positive effects with technology transfer, the net effect on local pollutants could be positive . Hence, we need to find methods to solve the problem of raising transport economic activities and serious environmental pollution creating as the same time occurrence.

Globalisation helps to facilitate greater division of labor, and to exploit its comparative advantage more completely. In longer term, globalization also stimilates technology an dlabour transfers, and allows the dynamism that accompanies economic activities to stimulate the development of new transport technologies and short time transport processes that lead to global welfare improvement.

On shipping transport industry aspect, shipping will increase ocean pollution, when international shipping activities are increasing. Trade and shipping encourages energy use in shipping is coupled with the movement of waterborne commerce. The estimates depending on the transport goods number of at-sea or in port days much increase globally every day. The energy demand of international shipping fuel sale number and domestically assigned fuel sales number also increases for global fuel usage. Estimates of ocean going ships now consume about 2% to 3% and perhaps even as much as 4% of world fossil fuels.Hence, when global shipping energy fuel usage number increases, because global shipping trading activities number increases. It will bring the environmental pollution to ocean level increases.

On air transport industry aspect, their travellers' catching air plans travelling needs and businesses' goods transport air delivery service needs are increasing from the requirements for high quality , fast and reliable international transport. Moreover, the networks that airline companies operate have changed often to hub-and spoke networks, many new often low -cost companies have entered the air freight market, any long time air journey is needed, e.g. Australia airline expands its one new air journey flies to UK, it needs two days flying time. It means that every flight to UK from Australia , it needs to use more fuel to fly. Then , air pollution will increase also.

On road transport industry aspect, global road transport cost and transit times, traffic jam occurrence chances also increase because when the road building number is increasing globally. So, it will cause traffic jam and long journey time spending , even fuel usage spending number is also increased. Then, accident occurrence chance is raised. Hence, global business or entertainment transport activities number increasing , it will bring much negative impact on environmental pollution, traffic jams number increases, long journey spending time increases, fuel usage number increases. Although , frequent transport activities may bring GDP income.

On transport service industy aspect, but is also brings negative influence to standard of living. It means that when transport fuel demand increases, transport activities number increases, GDP income on relative any transport activities needs industy , e.g. logistic demand needs, when lorry drivers need to drive lorries to deliver goods from one warehouse to another warehouse or supermarket or office etc. different business places on the road driving activities increase. But, it also bring air pollution , traffic noise and traffic jam etc. transport problems to road and natural environment and raises worse standard of living , bad emotion to working people or learning emotion to students , due to frequent traffic jam causes , low efficiency and productivity to workers, even student individual learning time can be reduced if they need to spend long time to wait bus, ferry, rail, underground train to go to schools , due to frequent long time traffic jam occurs on the roads to influence they can not go to schools on time often when they are catching buses to go to schools absolutely in busy transport time.

Thus, although any countries need to consider how to design their transport system, e.g. how to e.g. how to choose the right locations to build roads to let many cars can be driven available easily when the morning and evening (office and school transport busy time, e.g. 6:00 to 9:00 AM morning, 6:00 to 9:00 PM in the evening transport time usually because these two transport periods are usually , there are many students and working people need to catch any public transportation or drive cars tools to go back homes. So, enough roads number and long and not narrow road area must be needed to design in order to let enough cars be driven on the roads in the transport busy times to the countries have many big cities or have high population , such as UK, US, China, India, Hong Kong. They have many people , but drivers and cars numbers both are increasing. So, efficient road design and road number are also needed to increase in order to let drivers can transport goods to deliver, students and working people can catch any public transport tools to arrive any destinations on reads in the short time rapidly in order to avoid to spend long time transportation time and late to arrive any destinations in possible occurrence. So, any sudden traffic jam is not hoped to be caused by easy traffic accidents occurrence any time.

Hence, global efficient road transport system is needed, when global transport activities are increased, because any road logistic transport activities are increasing, they will also influence the students and working people when they also need to catch any public transport tools or drive themselves cars to go to working places or schools on the roads at the same busy transport time between 6:00 to 9:00 AM morning busy transport time and between 6:00 to 9:00 PM evening busy transport time. Because these both times will be have many students, working people , they need either go to offices or schools or go to homes. Hence, if the country had many lorry drivers need to drive their lorries to deliver goods on the roads in the transport busy morning or evening time in the same driving time on the roads. It will increase the risk to cause frequent traffic jam or traffic accident occurrence easily in possible in the country. So, any countries' governments can not neglect how to design roads and choose anywhere are the roads suitable locations to be built as well as anywhere land useful number to build road location choices in order to solve geographical traffic jams occurrence chance.

Hence, globalization of transport activities may bring geographical GDP growth, but it also bring traffic jams and traffic accidents occurrences, hearing impairment due to traffic noise, air pollution, traffic crashed, bad working emotions to workers and bad learning emotions to students, due to spending long transport time when traffic jam or traffic accidence occurs more easily.

However, transportation is an important tool if a country's progress. Rapid economic growth and increasing level of urbanization enhances a person's living standard have, it leads to a greater travel demands. Hence, governments ought not neglect have to design its roads , measure every road's length or width whether it has how many cars need to drive in morning or evening transport busy time for students, working people and delivery goods drivers of public transportation tools or private transportation tools easy driving needs in order to avoid frequent traffic jams or traffic accidents occurrences in possible.

Moreover, any governments also need to solve these issues, if they hope to develop their transport system successfully. These issues include : What mode of transportation to cost-effective in meeting a region's transportation needs to the country? How should a state department of transportation prioritize its highway delivers to maximize economic growth? What is the trade-off between additional growth in urban area and the cost of expanding transportation systems to accommodate greater growth? What effect does the expansion of transportation systems have on the need to invest in other types of transport modes? For example , the transport expansion may include the construction of additional highway segments, rail lines, runways, or additional sea, air, rail or bus terminal capacity using traditional technology; highway may include the additional of lanes to an interstate highway system; the conversion of an existing two-lane road to a four lane limited access highway, replacement or widening of bridges, and the extension of an existing road. Airport examples, include runway lengthening, apron expansion, and additional terminal gates.

On the other hand, enhancement to new transport technologies may bring efficiency of the existing highway system, examples may include intelligent highway systems, congestion pricing, intermodal freight facilities, geographic positioning systems, and instrument landing systems to mention of a few major transport innovations. So, transport policy makers need to understand the effects of these new transport mode innovations on economic development or GDP growth on transport activities growth transportation services and a more efficient use of limited land supplying scarce resources , air quality ,and noise pollution, traffic jams, long spending transport time to students, working people, entertaining people, even deliver goods lorry drivers their every day essential driving activities or catching public transportation tools needs problems. For example, the concept of intelligent highway systems needs increase trend. In simply , vehicles are being linked to each other and to traffic control devices to improve the efficiency of the total highway system. Similar types of innovations in intelligent traffic management are increasing needs for air, sea, and rail systems. The question is that whether intelligent highway systems can attribute of highways on economic development, raising on productivity of reducing highway congestion or improving pavement condition.

In fact, many developed countries' transportation system is mature. The nation has gone beyond the frontier of building, the interstate highway system and connecting most cities (markets). Tweaking the system with additional lanes and the new intelligent highway systems are useful in China, US, UK, because they have many cities. SO, road efficient traffic congestion control is needed when many students, working people, delivery goods transport people need to drive cars or catch cars on every city's roads in the transport busy time between 6:00 to 9:00 AM morning transport busy time as well as between 6:00 to 9:00 PM evening transport busy time.

However, transportation investment must be needed, if the country hoped to have good economic productivity, efficient transport service can bring good effects on the flows goods and people on roads every day when they use the country's transport system. So, any countries need to collect data, they can not be lack of enough transport information in any time that links anywhere locations of any drivers to the locations of the transport system that provide them with services in any time, e.g. every day morning and evening transport busy time, radio can report the real transport time of any roads traffic jam or traffic accident message to let drivers to listen to know whether anywhere roads are occurring traffic accidents or traffic jams or when the road traffic accident or traffic jam is solved to let the drivers can know whether when the roads can be opened to drive again. So, real time road transport message information is needed to report by radio, in order to let any drivers to know whether they ought choose to drive themselves cars on the road when they need to choose anywhere road to drive to the destination if they can know when the road has traffic accident or traffic jam occurs. They won't drive their cars on the road in the moment immediately.

On conclusion, globalization can being frequent transport economic activities. So, road , air, sea, transport service users' transport service needs are also increased. Every country ought not neglect how to innovate their transport service in order to satisfy their transport needs to achieve economic growth, efficient and short transport time spending, productivities increase, reducing air pollution, traffic noise , raisins standard of living on transport influence aspect to satisfy working people, students, entertaining people, delivery goods transport users' efficient road transport time behavioral spending aspect.

On conclusion, when one country's electric public transport tool service increases, it may cause gas need decreases and gas business will experience decline stage cycle stage rapidly.

Artificial Intelligent In Road Transportation Strategy

● How artificial intelligent vehicle may interact intelligent transportation tools

Can artificial intelligence (AI) and machine learning (ML) be used in the search for new " consumption" behavioral type variables that affect consumer individual or transportation service organization individual different transportation tools choices, such as road or sea or sky transportation tools? Can artificial intelligent vehicle may interact intelligent transportation tools market development?

Consumers usually have bargaining and on risk choice when they are already shopping, such as who need to accept to use any (AI) new technological products to replace human traditional behaviors, such as intelligent non-manual driving transportation market, e.g. cars are needed to be driven by human drivers on road, but it has bargaining and on risky choice, when non-manual (AI) vehicle buyers who need to depend on non-manual artificial intelligent (ML) system assists them to drive their cars on the roads.

So, any non-manual driving auto car buyers must need to believe (AI) non-manual driving vehicles (ML) systems can make accurate driving judgement to reduce or avoid any traffic accident occurrences more than human drivers' driving judgement when the (ML) systems are driving their cars on the roads. Then the intelligent vehicle manufacturers will have possible to sell their non-manual driving vehicles success.

This is the first reason or idea influences consumer individual choice to buy any kinds of (AI) non-manual driving vehicles, when consumers believe (ML) systems are more safe and make more accurate judgement to compare human or computer systems, when they are sitting in one non-manual auto driving vehicle on the road.

The another second reason or idea is that some common limits on driving consumer prediction might be understood as the kinds of errors made by poor implementation of machine learning.

Supposing driving consumers believe (AI) machine learning ability is worse to compare to human learning ability. It will also influence driving consumers do not accept to use any (AI) non-manual auto driving vehicles to replace every driver is essential on driving by himself/herself on the road. The third idea or reason is that it is important to influence driving customers believe how (AI) non-manual auto driving technology is used in them can both overcome and exploit human driving skill and safe limits and raise more auto driving safe judgement to compare human driving safe judgement.

However, how to predict any kinds of (AI) non-manual driving vehicles future consumption effort, due to different kinds of (AI) non-manual driving transportation vehicles which have different unique functions and designs to be used by different kinds of road transportation or driving demand of consumers. For example, lorry drivers need non-manual intelligent system can help them to drive fast, but safe to assist them to transport cargo to arrive destinations from their factories or offices. Otherwise, private car driver expects whose (AI) non-manual driving vehicle can auto drive to send to whom to arrive destination in safe way and non-too fast and non-too slow speed in order to avoid accident occurrences.

So, a different road intelligent consumer demand is to define whose individual driving behavior and driving habit and driving attitude and driving judgement and driving speed demand to decide how to design whose intelligent vehicle to satisfy those driving demand more generally, as simply being open-minded about what variables are likely to influence every consumer economic choice, when who decide either to buy any kinds of (AI) products or not to buy any kinds of (AI) products to replace the different demand of consumers their different (AI) useful demand.

Hence, for these three (AI) products group of stakeholders, such as home (AI) consumer group, firm (AI) consumer group and government (AI) consumer group . These consumer groups may consider whether different kinds of (AI) products can give what is special beneficial interest to them to use. These variables can be measurable properties of choices to influence them to choose to buy any (AI) kinds of (AI) products to use, e.g. psychophysiological, biological, social influences, consumer's wealth, moods and personality, (AI) product price etc. variable factors which will influence them to decide to attempt to buy any kinds of (AI) products to use.

If behavioral economics is as open-mindedness about what variables might predict. Then , (AI) machine learning system is a way to do behavioral economics because it can make use of a wide set of variables and select-which ones predict.

In behavioral economic view point, when general consumer overall demand to the product is much than the other similar (AI) non auto driving vehicle products, such as any kinds of (AI) non-manual auto driving vehicles and any kinds of manual driving vehicles case, then any kinds of (AI) non-manual auto driving vehicles will be more attractive to cause many manual driving vehicle buyers choose to buy (AI) non-manual auto driving vehicles. Hence, it seems if any kinds of (AI) non-manual auto driving vehicle products can make more attractive variable efforts to influence overall driving consumers to feel that they have more needs to drive non-manual auto vehicles to compare more than driving manual driving vehicle.

What is the main variable effort to intelligent vehicles to attract driving consumers to choose to accept to drive them ? However, I believe that (AI) machine learning system is a main factor to raise overall driving consumers' acceptances to drive it to replace manual driving vehicle. If it can persuade or prove (AI) machine learning system ability and judgement effort is more accurate than human or computer learning effort or judgement effort, then it is possible that any kinds of (AI) non-manual driving vehicle products will be accepted to drive on the road in popular.

Machine learning system is able to find prediction value in details of how the bargaining occurs. This discovery is the beginning of the next step for driving consumer individual driving behaviors or driving habits. It raises questions that include: What variables predict to influence driving consumers to change whose driving habits or driving attitudes? How can driving consumer individual emotion, face-to-face talking with whose friends when they are sitting in the non-manual driving vehicle to influence whom driving habit or driving attitude to be changed ? Do driving consumers consciously understand why those habit driving attitudes variables are important when they are sitting in one intelligent vehicle? Can (AI) driving machine learning methods capture the effects of motivated cognition to influence driving consumers decide to buy any kinds of (AI) non-manual auto vehicle products more attractively. So, it seems (AI) driving machine learning method is a main variable factor to influence driving consumers to feel who have more confidence to drive them more than any other kinds of similar manual driving vehicles on the road.

Consequently, (AI) driving machine learning system will be one important psychological method to influence driving consumers to choose to buy (AI) auto driving vehicle products to replace manual driving vehicles. The reason is because human and driving machine learning system both which will have limited variable factors to influence general different countries (AI) driving consumers' need desire to be raised.

   ● Why can (AI) driving machine learning system main factor influence driving consumer individual desires ?

Driving consumer expectations are hard to measure or predict driving attitudes and driving behaviors in (AI) non-manual driving vehicles market. Artificial intelligence is another kind of computer science development to apply intelligent vehicle market. Why do driving consumers feel need to buy any kinds of (AI) auto driving vehicles to drive to replace manual driving vehicles on the roads? What are (AI) auto driving features different to manual driving features?

(AI) is the recreation of cognitive functions in computers; it enables machines to perform tasks like humans and perhaps even better than human. In the real world, scientists develop the technological singularity, in which a superintelligence emerges with unfold human consequences.

Professionals in many industries are intensely interested in the specifics of what (AI) can do today, and how can it helps. They are considering the impact of applied (AI), in which computers are used to address a particular problem, extracting and utilizing patterns found in large volumes of data. Of all (AI)'s subfields, machine learning is attracting the most attention. I shall explain why (AI) machine learning system is the main factor to lead consumers feel need to buy any (AI) products to use. Such as below:

For smartphone, fraud detection to medical diagnosis etc. applied (AI) technological products examples. (AI) machine learning systems can help any one of these products to do any exceed general computer learning systems which (AI) learning systems can do any skills to supply (AI) users to use to compare computer learning systems can not do any skills to supply compute users to use. It seems that (AI) machine learning system is the unique feature to attract consumer consideration in technological product market.

An term for different types of learning, and can be accomplished using different techniques. This has led to a perception that all marketing teams should have (AI) to bring a unified personalized customer experience, when consumers choose to buy any (AI) products to feel what are the different or unique characteristics to compare general computer products. Such as (AI) product has this unique machine learning characteristics, we can predict (AI) and machine learning is connected to influence consumers to feel needs.

Furthermore, over the same time period, and in contrast to predictions for roles in many industries. (AI) won't take the place of marketers and merchandisers themselves although it is already a new value to analytical and strategic marketing skills to persuade consumers to buy any (AI) products. It means different kinds of (AI) products will have different machine learning effort and unique characteristics to attract consumers to choose to buy them to use. Such as, when intelligent vehicles need have unique road driving or sea transportation or flying machine learning system when they are applied on these three kinds of transportation tool aspects.

They need have good response safety driving and immediate response learning systems to avoid any boats or air planes or vehicles to crash to them to reduce accident occurrences immediately on any one of either road or sky or sea journey environment.

What is the reason why (AI) driving machine learning system can influence good at making sense to driving consumer desire? Only humans (drivers) , preferably experienced, well informed humans can understand their driving customer needs and decide how to design or reengineer any (AI) intelligent vehicle product functions. (AI) intelligent vehicle can give these professionals the means to do this better to compare manual driving immediate response control function when any vehicles are driving or they will stop immediately to close / near to them in order to reduce crash occurrence on the road, and then maximize relevance through real-time customization of the non-manual auto vehicle driving user experience.

For example, as ever, senior decision makers need to be informed, decisive and results-oriented or risk losing out. Harvard Business Review indicated : Over the next decade, (AI) won't replace managers, but managers who use (AI) will replace those who don't. Such as intelligent vehicle won't replace drivers, but drivers who use intelligent vehicles will replace those who can not control how to drive their vehicles in the most safe way. So, (AI) driving machine learning system will have possible to do any drivers' (human's) driving judgement, driving analytical mind and driving effort to be more accurate than manual driving skills. Such as how to control to drive the intelligent vehicle in the most safe way. It is general manual driving skill can not achieve to drive in the safe way.

For another (AI) digital commerce example, (AI) and machine learning are the most exciting developments in marketing and merchandising to be applied to digital commerce, such as making better decisions through trend and cluster analysis, deploying product and content in mutually reinforcing combinations, increasing customer engagement and satisfaction in real time.

Hence, the key attraction in digital commerce circles is that machine learning is designed to be self-optimizing. Optimizing for revenue example will surface are increasingly profitably selection of products (within the brand parameters selected).

When to apply (AI) capabilities and what value (AI) is delivering for customer and company like. Unlike any technology before it, (AI) is analytical and predictive capabilities offers the prospect for each and every individual. It can maximize real time and engagement. Effective tailored (AI) technology, such as digital experience cloud technology is available now. And once integrated, (AI) starts learning and delivering incremental value from day one. So (AI) could transform the digital experience to any business organizations.

Hence, (AI) driving machine learning system can be applied to road driving skill aspect. When intelligent vehicles are invented to own the most safe driving judgement skill and they can know when either they may auto drive fast speed, when they are feeling to know when there are not many vehicles are moving close/near to them or when they need auto drive slow speed, when they are feeling to know when there are many vehicles are moving close/ near to them. Then driving consumers will have more confidence to choose to buy any kinds of intelligent vehicles to replace manual driving vehicles to drive on the roads.

● Non-manual driving transportation tool market development

If Non-manual driving vehicle manufacturers expect their (AI) automatic vehicles can attract drivers to buy. I feel them to need to consider how (AI) driving machine learning system can achieve these requirements in order to satisfy manual driving vehicle drivers' requirement to change their traditional driving habit to choose non-manual driving needs. It means (AI) driving machine learning systems can help them to drive vehicles to replace manual driving vehicles on the road. This is the main factor to influence car buyers choose to buy intelligence driving vehicles replace to manual driving vehicles. I believe (AI) non-manual driving vehicle machine learning systems, need to be designed as below:

(1) Improving driving safety by preventing accidents from happening.

Every year, drivers are facing a large number of casualties, due to traffic accidents. The amount of killed and injured road traffic related accidents is increasing every year. The real cost of an accident can go well beyond the limits of immediate material destruction, and is impossible to evaluate.

Hence, researchers and car manufacturers are looking for solutions in order to reduce the amount of accidents. They already developed a considerable set of technologies in order to decrease the amount of casualties. Most of them (like airbags, seat-belts, anti-lock systems, shock absorbing car bodies) are efficient in decreasing the impact of an accident, and in protecting the passengers of the cars. The technologies already saved a lot of lives, but they are rarely able to avoid accidents because they do not anticipate them. Moreover, if they are protecting in many cases, the passengers of the car, they do not prevent most traffic participants, like pedestrians on bicyclists from getting injured. it causes (AI) non-manual automatic car manufacturers need to consider how to design machine learning safety system is to prevent accident from happening instead of just reducing their impact.

This can only be possible using intelligent systems that can observe the driving environment, reason and decide if there is a danger, determine how to avoid it and act if necessary

(2) Reducing energy consumption by optimizing the driving.

Nowadays, global air pollution is serious. (AI) non-manual driving car manufacturers need to concern how to design (AI) machine learning system can reduce degree of air pollution to be the most minimum level to compare to traditional manual driving vehicles.

The reduction of energy consumption if certainly one of the main challenges. Transportation is one of the major factors in fossil energy consumption, and it is also responsible for a large amount of CO_2 pollution. It is difficult to ask individuals to voluntarily limit the use of their vehicle of they do not have a strong incentive to do so. Specially in regions where vehicles are needed to drive to go to work every day. It stands to reason that if it is difficult to decrease the amount of vehicles, part of the solution is to make them more energy efficient.

Hence, non-manual driving car manufacturers need to design how to improve engines, which are more optimized and need less fuel to operate, and hybrid and electric cars have been developed and are continuously being improved. But we can go beyond these solutions that do not take into account the environment in which a vehicle is driving. A growing number of scientific contributions presented intelligent systems used in order to improve energy efficiency and reduce fuel consumption, based on the optimization of the way (AI) non-manual driving (AI) vehicles are performing. Such as recharge batteries and electric engine will be predicted the popular fuel in order to limit fuel consumption to future (AI) non-manual driving vehicles. They can reduce air pollution, consume less fuel for (AI) non-manual driving vehicles.

(3) Improving comfort by anticipating (AI) non- manual driving vehicle drivers.

Finally, another application for intelligent vehicle is the improvement of driving comfort. Car industry is very competitive market. Many potentials (AI) intelligent vehicle customers need to enjoy to sit more comfortable intelligent vehicles, who will be attracted by (AI) comfortable systems improving when driving, so part of the research in intelligent systems from cars focuses on how to improve the driving experience, i.e. make it easier and more enjoyable, more comfortable to compare to traditional manual driving vehicles.

As an example, lane keeping assistant systems are technologies that actively keep the vehicle in the lane in highways of the driven drifts out of it. Automatic speed regulation keeps the car at a certain speed without requiring to touch the gas pedal. This can be really interesting for, e.g. (AI) non-manual driving truck drivers that spend a lot of time on highways. But these technologies have a limitation in the case of automatic speed regulation, this technology can not copy of a vehicle ahead drives slower than the desired speed, or if another vehicle cuts into the lane.

This case requires the driver to have a constant focus on the road. In order to achieve more comfort, it is better of the system can adapt to changes in its dynamic environment: let the (AI) intelligent vehicle adapt to the speed of the man-manual vehicle, or autonomously change lane when requires. Again, this requires knowledge about the environment, detection capabilities, reasoning and action planning. Intelligent systems can be used in order to create more attractive and more comfortable and more safe, less energy consumption and less fuel expenditure by intelligent vehicles.

Factors influence public transport service industry reaches
life cycle decline stage

In our future road public transport service development. Does underground train improvement bring another new public transport service experience to let passengers to experiece another new road public transport service replace traditional bus, tram, train, taxi , rapid speed train etc. public transport tool service by this kind new " exceed sound speed" underground train public transport tool? Can this kind of " exceed sound speed" underground train public service transport tool replace traditional bus, train, tram, taxi, road piblic transport tools ? Will traditional road public transport tools experience to reach decline life cycle service stage from maturity life cycle service stage in soon future possible, if this kind of " new exceed sound speed innovation underground train is invented ?

What is exceed sound speed underground train ? It can run exceed sound speed to catch above four to eight passengers to sit in the small size circle shape underground train from one distination to another destination in short time. For example, it can run at exceed sound speed at underground from US Washington city to New York city, in the future, it will be possible one kind of small circle size underground train, it may only catch about one to eight passengers every journey, when this kind of new exceed sound speed underground train was really invented. Can it replace traditional slow speed underground train and road public transport tools to be accepted by many passengers?

In this US future new exceed sound speed small size underground train public transport tool case, it only needs spend half hour to transport passengers from US Washington to New York city rapidly. In general, underground train speed needs about three hours from Washington to New York city distance. So, it can shorten time to let passengers to avoid any delay. The question is that : Can it influences future global public transport service life cycle stage to reach decline life service cycle life in short time, if this kind of new exceed sound speed small size underground train public transport tool is invented in success? I shall attempt to answer whether future new sound speed rapid small size underground public tranport service train invention, it will influence other traditional public transport tools to reach the decline life service cycle stage rapidly in short time as below:

In our traditional public transport development history, since 1900, human had been beginning to consider every country ought own themselves public transport fools, e.g. for passengers service. So, passengers can pay cheap ticket to catch either bus, or tram, or train ot ferry, or taxi, or underground train from one destination to another destination in short time conveniently. So, public transport tool needs had been popular increasing, because there were not many people like to buy cars to drive when any kinds of public tranport tools are invented in 1900 beginning. The reason may be that they feel expensive gas expenditure and cars will need to repair or become old etc. different reasons. So, from 1900, public transport tool service tools may be whole public transport service industry's birth life cycle service stage. In this stage, global any passengers had been attempting to choose to catch either bus, trains, trams, taxi, underground trains etc. public transport tools to go to anywhere conveniently. They would compare whether public transport service can provide comfortable feeling and rapid transport service quality to be better than purchase one car to drive.

Hence, in this global public transport service birth life cycle stage, global human had been attempting any kinds of public transport tools catching feeling whether which one kind could bring more comfortable service feeling , e.g. bus service is better or tram service is better or train service is better or underground train service is bettr or ferry service is better. Hence, in global whole public transport industry tools will be compared by all passengers . Passengers will choose the best kind of public transport tool to catch in any time when they feel need. Hence, bus, taxi, train, tram, underground train, ferry transport service performance level must bee very high to avoid their passengers to make decision to choose another kind of public transport service to replace them.

From 1900 to 1950, global public transport service had been experiencing fair or birth stage competition because any one passenger had been attempting to choose which kind of public transport tool to replace purchase car need. After 1950, global public transport service had been experiencing growth life cycle service stage. Because many people began to feel different kinds of public transport tools prices are cheap and reasonable . So global had had many different transport tools to replace purchase cars needs to anyone. Also, bus, taxi, ferry, train, tram , underground train number and transport service frequent time will need to increase in order to satisfy increasing passengers transport service needs in transport service market.

After 1990, global transport service industry had been experiencing mature life cycle service stage, instead of non owning car people must need to catch any kinds of public transport tools to go to aywhere, even owning car people, when they feel that they often drive cars, frequent driving car behavior may bring high gas expenditure in long time. So, when they feel any one kind of transport tool can transport them to go to anywhere conveniently in short time. On the day, they will not drive themselves cars to go to anywhere, they will choose any one kind of public transport tools to go to the destination on that day, because they do not want to spend much gas expenditure or avoid traffic jam or accident occurrence when they need to go to the destination in shor time.

So, in this mature public transport service life cycle stage, global any one includes owning car person and non owning car person, we had been accepted to choose any one kind of public transport tool to replace cars to go to any destinations conveniently. Because bus stations number increased, bus number increases, bus can arrive in short time, taxi, train, tram , ferry , underground train public transport tools services can follow bus service to provide accurate shorten arrival time, comfortable catching environment, reasonable price, none delay arrival time, high passengers transport service quality to let global any one passenger to feel satisfactory. Hence, after 1980, global public transport service had been experiencing mature life cycle service stage.

Global public tranport service needs had been increasing. At the same time, when any one kind of public transport tool is popular to be accepted to choose to catch by any one passenger. In this suitation, if one kind of public transport tool is improved, e.g. shorten transport distance, arrival destination time can be decreased, price is reasonable cheap, such as Japan rapid speed train, China, prior rapid speed train etc. These rapid speed electric trains can transport many passengers from one station to another station in short time. So, in road train service industry, nowadays, it is experiencing mature life cycle service stage. It means that any passengers will be influenced to catch this kind of rapid speed train in prefer to compare tram, traditional old speed train, bus, ferry to catch.

However, in the future, it is possible that one kind of underground train may be invented successfully. It is short circle size underground train, it can catch one to maximum eight passengers only for every journey in underground. Nowadays, US scientists had been attempting to manufacture this kind of " exceed sound speed'" underground train, if it can be invented in success, it may catch maxium eight passengers from Washington to New York city within half hour time . In general, traditional US underground train needs two to three hours to catch passengers from Washington underground train station to New York underground train station. So, if this kind of " exceed sound speed" underground train is invented in success, it will be possible to influence global public transport train, tram, bus, ferry, taxi, public transport tool passengers number may be influenced to reduce, due to its fee is reasonable cheap, more comfortable, rapid destination arrival and on time arrival transport service etc. factors.

The question is that: How this kind of " exceed sound speed underground train tool" bring positive or negative changes to influence global public transport service life cycle stage?

Nowadays, rapid speed train or underground train public service transport tool had changed traditional gas energ train or electric train transport service need to mature life cycle stage. Since electric train or rapid speed train invention. This kind of public transport had provided one kind of more comfortable and rapid transport service choice to any passengers. So, train or underground train transport tool compares to general bus, tram , ferry to experience rapid mature life service cycle stage. Many passengers many feel to catch underground train or train in preference because their ticket prices are reasonable cheap and they are provided rapid short time journey to arrive any destinations any any countries. For London underground is a rapid transit system serving greater histry . These two ran electric trains in circular tunnels having diameters.

In 1933, most of London's underground railways, tramway and bus services are accepted in popular . Hence, UK, LOndon railway public transport tool has developed long time. The average speed on the London underground is 20.5 miles per hour, including station stops. On Metropolitan line, trains can reach over 60 mph. The shortest distance between teo adjacent stations on the network is only 260 metres and the longest is 6.3 kilometres.

Nowadays, the fastest underground train is the Victoria line, it can reach speeds up tp 50 mph because the stations are further apart. The metropolitan line has the fastest train speeds, sometimes reaching over 60 mph. IS light rail faster than buses? IN fact the data is from the National trainsit database website and it shows that it costs almost twice as much, one average to move one light rail vehicle per hour versus onw bus. Hence, light rail must be faster than buses, comparing rail versus bus trainsit transport service life cycle stages, rail versus may reach mature transport service life cycle stage. Otherwise, bus transit transport service life cycle stage will be possible to be influenced to experience decline life service cycle stage from nowadays mature stage. The reason is that future " sound speed underground rail transport will be possibe to invent successfully. Then, this kind improved exceed sound speed underground train transport tool may replace to traditional electric train or underground electric rail, when any countries passengers can accept to choose to catch this kind of developed " exceed sound speed" underground rail tranport tool in habit.

In fact, underground rail versus bus tranit focus primary on vehicle travel speeds and operating, per capita vehicle travel grew rapidly between 1970 and 2000. If one day, US " exceed sound speed" underground short size rail is invented successfully., it will change the whole traditional public tranport service industry mode to persuade passengers to enjoy this kind " exceed sound speed feeling" and choose to catch this kind public transport service in preference, due to they can enjoy rapid short time destination arrival journey, and it can bring benefit to transport providers for lifecycle saving energy and emission carbon pollutants reduces. It may reach the rail public transport tool invention to the topest mature life cycle service stage, if this kind of exceed sond speed underground train can be invented successfully. It means that rail transport service industry only needs to spend less developing time to reach the mature life cycle service stage from birth and growth life cycle service stages .

In global whole public transport service life cycle development stage, underground rail transport tool is the most rapid experiencing the topest mature life cycle service stage of only one kind public transport tool to compare bus, ferry, tram , train . Although, transport infrastructure has long operational life, there are too many urban public transport networks, including light rail (metro and tram), but if the kind of new " exceed sound speed" underground rail can be real invented. Then, in underground rail public transport tool development history, it will help underground electric rail development to let any passengers to feel more comfortable, most rapid, reasonable ticket price and convenient underground journeys in every day.

Hence, if it can be invented successfully, it will not only help whole rail transport service to reach mature life service cycle stage or it will be future the best or the most comfortable one kind of using public transport tool choice to global any passengers by 2041. Because when it could real be invented in success, it proved that it may fight physical barriers and fast moving or elevated sound speed levels can cause that any passengers can feel more comfortable and none long time distance to arrive destination anywhere. For example, if this kind of exceed sound speed underground short size rail transport tool can transport US passengers from tunnel to go through ocean to another countries stations. Then, any one does not need to catch airplane transport or ship to go to another country easily. They can catch it to go through ocean underground tunnels to any country from ocean in short time also. So, instead of this kind of sound speed underground rail can replace traditional tram, train, transport service on the road, even it can also replace airplanes and ships, ocean and air transport service by 2041 in the future. So, its transport inventio may change global traditional transport mode, it can provide underground ocean tunnel and underground and tunnel transport channels to arrive any underground road tunnel transport channels to arrive any destinations conveniently. Then, it can bring shop and airplane transport service changes to let wholc passengers to have more one kind of new transport tool choice, such as underground exceed sound speed rail feeling need. So, ship and airplane transport service life cycle may also be influenced to experience decline life cycle service cycle stage after 2041, if this kind of exceed sound speed short circle size underground rail could be invented in success to catch any countries passengers spend short time to catch it to go to another countries' underground rail stations from himself/herself country's underground rail station by ocean tunnel conveniently.

Consequently, future exceed sound speed underground short circle size rail public transport tool invention may influence other kinds of public transport tools to experience and reach decline life cycle service stage early after 2041, if it can real invent successfully by 204. Hence, it explains that why bus, tram, train, ferry, airplane transport tools need to continue to invent or improve rapid flying speed or rapid flight speed and comfortable feeling quality in order to fight this kind of future new exceed sound speed underground rail transport tool to avoid rapid decline life cycle service stage easily after 2041. So, " this kind of exceed sound speed small circle size underground rail" transport tool invention " it will bring global other different kinds of road and sea and air transport tool will face decline life service cycle stage early after 2041 in possible.

So, future any electric vehicle and electric public transport tools are popular to let any countries passengers to choose to catch in prefer or buy to drive on the road in preference, then it will bring serious negative influence to global gas energy businesses reach decline stage cycle stage rapidly.

● Does oil price sudden high rising factor influence global oil industry rapid reaches decline life cycle stage?

Can sudden oil price sudden raising factor cause global oil industry rapid reaches decline life cycle stage? For example sudden crude oil price raising of last year from US$40 to US$150 , even $200 or higher per barrel. Why did it happen to cause global oil industry reaches decline life cycle stage in possible? When global economic growth, if it influences global oil price raises, such as the case crude oil price sudden rises to US$150, even more from US$40 per barrel. Due to global crude oil demand increases, but crude oil supply is shortage. SO, it causes crude oil price increases high percentage from US$40 to US$150 , even higher per barrel. Because crude oil is shortage, global crude oil supply reduces , but global crude oil consumers number is increasing.

Consequently, it causes global crude oil price may have influential increasing number. IS it good or bad to oil manufacturers when they sell too high crude oil price to global crude oil consumers? Although, it seems that raising crude oil price may help them to earn high profit, it will cause many crude oil users feel crude oil prices are too high. So, they will attempt to choose to use other kinds of oil energy to replace it, when other kinds of similar crude oil energy products can also satisfy their energy needs. Can too high crude oil price influence crude oil industry rapid reaches decline life cycle stage? I shall attempt to explain as below:

It is correct that say they the price is linked to the supply and demand balance, the essential is to explain oil price movements by use of the classic model of economics, price=f(demand, supply). We need to find out the commodity whose supply and demand is determining the dynamics of oil. It is therefore reasonable to question whether the economic model utilized really models or if it is applied in an incorrect way to the oil market. Or rather, that the technological complexity of this crude oil market does not allow it to be modelled on the simple relationship between demand and supply at a global level.

Econometric models to crude oil is more suitable, which are suitable for the commodities (coffee, copper, gold etc.) , where the production and technological transformation processes are less complex. SO, it implies that crude oil business life cycle stage development factor ought be influenced by its unpredicted refining crude oil manufacturing technological factor as well as it influences that this kind energy product needs how much time to reach growth life cycle stage from birth stage or reaches mature life cycle stage from growth cycle stage, even it will be influenced to experience the decline life cycle stage by any kinds of unpredicted new energy invention. So, if future one new energy invention may be used to replace crude oil raw material to produce any kinds of energy products . Then, global crude oil demand may be influenced to decrease by this kind of new energy invention. Consequently, it may cause global crude oil industry will experience the decline life cycle stage.

We refer new to the crude oil market (raw material), to the finished products market(gasoline, diesel, jet fuel, fuel oil, chemical feedstocks) and to the financial market for crude and finished products (futures). We should always remember that in our cars an in airplanes do not use crude oil, but finished products, which are increasingly difficult to produce. We can not also neglect the dramatic developments of the future market and its prodominant role in the world economy. So, if in our future energy development, scientists can invent one kind of energy which does not need to use crude oil (raw material) to finished any kinds of oil produces. Then, global crude oil industry , it will be possible influenced to rapid reaches life cycle stage.

Hence, it seems that , in short time, sudden crude oil increases price, it won't influence oil users do not choose to use its finished products, such as gasoline, fuel oil, jet fuel etc. Because nowadays, crude oil raw material product is still main global energy market raw material leader. But, if one day, scientists can discovered one kind of natural energy resource can replace crude oil to refine or manufacture any kinds of energy products easily. Then, it may influence global crude oil needs reduce, when new energy manufacturers began to accept this kind of new natural energy resource to manufacture any kinds of new energy products.

Consequently, global crude oil market may be influenced to rapid experience the decline life cycle stage. SO, it explains crude oil price sudden changes to rise much, it can not influence global crude oil market to experience decline cycle life stage easily, because each and all these different kinds of finished oil products markets respond to different behavioral patterns and they are operated by bodies to with differing interests, culture and business objectives. A model that does not take into account the inter-relations between above these different kinds of finished oil product markets and their individual dynamics is incapable of describing what happens to oil prices.

When the analyst is confronted by the unequivocal event of a crude oil price ccariation, and having only the classic model of the global demand/ supply, he can only create a scenario of probable events (input to the model), which , when , processed, might generate the variation in price which actually took place. If the crude oil rises, it is clear that there must have been an increase in crude oil users' demands or a reduction in crude supply in the time.

In the absence of reliable information, it is thus very easy to reach the mistake conclusion that, e.g. China and India the distance enemy, the invisible hands are becoming the critical factors for our planet. And that certainty OPEC (the conflict of civilizations) is yet again, for political reason, not producing enough crude. It seems that highly likely that both would wish to create problems for the west by raising prices. So, shortage of crude oil supply or increasing drude oil users number, which won't be the main factor influence drude oil rising price. Crude oil variable price may be influenced by other factors, such as of future one kind of new natural resource energy product may be invented to replace crude oil. Then crude oil won't have any market worth in global crude industry market.

Consequently, global crude oil manufacturing industry will be influenced to experience decline life cycle stage by future any one kind of unpredicted new natural resource energy product invention in possible. On conclusion, it seems that crude oil price changes , it does not depend on demand and supply side mainly, there are many other invisible hands issue to influence global crude oil changes. Also, crude oil price sudden rises too much, it can not influence crude oil users number decreases. Unless one kind of undiscovered new enery product may be invented to replace crude oil. So, it may cause global crude oil market will experience decline life cycle stage in possible.

www.ingramcontent.com/pod-product-compliance
Lightning Source LLC
Chambersburg PA
CBHW052000150726
47999CB00004B/1457